AF522056

INDIA BOOKVARSITY

LOTUS CHOICES

Editor: Mahendra Kulasrestha

Classics Revived
for an
Ultra-modern World

CULTURE INDIA

'An encyclopaedia of ancient Indian Culture'

—*Journal of American Oriental Society*

Published by

CULTURE INDIA

A compendium of
Indian philosophy,
religion, arts,
literature and society
contributed by
authorities in various areas

Edited by
MAHENDRA KULASRESTHA

Source :
Part II of the Tagore Centenary
Volume, published by V.V. Research
Inst., Hoshiarpur, Pb., 1962

Culture India

ISBN 81-8382-031-1

Published by:
Lotus Press
4263/3, Ansari Road, Darya Ganj, New Delhi-110002
Ph.: 30903912, 23290047
E-mail: lotus_press@sify.com

Lasertypeset by: Sai Kripa Computers, Delhi
Printed at: Gyan Sagar, Delhi

Editorspeak

Towards an Earth Citizen

This work was published in 1962 as a part of the *Tagore Centenary Volume* sponsored by the well-known institute of Indology, V.V. Research Inst., Hoshiarpur, Pb., under its Woolner Indological Series. Planned and edited by the present Editor, it had contributions by famous authorities in various fields, who, in order to pay their genuine homage to the great poet and visionary Rabindra Nath Tagore, willingly joined and put in their best in their articles. Prof. Humayun Kabir, the then Education Minister of India, provided the Foreword. He also contributed a perceptive article on Muslims in India. No wonder, it came out as a significant one-volume holistic work which, on publication, was commended by everybody. It was noticed and reviewed in many Western countries and was used by scholars and educated general readers, as well as universities, as an easy-to-understand tool to study the manysided and quite complex, because of its several religio-philosophies, Indian culture.

Time passed and after the demise of its dynamic director, Acharya Vishwa Bandhu, the Institute fell on hard days. The book went out of print though its quality and utility did not fall, it rather increased with the change of times in favour of India, her culture and values. Since the Editor was/is still alive, he, when he started the INDIA BOOKVARSITY to revive classical works on aspects of Indian culture, to inform, educate and stimulate the new generation, Indiaspora, as well as those interested in Indian culture worldwide, he thought it in the fitness of things, nay, his duty to republish the work. The learned scholars, our contributors, are no more, all of them—our respectful homage to them!

The articles were either written specially for this volume or selected from the major works of the authorities and approved by them. A few articles present something very new regarding Indian culture—such as the one by Dr. Suniti Kumar Chatterjee. He skillfully presents the racial combination of Indian society—a new research done and promoted by him—which convincingly explains the variegated characteristics of Indian people, their customs, thought processes and expressions in the arts, literatures, etc. His second article presenting a running survey of all the literatures of India, is also very effective. The articles on Indian music and dances, by Priya Chatterji Tandura, a practitioner who married an Italian and settled down in that country, and the famous danseuse Ritha Devi, are most comprehensive and full of information. The religio-philosophical aspect has been suitably taken care of. The contribution of South India in various areas, generally neglected in most volumes of a similar nature, is given its fullest due.

Another remarkable contribution, on Indian painting, is by the famous son of the celebrity artist, Nicholas Roerich, Svetoslav Roerich, himself an artist of great merit, and the husband of the never-to-be-forgotten actress, Devika Rani. The Editor will never forget the genuine love and interest shown by both of them in the venture.

I would like to recommend to the reader Dr. Indra Sen's article on Sri Aurobindo's 40-yr. long experiment in creating the evolved human species through his new Integral Yoga, which, though did not succeed, but drew the enlightened world's attention to its possibility. Such a thing could have happened in India only, and still remains a possibility — a prospect which will change life fundamentally.

If we compare India with Europe, we will be quite surprised. Religion is generally one in both the lands, but the sub-areas are independent countries in Europe while they are states or provinces in India—though their number is generally the same, about 25, in both. That reflects on the unifying, all inclusive, live-and-let-live character of India's culture. Perhaps this is a model for the future of the world, a globalised world, where every human being is an Earth Citizen—this significant concept was discussed threadbare a decade ago at an international seminar held under the auspices of the Indira Gandhi Memorial Trust, New Delhi, under the head 'The Making of an Earth Citizen', later on published in book form.

The ultimate ideal of *Culture India* is the *Making of an Earth Citizen.* Perhaps the 21st century of Millennium Three is the time to achieve it.

Contents

Philosophy, Religion, Culture

History and Society

Literature and Arts

'Hindu religion has no Pope, no ecclesiastical hierarchy, no compulsory dogmas. It is a religion that has refused to be shackled by a particular religious book. It does not have fundamentals, so there is no Hindu fundamentalism.

'Hinduism is a civilisation. America called itself a melting pot, then India could well be called a thali. *All the flavours are separate on the steel plate but they all combine on your palate.'*

—Shashi Tharoor,
renowned writer and
Under-secretary-General
of the United Nations
(Nov. 2005)

1

The Song of India

Heart of mine, awake in this holy place of pilgrimage,
In this Land of India on the shore of vast humanity.

Here do I stand with arms outstretched to salute man divine,
And sing his praise in many a gladsome paean.
These hills that are rapt in deep meditation,
These plains that clasp their rosaries of rivers,
Here will you find earth that is ever-sacred;
In this land of India, on the shore of vast humanity.

We know not whence and at whose call, these myriad streams
Have come rushing forth to lose themselves in this sea—
Aryan and non-Aryan, Dravidian and Chinese
Scythian, Hun, Pathan and Moghul, all merged into one body.
Now the West has opened her doors, bringing their offerings,
They will give and take, unite, and will not turn away,
In this land of India, on the shore of vast humanity.

Come O Aryans, come non-Aryans, Hindu, Mussalman come,
Come ye Parsees, come O Christians, come ye one and all,
Come Brahmins, let you be hallowed by holding all by hand.
Come ye all who are shunned,wipe out the dishonour,
Come to the crowning of the Mother, fill the sacred bowl
With water that is sanctified by the touch of all
In this land of India, on the shore of vast humanity.

2

The Philosophy of India

Spiritual life is the true genius of India. Those who make the greatest appeal to the Indian mind are not the military conquerors, nor the rich merchants or the great diplomats, but the holy sages, the rishis who embody spirituality at its finest and purest. India's pride is that almost in every generation and in every part of the country, from the time of her recorded history, she has produced these holy men who embody for her all that the country holds most dear and sacred. Though they generally remain away from the main stream of life, kings and commoners pay reverent homage to them and take their advice in the problems of their personal lives as well as in public affairs. By their lives they teach us that pride and power, wealth and glory, are nothing in comparison with the power of spirits. It is those who scorn their own lives that raise life above our scorn.

Religion is a matter of experience. It is not an awakening from a swoon, but a transformation of one's being. It is not an addition to one's intellectual furniture, but an exhaltation of one's personality into the plane of the universal spirit. It is *Brahma-darshana*—insight into reality—a direct awareness of the world of values. Religious experience is not to be confused with the pursuit of truth, beauty, or goodness. It is a life of adoring love transcending these. The Divine is not a mere sum of knowledge, love and beauty. The

Ultimate Reality which responds to our demands is more than rational. Religion means awe more than service, holiness more than virtue. We worship not what we can, but what we cannot, understand. So, it is spiritual discovery not creation. The men of experience feel the presence of God and do not argue about it. The shoals and shallows of existence are submerged in a flood-tide of joy.

Though the experience is beyond reason, it is not opposed to reason. While the Upanishads emphasise the direct awareness of the world of spirit, they also adduce reasons in support of the reality of spirit. Their approach is both objective and subjective. Each order of reality is truly apprehended from a standpoint higher than itself. The significance of the physical world *(anna)* is disclosed in the biological *(prana)*; that of the biological in the psychological *(manas)*; that of the psychological in the logical and ethical *(vijnana)*. The logical finds its meaning in the spiritual *(ananda)*. The drift of the world has an underlying tendency, a verifiable direction towards some implied fulfilment. If the vast process of the world leads us to the spiritual, we are justified in finding in the spiritual the best clue to the understanding of the world.

It is now admitted that the forms and properties of matter, animals and plants, in their varied classes and orders, human beings with their power of choice between good and evil, did not come into existence in their present form by a direct act of Almighty God, but assumed their present forms in slow obedience to a general law of change. The higher exerts a curious pressure on the happening of the lower and moulds it.

Modern philosophers confirm the suggestions of the Upanishads on this question. Professor Lloyd Morgan, who studies the problem from the biological side, affirms that while resultants can be explained as the results of already existing conditions, emergents like the advent of life, mind and reflective personality, cannot be explained without the assumption of divine activity. The progressive emergence, in the course of evolution, of life, mind and personality, requires us to assume a creative principle operative in nature, a timeless reality in the temporal.

When we consider the nature of cosmic process with its ascent from matter to spirit, we are led to the conception of a Supreme Being who is the substantiation of all values. These values are not only the revealed attributes of God, but the active causes of the world. Till these values are realised, God is transcendent to the process, though He inspires it. He transcends all creatures as the active power in which they take their rise.

An analysis of the self yields the same result. The Upanishads undertake an analysis of the self and make out that the reality of the self is the divine universal consciousness. It is needless to repeat here the careful accounts which the *Chhandogya* and *Mandukya* Upanishads relate. Some modern thinkers arrive at similar results. The *jivatman* is not a substance, but an activity, what Aristotle calls *Energeia* or self-maintaining activity.

We must seek for the sources of substance not in the external persistence in space, but in the internal continuity of memory. The question, why do the contents of the mind hang together, how are they unified, Kant answers by referring us to the transcendental subject, to which all experiences are finally to be referred. This transcendental self is the *Paramatman*, functioning in all minds. It is not capable of existing in the plural. There is only one transcendental self and our empirical selves are psychical facts, streams of change.

Those who live in God do not care to define. They have a peculiar confidence in the universe, a profound and peaceful acceptance of life in all its sides. Their response to Ultimate Reality is not capable of a clear-cut, easily intelligible formulation. An austere silence is more adequate to the experience of God than elaborate descriptions.

The Upanishads often give negative accounts of the Supreme Reality. God is nothing that *is*. He is non-being. Pagans like Plotinus and Christians like Nicholas of Cusa support the negative theology of the Upanishads. This negative theology also gives us a knowledge of Divinity. It affirms that Divinity is not perceived by the categories of reason. It is grasped by the revelations of spiritual life.

When positive accounts are given, we abandon concepts in favour of symbols and myths. They are better suited to life which is inexhaustible and unfathomable. God is regarded as father, friend, lover. Infinite power and infinite love are both revelations of God. God is infinite love that pours forth at every time and every place its illimitable grace on all that ardently seek for it. The divine solicitude for man is easy of comprehension when we look upon the Divine as Mother. She wishes to possess us and so will pursue and track us down in our hiding places.

The positive descriptions are variations of the central theme that God is a person. The negative theology makes out that even personality is a symbol. In later Vedanta, a distinction is drawn between the Absolute Brahman and the personal Ishvara. Shankara says: 'Brahman is realised in its twofold aspect: In one aspect it is endowed with the *upadhis* (adjuncts) of name and form that are subject to modification and cause differentiation; and in the other it is just the opposite (bereft of all *upadhis*) i.e., the transcendental Reality.

Brahman and Ishvara, Absolute and God, are not contradictory, but complementary to each other. Each is the perspective offered to the mental standpoint of the seeker. Religious experience also lends support to this dual conception. It has normally two sides, an experience of personal intercourse with a personal God as well as a sense of rest and completeness in an absolute spirit which is more than personal. If the latter alone were experienced, we should not lapse from the condition of absolute freedom. It is because our natures are rooted in the world of space-time as well, that we look up to the Absolute as something different from us, with whom it is possible for us to have personal relations. There are experiences of men who are convinced that they are working with God, thinking and striving under pressure from him. For them God is not an unchanging Absolute, a Being perfect in nature and realisation. God is aiming at something through the medium of the human. There is a sense in which God has real need of us and calls us to share in his increasing victories, and another in which God is timeless and completes our being. When we emphasise the former aspect, we call it the Supreme God; when we lay stress on the latter, we call it the Absolute.

Since Brahman is apprehended by us it is clear that we have in us a quality which apprehends it. It is we that possess the ineffable consciousness of the eternal. The soul it is that becomes aware of Brahman. The Absolute is spirit. Though unspeakable in its transcendence, the Supreme is yet the most inward part of our being. Though Brahman in one sense entirely transcends us, in another sense it is intimately present in us. The Eternal Being, Brahman, is spirit, Atman.

Off and on, in some rare moment of our spiritual life, the soul becomes aware of the presence of the Divine. A strange awe and delight invade the life of the soul and it becomes convinced of the absoluteness of the Divine, which inspires and moulds every detail of our life. To bring out that God is both transcendent and immanent, that He is a presence as well as purpose, the conception of Ishvara is used. He is the lord and giver of life, in this world and yet distinct from it, penetrating all, yet other than all. Ishvara is the Absolute entering into the world of events and persons, operating at various levels but most freely in the world of souls. The religious sense that spiritual energy breaks through from another plane of being, modifying or transforming the chain of cause and effect, finds its fulfilment in the concept of Ishvara. As the Upanishad has it: 'The divine intelligence is the lord of all, the all-knower, the indwelling spirit, the source of all, the origin and end of all creation.'

In Hinduism the descriptions of the Supreme are many-sided and comprehensive. A catholic religion expresses itself in a variety of forms and comprehends all the relations which exist between man and God. Some of the great religions of the world select one or the other of the great relations, exalt it to the highest rank, make it the centre and relate all else to it. **They become so intolerant as to ignore the possibility of other relations and insist on one's acceptance of their own point of view as giving the sole right of citizenship in the spiritual world. But Hinduism provides enough freedom for a man to go forward and develop along his own characteristic lines. It recognizses that the divine light penetrates only by degrees and is distorted by the obscurity of the medium which receives it. Our conception of God answers to the level of our mind and interests. Hinduism admits that religion cannot be compressed within any juridical system or reduced to any single doctrine.**

Idolatry is a much abused term. Even those who oppose it are unable to escape from it. The very word brings up to our mind thoughts of graven images, strange figures of frightful countenances, horrid animals and shapes, and so long as the worshippers confuse these outer symbols with the deeper divine reality, they are victims of idolatry. But as a matter of fact, religion cannot escape from symbolism, from icons and crucifixes, from rites and dogmas. These forms are employed by religion to focus its faith, but when they become more important than the faith itself, we have idolatry. **A symbol does not subject the infinite to the finite, but renders the finite transparent. It aids us to see the infinite through it**. But the different religious groups, bound within themselves by means of rites and ceremonies, militate against the formation of a human society. Intuitive religion rebels against these communal and national gods, confident in the strength of the one spirit whose presence works and illuminates the whole of mankind.

The idea of *karma* has been with us from the beginning of philosophic reflection. Surely 'one becomes good by good action, and bad by bad action.' When a man dies, the two things that accompany him are *vidya* and *karma*. 'According as one acts, according as one conducts, so does one become.' Evolution of life goes on until salvation is attained.

Salvation or *mukti* is life eternal and has nothing to do with continuance in endless time. No adequate account of *mukti* can be given since it transcends the limitation with which human life is bound up. So the question of the nature of salvation, whether it is individual or universal, has no relevance or meaning when applied to life eternal, which is altogether a different life.

Sankara admits that the world-appearance persists for the *jivanmukta* or the *sthitaprajna* of the *Bhagavad-Gita*. The *jivanmukta*, though he realises *moksha* or *Brahmabhava*, still lives in the world. The appearance of multiplicity is not superseded. It is with him as with a patient suffering from *timira* that, though he knows there is only one moon, sees two. Only it does not deceive the freed soul, even as the mirage does not tempt one who has detected its unreal character. Freedom consists in the attainment of a universality of spirit or *sarvatma-bhava*. Sankara's view of the *jivanmukta* condition makes out that inner perfection and work in the finite universe can go together.

Two conditions are essential for final salvation: (1) inward perfection attained by intuition of self, and (2) outer perfection possible only with the liberation of all. The liberated souls which obtain the first condition continue to work for the second and will attain final release when the world as such is redeemed. To be saved in the former sense is to see the self all in all, to see all things. To be perfect is to be oneself, so that all might be saved. Commenting on the *Mundaka Upanishad* text (III. 2.5), Sankara says: 'He who has reached the all-penetrating Atman enters into the all.' Kumarila in his *Tantravartika* quotes Buddha as saying: 'Let all the sins of the world fall on me and let the world be saved.'

The liberated individual has the consciousness of the timeless infinite and, with that as his background, takes his place in the temporal world. He has what the seers called *trikaladristi,* an intuition of time in which past, present and future exist together for ever in the self-knowledge and self-power of the Eternal. He is no more swept helplessly on the stress of the moments. He lives in the consciousness of the universal mind and works for the welfare of the world in an unselfish spirit.

3

Culture: A Fusion of Four Races

The people and culture of India form a component, a mixture of at least four distinct types of humanity, which may loosely be called 'race'. With their various ramifications presenting distinct anthropological groupings, all may be brought under one or the other of the four kinds of 'Language-Culture' which we find in India from very ancient times .The Indian people is a mixed people, in blood, in speech, and in culture.

It has generally been accepted by competent scholars, both in India and abroad, who have been investigating into Indian civilisation, that **the fundamental trait of this civilisation may be described as Harmony of Contrasts, or as a Synthesis creating a Unity out of Diversity. Perhaps more than any other system of civilisation, it is broad and expansive and all-comprehensive, like life itself, and it has created an attitude of acceptance and understanding which will not confine itself to a single type of experience only, to the exclusion of all others.**

The name of the dominant race, Arya, very soon lost its narrow ethnic significance or application and became rather a word to denote nobility and aristocracy of character and temperament. With the general acceptance of the Aryan language in North India and with the admission of its prestige in the South as well, the fact that this language was profoundly modified within India by taking shape in a non-Aryan environment, reconciled the Dravidians and others to come under the tutelage of Sanskrit as the sacred language of Hinduism and as the general vehicle of Indian culture.

The oldest people to come into India belonged to the Negrito or **Negroid** race, who arrived in the eolith stage of their culture from Africa along the coast lands of Arabia and Iran and settled in Western and Southern India and spread over to Northern India, and passed on to Malaya and Indonesia. They were mostly killed off or absorbed by subsequent arrivals in India. They survive in a few tribes in South India where they now speak dialects of Tamil, and traces of them are found among the Mongoloid Nagas in Assam. A small number still retaining their language is isolated in the Andaman Islands which they reached in pre-historic times in their dugouts from the south-western tip of Burma, namely, Cape Negrais. The Negroids evidently passed away, leaving hardly any trace in Indian civilisation and among the Indian people.

After the Negroids there came to India from Palestine, the medium-sized, long-headed, snub-nosed and rather darkskinned **proto-Australoids**. Some of these passed out of India and found themselves as far as Australia, where their descendants still live as the Australian aborigines. Those who stayed on in India evidently became characterised into the Austric people, and developed their language and culture on the soil of India. Everywhere there has been mixture of the Austric people with those of other races—Negroids and Caucasoids. The Austrics of India were known in ancient India as Nishadas, and possibly also as Nagas as well as Kollas and Bhillas in post-Christian times. They were a dark-skinned people, speaking languages and dialects allied to Santhali, Mundari, Kurku, Gadaba and Savara, and to Khasi and Mon-Khmer dialects.

These Austrics were spread all over India, and they form the most important element among the lower classes or castes throughout the country. In the great plains of North India, they have merged into an Aryan-speaking people and have lost their name and their language. They gave some basic things in the material and spiritual domains to Indian civilisation, like the stick or hoe cultivation of rice and of some plants and vegetables, the domestication of the fowl, the taming of the elephant, the weaving of cotton, and some notions about future life which later were sublimated with the help of other elements into the doctrine of transmigration and *samsara*.

The **Mongoloid** peoples, with a number of different racial elements possessing certain common physical characteristics (yellow or yellow-brown skin, narrow or slant eyes, high cheek-bones, flat noses and paucity of hair on face), came into India probably before the Aryans who knew them as Kiratas. Evidence of their presence as far down as Mohenjo-Daro has been found. They entered into India from the east, along the course of the Brahmaputra river and its eastern tributaries, and also by way of Tibet, crossing the eastern Himalayas. They formed wide settlements throughout Assam, Bhutan and Nepal and also in East and north Bengal, north Bihar and the regions to the south of the Himalayas in north India right up to Kashmir. Some of them appear to have penetrated even further to the south—into Orissa and central India. The participation of the Kiratas in the common civilisation of India has been confined to the north and northeast only. But nevertheless, we have to take note of them as an important element in the formation of the Indian people in the extreme north, east and north-east, and in their participation in the development of Indian civilisation.

The next 'Language-Culture' group which came to India is believed to be the **Dravidian**. There is strong reason to think that the original Dravidian speakers came to India from the East Mediterranean region, from Asia Minor, and they were mainly a people of the Mediterranean race, mingled with other racial elements like the Armenoid which came with them—all of these apparently united by a common speech. These primitive Dravidian speakers of Mediterranean origin brought with them elements of religion and civilisation into India probably before 3500 B.C., and groups of them were settled in Mesopotamia and Persia—Iraq and Iran—before they became established in India. **They were a highly advanced people, and the city civilisation of India, as opposed to the village culture which was the creation of the Austrics was their great contribution.** The pre-Aryan people of the Punjab and Sindh, known to the Aryan invaders as Dasa and Dasyu and later as Shudra, who are believed to have built up the great city cultures like those of Harappa and Mohenjo-Daro, are now generally regarded as having been Dravidian in speech, religion and social and political organisation. The Brahuis of Balochistan appear to be just a remnant of a Dravidian-speaking bloc in Sindh, south Punjab and eastern Iran.

These Dravidian barbarians of unknown provenance, were in possession of the country when between 1500-1200 B.C. equally rude semi-nomad **Vedic Aryans** came into the field and established themselves as conquerors over all the pre-Aryan population. The Dravidians appear to have lived side by side with the Austric speakers in the great river-valleys of north India from Punjab to East Bengal and Assam, and with the Mongoloids also in the sub-Himalayan tracts. But they were able to make their language and culture paramount throughout the whole of central India and India to the south of the Vindhya mountains, many centuries before the Christian era — although the Dravidian speech retreated here also before the Aryan in post-Christian times. Place-names of non-Aryan origin all over northern India, where they are capable of analysis, suggest Dravidian and Austric as well as Sino-Tibetan elements, which are indicative of the presence of speakers of these languages in the land. **But the Dravidian is the most important of the non-Aryan elements in the civilisation of India and the basic culture of India is certainly over 50% Dravidian although expressed in the main through the Aryan language.**

Finally, we have the **Indo-Aryans**. The Indo-Aryans—Aryans, as they called themselves—were a section of the great Indo-Iranian (or Aryan) branch of the Indo-European speakers who became a powerful force and leaven in the civilisation of Middle and Western Asia and of Europe from about 2000 B.C. The original Indo-Europeans were characterised in the dry highlands to the south of the Ural mountains, probably before 3000 B. C. Groups of them went west, and in the moist lands of what is now Poland, developed the second phase of their culture which was the one which passed on further west into Eastern and Central, Northern and Western, and also Southern Europe. In all these lands the original Indo-European speech and civilisation were transformed into those of the Balts and the Slavs, the Celts and the Germans, and the Italians, Illyrians and Hellenes.

The Aryans are believed to have left the original homeland to the south of the Ural Mountains and to have come down, according to the two schools of opinion, either to Central Asia, or to the Caucasus regions and from there to Northern Mesopotamia. They left traces of their presence in the records of the local people in Mesopotamia and Eastern Asia Minor which have been unearthed and read, and these records give names and words in the Aryan language representing a pre-Vedic and pre-Avestan form of the speech. Some of their tribes pushed on to the east and settled in Iran, and others went further to the east and through eastern Iran they found themselves into India, and here we meet with them first, as Vedic Aryans. **The language they brought became an instrument of the greatest power in the setting up of Indian civilisation. It was the Vedic language, the Old Indo-Aryan speech which later on as Sanskrit was transformed into one of the greatest languages of civilisation, in which the composite culture of ancient India found its most natural vehicle.**

We have thus (not taking note of the extinct Negroid) these four great speeches and the culture-worlds of which they were the expressions, which came into contact, conflict and compromise with each other in ancient India when the ancient Indian or Hindu people was being formed between about 1500 and 1000 B. C. According to F. W. Thomas **it was 'the Vedic or Aryan period which witnesses the creation of the Indian Man'. A certain unique cohesion has been given to it by a philosophy which rises above the contradictory elements which have been sought to be accomodated to each other**. The persistent efforts of the best intellects of the country for all these 3000 years, from the time of 'the creation of the Indian Man' to harmonise everything with this synthesis, has been most remarkably successful.

Thus our great heritage, the Aryan speech, together with the Nordic and other Western elements in our population, particularly the mentality that is behind our Aryan speech, is our great link with Indo-European-speaking Europe and America. Our Dravidian elements are another link with the basic culture and people of Western Asia and the Mediterranean area; and the Austric bases of our people and culture have intimate connections with South-Eastern Asia, Indonesia and beyond. Through our Kirata or Mongoloid background in Northern and North-Eastern

India, we are not only neighbours but also kinsmen of the peoples of Eastern and Central Asia. Finally, through Indian Islam which has been a potent leaven in our civilisation for the last 750 years, we have more than a mere contact with the Arab and other Islamic lands; and during the last 300 years we have absorbed racial and cultural elements from modern Europe as well: the Luso-Indians, Anglo-Indians and other Indians of Eurasian origin, with the different forms of Christianity which they profess, represent this latest phase of the Indian people.

There has not been much mixing in people like pure-blooded Kashmiri Brahmins, Mongoloids like the Garos and Nagas, and Austrics like Santhals. **The Common Indian Man is ordinarily a brown man, pale or dark, either individually or in groups; he is not pure white, as the Aryan was, or pure yellow like the Kirata or black like the Nishada**. Although broadly he can be classified as long or middle or short-headed, straight or broad or flat-nosed, a general family likeness which marks him off from neighbouring peoples—Iranians or Burmese, Malays or Arabs—is discernible among the ordinary run of Indians, if he does not in his physical make-up go to any of the extremes.

No part of India was free from this racial admixture. Constant streams of North Indian Hindus, after the formation of the Hindu people, were going to the extreme east, to the Brahmaputra valley and Manipur, and even beyond, carrying Brahmanical civilisation with them. They were going to the Deccan and South India, as Brahmins and Kshatriyas, as merchants and settlers, soldiers and adventurers, and were merging into the Dravidian-speaking people in the more advanced areas. We may note the Nambudri Bramin leaven among the Nayars of Malabar as typical. In this way North and South and East and West in India were brought together by racial fusion. The 'Indian

Man' also pushed beyond the frontiers of India, by both land and sea.

As a pre-requisite to racial fusion, there must be first, linguistic assimilation; mingling of blood by marriage can only take place on a large scale when people of diverse origin accept one common language and conform to the culture-type of which that language is the expression. The Aryan's language supplied this need for a common speech to the Dravida, Nishada and Kirata, and the want of linguistic unity or cohesion among the non-Aryan peoples of ancient India gave to the language of the Aryan its great opportunity, apart from its prestige as the language of puissant *Conquistador* and from the inherent strength, expressiveness and beauty of the language itself.

It would appar that all non-Aryans within the framework of the Aryan (Brahmin) dominated society which was being developed were at first given the general name of Shudras and were relegated to an inferior position with considerable disabilities. But wealthy Shudras and those of them who were artisans and craftsmen and not merely tillers of the soil or followers of unclean trades, when they became Aryan-speakers, frequently got access within the group or caste of the Vaisyas, or were given at least equality of status with them.

Varna: or skin-colour—white or yellow or brown or black—was the basis of division of the diverse types of humanity in the first period when Aryan and Dasa, Kirata and Nishada, stood face to face with each other. Later, it became unmeaning with the invasion of the coloured elements into Aryandom, although tradition harking back to these very early times is still suspicious in present-day India of a black Brahmin and a fair Shudra. The skin-colour became irrelevant with racial mixture and there was a new theory of caste in which the original racialistic notion of the Vedic Aryan was lost; and it was only birth within a recognised profession or guild, that formed the essential argument for caste. The economic aspect rose superior to the racial, the social to the biological. Caste has been supported or tolerated by the Indian people as it generally helped the stability of their economic existence, all racial implications being lost.

Caste began to crystallise and become rigid with the establishment of Muslim state by the Turks. The Hindu states were destroyed and the Hindu social order under Brahmin domination lost its natural patrons in the Hindu aristocracy, yet Hindu culture was too strongly ingrained in the people to permit their being swept away by the flood of Muslim aggression. With its inherent force of inertia and its spirit of bowing before the storm, with the innate spirit of harmony among the various castes, **the Hindu body-politic resisted the threatened disintegration of itself through this Muslim impact by its method of a general non-co-operation. This non-co-operation was of a passive sort, and it meant having nothing to do socially with that unappreciative and unsympathetic foreign ruler, the Turki Muslim, and sometimes his client the *renoncant* Indian Muslim, and each caste unit in Hindu society offered opposition in a piecemeal fashion by stiffening itself up in self-defence and by becoming more rigid within itself.** This rigidity and non-co-operation became a force not only against the foreigner, but also vis-a-vis the other castes within its own world. With the passing of centuries this rigidity grew stronger and during the last two centuries, certain other new factors came in, which strengthened the present-day caste ideology which would regard miscegenation to be pernicious and reprehensible in a divinely ordained social order. The new factors were the growth of individualism in the place of collectivism; the tendency to the new type of economic exploitation; and a revival of orthodox notions and attendant snobbery with fantastic ideas of personal purity and caste pride.

In the development of the Aryan language in India, Austric (Kol or Munda, and Mon-Khmer) languages have exerted a considerable influence, particularly in vocabulary and idiom. The French orientalist Jean Przyluski has shown how a number of common words in Sanskrit like *karpasa, tambula, kadali, kambala, bana, langala, lakuta* etc. are of Austric origin, In the evolution of at least two modern Indo-Aryan sister-speeches in Bihar, the Maithili and the Magadhi, there has been a very likely influence of the Kol languages. The subject of the modification of the Aryan speech by the Kirata dialects has not been taken up properly, but it is very likely that a respectable Kirata vocabulary exists in indo-Aryan place-names and ordinary words, and there are Kirata influences in some present-day Aryan speech-habits also.

The nature of Dravidian influences over the Indo-Aryan is not superficial or just literary, but it is that of a substratum, profound and at the same time wide in scope. There has been through some 3,000 years a gradual approximation of the Aryan speech towards the Dravidian, in its system of sounds, in its trend in morphology, in vocabulary, and above all, its syntax or order of words. **In syntax, which is regarded as being of greater importance than Phonetics or Morphology, we find that Indian Dravidiandom and Aryandom are one. A sentence in a Dravidian language like Tamil or Kannada ordinarily becomes good Bengali or Hindi by substituting Bengali or Hindi equivalents for the Dravidian words and forms without modifying the word order.**

We find that the Aryan speech has been borrowing words from the Dravidian even since the former made its advent into India. The study of the Dravidian loan-words in Indo-Aryan forms an important subject of Indian linguistics. Some of the commonest words of Indo-Aryan are from this source.

In the Vedic period, there were just scattered islands of Aryan speech in the Punjab and Gangetic India, in a land of Dasas, Dasyus and Shudras, of Nishadas and Nagas, and of Kiratas. By the middle of the first millennium B.C. the tables were turned, and in the time of Buddha, the country from Gandhara to Magadha was mainly Aryan-speaking, with islands of Dasa or Shudra and Nishada or Naga speech in the countryside and beside the virgin forests of Northern India.

The non-Aryan languages gradually died out in northern India probably for these reasons: (1) the prestige of the Aryan speech which had established itself in the country and to which the allegiance of the conquered peoples was a matter of course; (2) absence of cohesion among the polyglot non-Aryans and the coming of Aryan speech to the forefront as a very convenient *lingua franca*; (3) the spirit of *laissez faire* and an evident policy of non-intervention and the policy of letting the non-Aryan speeches have their own way while ignoring them in all domains of serious study; (4) the liberal policy of Brahmins resulting in the gradual and unrestricted entry, mostly by the backdoor, of a large non-Aryan vocabulary first in Vedic and in the Prakrits and then in the Classical Sanskrit; (5) the fact that Sanskrit became the vehicle of a great composite culture, which helped to maintain its supreme position in the new Indian population, directed more or less by groups like the Brahmins boasting of a pure Aryan tradition; (6) the early development of a literature in Sanskrit through the collection of Vedic hymns and sacrificial texts, and through the redaction of masses of national legendary and semi-historical tales and traditions as in the Puranas, which gave to Sanskrit an immense advantage over other languages;

(7) the likely non-existence of any effective linguistic or cultural patriotism among the non-Aryan groups in Northern India, particularly when the Brahmins were able to give a theory of society which ignored the racial and linguistic aspects and included the whole of Indian humanity within a single scheme; and (8) the inherent beauty and force of the Aryan language which fulfilled the intellectual requirements of the Indian Man and satisfied his aesthetic sense.

The Aryans, while living in the drier and colder lands of Iran and Northern Mesopotamia, were, as a people, partly nomadic and partly agricultural, and they had built up a way of life which they had perforce to change profoundly in the country of India which in those days was much more wooded, even in Punjab and in Sindh, and much moister than Iran. Their food, dress and habitation, everything had to be altered according to the requirements of their new home and the climate.

The food of the Aryans as of their kinsmen the Greeks of Hellas consisted mostly of meat and barley and milk preparations of various kinds and honey was a great delicacy with them. They partook freely of , and offered to their gods as well, a kind of spirituous drink called *soma*, made from some plant which grew in the hills, which was pounded between two stones and mixed with milk. Barley they knew in their primitive homeland to the south of the Ural mountains, and wheat they would appear to have found in Mesopotamia; and either in Eastern Iran or in India they found the rice, and various kinds of lentils, which quickly became popular with the Aryans in India, more than wheat. The typical Indian food at the present day is rice (or wheaten bread in the Punjab and in the Upper Ganges Valley, or some kind of inferior grain like the millet in the poorer areas) eaten with lentils of various sorts, seasoned with butter or oil and with spices, and with some milk product, if that can be afforded. In the coast lands and in the predominantly Mongoloid eastern tracts, however, the main diet consists of rice and fish. The old Aryan habit of eating meat regularly and plentifully, gradually became restricted or abandoned, through milk as well as vegetarian food being plentiful in the land and more suited to the warmer climate of India, and through ideas of non-injury to life (*Ahimsa)* which came to dominate the life of the mixed Indian people from after 1000 B.C.

The dress of the Vedic Aryans consisted of garments of wool, linen and skin, with some prominent kind of head-dress for men, and wimples for women, as well as sandals of leather, and the whole body was fully covered. The dress of Persian men and women in Achaemenian sculpture may reasonably be taken to be representative of the old Aryan dress. It is likely that coming as they did from a cold climate, some sewn garments at least were in use among the Aryans. In India, although some very elaborate types of head-dress and ornaments (often made with cowrie shells) for both men and women are noticed in the art of the pre-Christian times, the basic dress consisted of two (or three) pieces of unsewn cotton cloth, one being used as the loincloth, one as a covering for the upper body and the third as a turban for the head. Women's dress had only two pieces—one for the lower limbs from the waist to the ankle, more or less in the style of the Indonesian *sarong*, and another as a covering for the upper part, but the breasts were generally left exposed, as in Malabar until recently.

The Vedic Aryan wore a beard and had long hair, and the hair for convenience was made into a knot at the top of the head. The Buddhist and Jaina, indicating a reaction against the Aryanism of the Brahmins, enjoyed complete shaving of the head and face, and this, with the addition of a top-knot, became later on the accepted custom among

Brahmin householders also.

The household furniture—pots, cups, receptacles and vessels, spoons and ladles, were at first mainly of wood among the Indian Aryans, as among their kinsmen like the Slavs, the Germans and Greeks of ancient times. Skins were also used for storing food and drink. The pre-Aryan people seem to have preferred earthenware, and for temporary use earthenware became generally adopted in Aryan-speaking Indian society as well. Bronze and copper vessels were known to the Aryans, and these also came to have a greater vogue in India when vessels of an enduring character were required. In Vedic sacrifices the old custom of having vessels, cups, goblets, spoons, ladles etc. of wood, and not of metal or terracotta, was continued as an antique practice and therefore sacrosanct.

4

Buddhism and the Upanishads

In Buddha's time, there were many wandering teachers, who went about from place to place giving an exposition of their particular doctrines and challenging their opponents to public discussions. Out of many such teachers the Buddha selected six teachers for his special attention. He criticised their doctrines in an unsparing manner. We thus come to know definitely that there were certain views which he did not accept. For instance, he was against the view held by Purana Kassapa,the doctrine of Ahetuvada or fortuitous origin of things. In other words, he did not believe that events can happen without a cause or that something can originate from nothing. If good and bad conduct happened just by chance—the soul remaining passive all the time—there was, in that case, no merit in virtune and no harm in murder. The Buddha did not accept the doctrine of complete indeterminism.

Nor did he believe in complete fatalism, as his criticism of the doctrine of Makkali Goshala shows. According to Goshala, things happen in a predestined way and human effort cannot do anything to hasten the process. This doctrine also, according to the Buddha, frees a person of all responsibilities and has a paralysing effect on moral effort.

The Buddha similarly criticised the extreme materialism of Ajita Kesakambali, according to whom all objects arise out of the combination in different proportions, of four material elements, the soul having no separate existence apart from them. It is born with the body and dies with the death of the body. The Buddha regards this theory of annihilationism as a perverse doctrine from the moral point of view.

He similarly criticised Sanjaya for his thorough, going scepticism, and Nigantha Nataputta for making certain definite statements about matters on which no such statements could be made on account of the limitation of human powers.

The last of the doctrines which he criticised was that of Pakudha Kaccayana who believed in a number of eternal substances, soul being one of them. Out of the coming together of these eternal substances under the influence of the principles of pleasure and pain, various objects and organisms in the world take their rise. While the objects appear and disappear, the elements of which they are constituted continue to exist for ever. The Buddha calls it the doctrine of eternalism and directs his criticism against it as well. According to him, there are no eternally-existing finite souls nor eternally-existing material atoms.

There were also many sages and thinkers who followed the Upanishadic way of thought. We meet with many divergent views in the Upanishads, but there was undoubtedly present a dominant Upanishadic philosophy as well. It is apparent that the Buddha did not criticise the main doctrines of the Upanishads as he had done in the case of other contemporary thought systems; nor has he made any direct reference to them. While he was enunciating his own doctrine of spiritual enlightenment, perhaps the term Upanishad had not yet become as well-known as it became later on. We know that the Gita owes much of its thought to the Upanishads, but there is no direct reference to them in it . There are, however, many points of kinship between the main doctrines of the Upanishads and those of the Buddha. There is every likelihood that the Buddha was influenced by the thought of the Upanishads in formulating his own system of thought. It stands to reason, that just as he had studied the views of the teachers whom he subjected to a critical examination, he had similarly studied the important Upanishadic thought.

The approach of the Buddha towards the religious problem is undoubtedly original; but it is strange to find that almost all of his teachings are found in the Upanishads as well, though the emphasis on the various points is differently distributed in the two systems. The Upanishads start with a theoretical enunciation of the nature of Ultimate Reality. In fact, for the thinkers of the Upanishads, this seemed to be the main problem and the other problems of life revolved round it as the planets revolve round the sun. The approach of the Buddha was different. He started with the practical problem of suffering and how to get rid of it. But though his approach was different, his basic ideas were largely similar to those of the Upanishads.

It can be said, without any fear of contradiction, that **the elements of a religious life are the same in both the systems, but they have been mixed together in different ways, according to the temperaments of the thinkers who gave birth to these systems.** Both the Upanishad thinkers and the Buddha expressed their disapproval in an explicit or implicit manner, of animal sacrifices and extreme asceticism.. Both of them welcomed persons of all castes to the search for spiritual enlightenment. Persons of all castes could become members of the order of monks founded by the Buddha. We find similarly in the Upanishads Brahmins, Kshatriyas and even low-born Shudras being freely admitted into spiritual discipleship, and in their turn becoming sages and teachers imparting their knowledge to other aspirants. We find in both systems an emphasis on sorrow and suffering; in both desire or *trisna* is regarded as the cause of bondage and sorrow, and which itself is due to *avidya* or ignorance. In both it is declared that the end of sorrow takes place on the dawning of true knowledge and this state of enlightenment is known as *nirvana* in Buddhism and *moksa* in the Upanishads. In both Buddhism and Upanishads belief is held in the impermanence of ego, in the law of *karman* and of transmigration from birth to birth till freedom from *avidya* and *trisna* is attained . Both of them enjoin a life of morality and goodness and the practice of certain yogic exercises of concentration as means of spiritual enlightenment.

The presence of so many points of resemblance cannot be dismissed as merely accidental or as a happy coincidence.One can safely conclude that of all the contemporary systems of thought, which Buddha found around himself, he was strongly impressed by the thought of the Upanishads. But an original and profound thinker as he was, he gave a new form to these common ingredients. The Buddha had been struck with the vanity and fruitlessness of metaphysical discussions, which were so plentiful in his time . In the Upanishads we, no doubt, come across discussions as to the nature of Ultimate Reality, but we also meet in them a realisation that mere metaphysical speculation leads nowhere, unless the aspirant persistently and earnestly follows certain spiritual practices. The Buddha did not deny the existence of Ultimate Reality, but he simply deprecated, from the point of view of practical realisation, too much pre-occupation with metaphysical problems. Here he differed from the Upanishads in as much as the latter show a deep interest in philosophical discussions.

The law of *karman* is an accepted principle is Buddhism. White deeds result in white fruits and black deeds in black fruits. Along with the law of *karman* goes the belief in transmigration. There is a form of literature in Buddhism known as Avadana, in which the stories of present and past lives of various persons are narrated and each story is followed by a moral to illustrate the principle that the joys and sufferings of each individual depend upon the deeds which he had performed in this life or in previous lives. *Avadana Shataka* is a collection of hundred such stories. There are stories of men and animals who had been reborn as gods in heaven as a consequence of their pious deeds. The moral of the story is always given in the following words: "So, O monks, the fruit of quite black deeds is quite black, that of quite white deeds is quite white, that of mixed deeds is mixed. Therefore, O monks, give up the black and the mixed deeds and take pleasure only in the quite white deeds....."

The *Jataka* tales are also a form of Avadana literature, in which all stories refer to the previous lives of the Buddha himself. These stories are also sometimes known as *karman* stories, because they narrate the consequences of *karmans* performed by an individual in his previous life. There is a collection of hundred stories known as *Karma-Shataka* written on the same lines as *Avadana Shataka*. It is found now only in its Tibetan translation. The underlying idea of all these stories is to convey the truth that the destiny of all men is governed by the forces set in motion by their own *karman* in past lives, whether they understand the law or do not understand it . The laws of *Karman* and transmigration as preached by the Buddha are on the same lines as expounded in the Upanishads.

The Buddhist doctrine of the impermanence of Self has landed some Western and Eastern scholars into a difficulty mostly of their own creation. A human being, according to the Buddha, consists of five *Skandhas: Rupa, Vedana, Samjna* and *Vijnana*. They are severally and collectively impermanent and transitory as they are devoid of Atman. It is known as the Nairatmya theory. In the second sermon given by the Buddha, he says to his disciples what they should think in regard to each one of the *Skandhas*: "This is not mine, I am not this, this is not *Atman*." From this it came to be inferred, that the Buddha did not believe in the existence of soul. So these authors tried to explain the Buddha's theory of *Karman* and transmigration in curious ways. We, however, know that wherever Buddha speaks of his own previous births, or the effects of *karman* performed in previous births, it is clearly mentioned that the same individual passes from one birth to another, and reaps the consequences of his own actions previously performed. There is no doubt that the Buddha and his followers accepted the continuity of personal identity between one life and the next. If the notion of personal continuity is left out, the whole idea of transmigration becomes absurd and altogether unreasonable. When Buddha describes one of his own previous lives as narrated in the *Jataka Mala*, he always says at the end of the story that he himself was the hero described in the story and no other. It is distinctly stated in the *Digha Nikaya*, that of the five *Skandhas* the last *Skandha*, i.e., *vijnana* or consciousness continues to exist after death and enters the mother's womb for the next rebirth." We are told in *Samjutta Nikaya* that Mara, the Deva of desire and death, could not find the *vijnana* of Godhika and Vakkali, after the death of those monks, though he looked for it everywhere. They had attained final and complete *nirvana* and their *vijnana* was not reinstated in a new embryo. *Vijnana* thus corresponds to the soul as this latter word is understood by most non-Buddha religious teachers.

But the Buddha did not regard this enduring entity from birth to birth as unchangeable, permanent or eternally self existent .We already know that he was against the view of the Samkhyas, the Jainas and others who accepted the existence of certain eternal substances. This point of view, therefore, seems to go against the view expressed in the Upanishads, namely, that the *atman* is immoral. Such statements occur in a number of places in the Upanishads. But the terms *atman* and *Brahman* are used interchangeably in all important Upanishads. It is quite possible that in some Upanishads the view may have been expressed like that of Pakudha Kaccayana, namely, that the individual soul is immortal and unchangeable; but the general trend of the teachings of the Upanishads is that the individual soul or ego is impermanent and is composed of consciousness and mental adjuncts. As long as the mental adjuncts or *upadhis* remain attached to consciousness, it transmigrates from body to body, the adjuncts gradually becoming thinner and thinner till their complete eradication, the illusion of individuality and egohood is destroyed and the soul realises its identity with the Universal Spirit. There is, thus, practically no difference between the Buddhist doctrine of the transient and unsubstantial ego and the Upanishadic view of individual soul. **The Buddha speaks of the components or adjuncts of ego as *Rupa, Vedana, Samjna, Samskaras,* and *Vijnana*. In the Upanishads they are described as the five *Kosas—Annamaya, Pranamaya, Manomnaya, Vijnanamaya* and *Anandamaya*. The terms used are different but the meaning is more or less the same.** As the ego reaches perfection the *Kosas* drop off and the ego loses its separateness in the Universal Reality. The idea of the absorption of the individual ego into Absolute Reality in Buddhist thought is brought home to us in its conception of *nirvana* or final deliverance.

Buddha gave no discourses on the existence of God. There were many teachers in the time of the Buddha who were fond of holding public discussions on metaphysical problems. It was clearly realised by the Upanishadic thinkers also, that the Ultimate Reality cannot be known by logical thinking but only by direct experience which comes as a result of living a certain kind of life and practising certain meditational exercises. The Upanishadic thinkers, however, in spite of this realisation, could not resist the temptation to engage in intellectual discussions about the nature of the Supreme Reality and man's relation to it. The Buddha, unlike the teachers of the Upanishads, firmly refused to have anything to do with philosophical questions and confined himself strictly to his practical programme of spiritual realisation.

It would be wrong to infer from this, that he had reached no conclusions of his own in regard to these problems or that his knowledge was only confined to the things which he taught to his disciples. Another thing is that he did not, at any time, make any positive denial of Supreme Reality. If he disbelieved in such a Reality nothing could have prevented him from making a definite declaration to this effect. Therefore the prima facie conclusion that can be drawn from the silence of the Buddha is that he had some sort of belief in Supreme Reality, but he forbore to express his views on it. He felt that if he, once in a weak moment, yielded to the temptation of taking sides in a controversy, there would be no end to it throughout his life-time.

Though he did not avow his faith in so many words, we have plenty of indirect evidence, which throws light on his belief in Spiritual Reality. The description of *nirvanic* experience which the Buddha gives in a number of places leaves no doubt on this point. The following passage from the *Udana* deserves to be quoted in order to clinch the point:

> "There is, monks, an unborn, an unbecome, an uncompounded; if, monks, there were not this

> unborn, unbecome, unmade, uncompounded, there would not here be an escape from the born, the become, the made, the compounded.. But because there is an unborn, an unbecome, an unmade, an uncompounded, therefore there is an escape from the born, the become, the made, the compounded."

It should be clear that the law of righteousness can operate only if the Ultimate Reality is spiritual. In a materialistic universe, moved solely by blind forces, there can be no scope for the law of righteousness or Dharma. This emphasis on Dharma or *Rta* and its identity with Reality or Satya comes right down from the Vedic times.

Gautama Buddha laid a rigorous ban upon himself in regard to metaphysical speculations, but the thinkers of the Mahayana school made free use of metaphysical speculations, which took them in the direction of idealistic systems of thought. Alaya Vijnana or absolute consciousness became the Supreme Reality and God came to be worshipped in the name of Dharma Kaya, and even as Vairocana, Amitabha, etc. It would be wrong to suppose that the idealistic philosophy was an innovation of the Mahayana thinkers, or that they introduced into Buddhism something which was foreign to the spirit of the original founder of the religion. They only made explicit, what was already implicitly present in the teachings of the Buddha. The ban imposed by the founder upon philosophical thinking could be observed no longer and so the latent spirituality in Buddhism which in the beginning was only hinted at as *nirvana* or Dharma, blossomed forth into a full-fledged idealistic system bearing a great resemblance to the Vedanta of Upanishads, so much so that Shankara, that great protagonist of later day Vedanta, borrowed many of his ideas from the Buddhist systems of thought.

5

The Incredible Jaina Philosophy

The history of Jainism goes back to an ancient period, and its doctrines have arisen out of early currents of thought of Eastern India which also gave rise to systems of philosophy like the early Samkhya and Buddhism. The metaphysical start is practically the same in Jainism and Samkhya, though the subsequent details are differently worked out; and the monastic institutions of Jainism and Buddhism show much that is common, though their philosophical outlook is not the same.

Reality, according to Jainism, is uncreated and eternal: and it is characterised by origination or appearance (*utpada*), destruction or disappearance (*vyaya*) and permanence (*dhrauvya*). Every object of reality is found possessed of infinite characters both with respect to what it is and what it is not. It has its modes (*paryaya*) and qualities (*guna*), through which persists the essential substratum through all the times. The basic substance with its qualities is something that is permanent, while the modes or accidental characters appear and disappear. Thus both change and permanence are facts of experience. The soul or spirit, for instance, is eternal with its inseparable character of consciousness, but at the same time, it is subjected to accidental characters like pleasure and pain and superimposed modes such as body etc, both of which are changing constantly. Gold, for instance, with its colour and density is something that is permanent though subjected to different shapes at different times.

The substances are real, characterised by existence, and they are six in number. They can be broadly divided into living (*jiva*) and non-living (*ajiva*). The *jiva* means soul or spirit. It is essentially a unit of consciousness and there is an infinity of them. The souls can be classified into those that are in bondage (*baddha*) and those that are free (*mukta*). Those in bondage may possess only one sense organ or more than one, the former being associated with earth, water, fire, wind and plants, and the latter differing among themselves according to the number of the senses.

The class of non-living substances is made up of matter (*pudgala*), principles of motion and rest (*dharma* and *adharma*), space (*akasa*) and time (*kala*). Though all these are characterised by existence, the constitution of time is slightly different: it has no extension in space, but is made up of partite units. Matter is the non-living stuff possessed of sense-qualities with varied functions and form; the principles of motion and rest facilitate all movements or static states in this physical universe; all these substances are accomodated in space; and it is the principle of time that marks continuity or change. These substances are eternally existing, uncreated and with no beginning in time. As substances they are eternal and unchanging, but their modifications are passing through a flux of changes . Their mutual co-operation and interaction explain all that we imply by the term 'creation'; and **Jainism, therefore, admits no intelligent Creator who can be credited with the making of this universe.**

Consciousness (*chetana*) is the very essence of the soul which is potentially endowed with infinite vision, infinite knowledge, infinite power and infinite bliss. But all these are suppressed in the case of mundane souls, because they are bound by subtle matter, namely *karman*, a sort of energy as it were, which obscures their power. The destiny of the soul in transmigration is governed by *karman*. Every thought, word or act of the individual fashions a certain state of the soul, as a result of which there is the influx of *karman* of various types and sub-types. The *karmic* matter shapes itself into a subtle body and clings to the soul and binds it in a circuit of births as gods, men, denizens of hell and sub-human beings. By cultivating pure thoughts and acts, the influx of *karman*, both good and bad, has to be consumed by religious austerities; when the *karmas* are completely destroyed, the soul becomes liberated with all its potential qualities fully developed. This liberated and perfect soul is an embodiment of infinite knowledge and bliss.

The doctrine of *karman* is an original and integral part of Jainism, and it goes a long way to prove how Jainism is older than Buddhism. **The Jaina *karma* doctrine is an elaborate system, most meticulously worked out showing how different *karmic* energies become operative or inoperative in the spiritual career of the mundane soul from its lowest state to final liberation.** It is made to explain all the vicissitudes of life. Just as the interacting eternal substances postulated in Jainism admit no Creator, so also the inviolable law of *karman* makes man the master of his destiny and dispenses with the favourite theistic idea that some divinity bestows on man favours and frowns.

The soul or spirit being essentially constituted of consciousness, the act of knowing is just the manifestation by the soul of its intrinsic nature. This consciousness is something like the sun's light, able to manifest itself as well as to enlighten other objects, unless obstructed by *karman*. Every soul thus is potentially omniscient. Omniscience is fully manifested in the case of liberated souls, while mundane souls have different degrees of limited knowledge due to the hindrance of *karmas*. The body, the sense organs, the mind (*manas*) are all material and the results of *karman*; and they counteract omniscience. The types of knowledge manifested in the soul mark in a way the stages of its spiritual development.

There are five types of knowledge (*jnana*): (i) *mati*, which refers to sense experience and covers perception through the activities of sense-organs (including mind) and the inferential knowledge based in these, (ii) *shruta*, which is the knowledge revealed by scriptures; (iii) *avadhi*, which is clairvoyant perception that enables one to perceive material objects and events of distant time and place, and which has varying scope and degrees according to the qualification of the individual; (iv) *manahparyaya*, telepathic knowledge, whereby one knows the thoughts in the minds of others, and when is the result of meritorious austerities etc, and (v) *kevala*, the unique or the perfect knowledge, which is revealed in the soul when the obstructive *karmas* are destroyed and wherein the process of knowing is without spatial and temporal limitations.

Understanding or the acquisition of knowledge (*adhigama*) is attained by means of *pramana* (instruments of knowledge) and *naya* (points of view). This five types of knowledge, noted above, constitute the *pramana*. In the last three types, the process of knowing is directly by the soul or spirit, without the aid of sense-faculties; and they are called, therefore, immediate or direct (*pratyaksa*) instruments. The last two and even a variety of the third (*avadhi*) are necessarily infallible. The first two are indirect or mediate (*paroksa*); herein there is no direct perception by the soul, but it is through the aid of the intervening medium of the sense-organs. These can be authentic as well as liable to error.

It is seen above that according to Jaina philosophy, the object of knowledge is a huge complexity, constituted of substances, qualities and modifications extended over three times and infinite space, and simultaneously subjected to origination, destruction and permanence. Such an object can by fully comprehended only in omniscience which is not manifested in the case of worldly beings who perceive through their organs of senses. But the senses are the indirect means of knowledge and whatever they apprehend is partial like the perception of an elephant by seven blind persons; each one touches only a part of the animal and concludes that the animal is like a log of wood, like a fan, like a wall, etc. The ordinary human being, therefore, cannot rise above the limitations of his senses; so his apprehension of reality is partial, and it is valid only from a particular point of view: this leads to the Nayavada of the Jainas. In describing different ornaments, one's attention is directed towards the modes or modifications of gold, that is the modal point of view (*paryayarthika-naya*); and when one describes gold with regard to its substance and inherent qualities,that is the substantial point of view (*dravyarthika-naya*). On par with these but in spiritual discussions we have the common sense or practical point of view (*vyavahara-naya*) and the realistic point of view (*niscaya-naya*). Going into further details there are seven *nayas*; some refer to the substance and others to modifications; and some arise out of the nature of the subject and some out of the verbal statement.

A thing, or the object of knowledge, is of infinite characters (*anekantatmaka*) which require to be analysed and apprehended individually; that is the function of the *nayas*. Individually the *nayas* reveal only a part of totality and it should not be mistaken for the whole. Because of this infinite-fold constitution of a thing, there can be infinite points of view; and the same are classified as seven, two, etc. **This *Nayavada* is a unique instrument of analysis. The Jaina philosopher has taken the fullest advantage of**

it not only in building his system by a judicious search and balance of various viewpoints, but also in understanding sympathetically the views of others from whom he differs and in appreciating why there is difference between the two. This analytical approach to reality has saved him from extremism, dogmatism and fanaticism, and has further bred in him a remarkable intellectual toleration, a rare virtue indeed.

It is not enough if various problems about reality are merely understood from different points of view. What one knows, one must be ale to state truly and accurately. This need is met with by the famous theory of *Syadvada* in Jainism. The object of knowledge is a huge complexity covering infinite modes and related to three times; the human mind is of limited understanding; and human speech has its imperfections in expressing the whole range of experience. Under these circumstances all our statements are conditionally or relatively true . So Jaina logic insists on qualifying every statement with the term *syat,* i.e., 'somehow' or 'in a way' to emphasise its conditional or relative character. Such a qualification is to be always understood whether a term like *syat* is added or not. A judgement, ordinarily speaking, can assume two forms, affirmative and negative, and as a reference to the substance (*dravya*), place (*kshetra*), time (*kala*) and shape or concept *(bhava)* of an object. An affirmative judgement predicates the characters possessed by a thing, while the negative one denies characters absent in this but belonging to others. Besides these two judgements, namely, 'Somehow S is P' and 'Somehow S is not P', Jaina logic admits a third kind of judgement, namely, that of indescribability, 'Somehow S is indescribable'.

This is of great philosophical significance. In view of complex objectivity, limited knowledge and imperfect speech, the Jaina logic admits situations which cannot be described in terms of plain 'yes' or 'no'. A thing cannot be described at all when no distinction of standpoints and aspects can be made. Some aspect can be affirmed or denied separately from a certain point of view, or both affirmed and denied successively. But when this predication is to be made simultaneously, one is faced with contradiction which can be wisely avoided by the third judgement of 'indescribability'. These three are the basic predication; and when they are combined successively and simultaneously, the maximum number of combinations is seven and not more. Naturally these should be able to answer every purpose however complex it may be. Thus we have the following seven conditional predications:

(i) somehow S is P; (ii) somehow S is not P; (iii)somehow S is indescribable; (iv) somehow S is P and is also not P: (v) somehow S is P and is also indescribable; (vi) somehow S is not P and is also indescribable; and lastly, (vii) somehow S is P, and also is not P, and is also indescribable.

The ultimate goal of Jaina ethics is the realisation of *nirvana* or *moksa* which consists in completely liberating the soul from the *karmas*. Right Faith, Right Knowledge and Right Conduct collectively constitute the path of liberation. To set the *atman* free from *karmas, karmic* influx has to be stopped and the *karmic* stock to be destroyed . This whole process demands purity of thought, words and acts; and it becomes possible by observing a code of morality which is less rigorous in the case of householders but more rigorous for monks.

There are these five vows (*vrata*): (1) abstention from violence or injury to living beings (*ahimsa*); (2) abstention from false speech (*satya*); (3) abstention from theft (*asteya*); (4) abstention from sexuality (*brahmacharya*); and (5) abstention from greed for worldly possessions (*aparigraha*). The principle of *ahimsa* is the logical outcome of the Jaina metaphysical theory that **all the souls are potentially equal. No one likes pain. Naturally one should not do unto others what one does not want others to do unto one. The social implications of this principle of reciprocity are profoundly beneficial. In no other Indian religion the doctrine of *ahimsa* is explained as systematically as in Jainism.**

Violence or injury is of three kinds: physical violence, which covers killing, wounding and causing any physical pain; violence in words consists in using harsh words; and mental violence implies bearing ill-feeling towards others. Further it may be committed, commissioned or consented to. A householder is unable to avoid all these in an ideal manner, so he is expected to cause minimal injury to others. In view of the routine of society in which we have to live, injury is classified under four heads: first, there is accidental injury in digging, pounding, cooking and such other activities essential to daily living; secondly, there is occupation injury when a soldier fights, an agriculturist tills the land, etc; thirdly, there is protective injury when one protects one's or other's life and honour against wild beasts and enemies; and lastly, there is intentional injury when one kills simply for killing them as in hunting or butchery.

A householder is expected to abstain fully from intentional injury and as far as possible from the rest. It is the intention or the mental attitude that matters more than the act. So one has to take utmost care in keeping one's intentions pure and pious and abstain from intentional injury. Binding, hitting, mutilating, overloading and starving animals are various forms of injury. The fifth vow has a great social significance. By limiting his possessions, the householder is expected to spend his additional earnings in helping the poor and needy by fourfold gifts: food, shelter, medicine and books. The detailed practical instructions to him are many; he is asked, among other's, to avoid the following: withholding food and drink from any animal or human being; spreading false views; divulging other's secrets; preparing forged documents; misappropriating deposits; receiving stolen properties; illegal traffic; using false weights and measures; adulteration, etc. These put a restriction on his profession and mould a humanistic outlook on society.

A layman progresses further in his spiritual career by observing seven more vows; (i) he limits the distance up to which he would go in this or that direction (*digvrata*); (ii) he abstains from wanton sinful activities (*anarthadanda-viramana*); (iii) he restricts enjoying consumable and non-consumable articles (*bhogopabhoga-parimana*). The next four vows take him still further in his practice of self-denial, self-control and renunciation: (iv) he limits the area of his activities (*desavakasika*); (v) with minimum possessions a layman retires to a quiet spot at stated times, and for the time being he renounces worldly attachment and aversion and cultivates the meditational mood of mental equipoise (*samayika*); (vi) on four days in a month, he observes complete fast and more rigorous, religious life (*prosadhopavasa*); and lastly (vii) he shares the food with guests, namely, the pious and holy persons that come to his house at the proper time and also renders them necessary aid in their religious practices (*atithisamvibhaga*). A close study of these vows reveals the fact that a layman is virtually participating, to a limited extent and for a limited period of time, in the routine of a monk without actually renouncing the world.

According to Jainism, **dying is as much an art as living. A layman is expected to live not only a disciplined life but also die bravely a detached death. There are elaborate rules about voluntary death (*sallekhana*) which has been practised not only by Jaina monks but also by pious**

laymen; and we have inmumerable inscriptions commemorating such deaths of pious Jains. The volunary death is to be distinguished from suicide which Jainism looks upon as a cowardly sin. When faced by calamity, famine, old age and disease against which there is no remedy, a pious Jaina peacefully relinquishes his body. With a pure mind, he rises above love and hatred, and relinquishes attachment and possessions; he forgives all and asks his kinsmen and attendants to forgive him before his life ends. After recounting and confessing his sins and avoiding all sorts of distractions, he sets his mind on a high pitch of peace. First he should stop taking solid food and take only liquid food for some time; then gradually he should pass on to pure water; and finally he should observe complete fasting and give up his body with his mind occupied by religious meditation.

In their outward form and equipment we see some different schools among the Jaina monks. The Digambara monk, who goes about naked, has a *kamandalu* (a gourd pot) to carry water and a bunch of peacock feathers for cleansing the seat etc. But if he belongs to the lower stage, he has the minimum clothing to cover his nudity. A *Svetambara* monk is clad in white robes, and he is equipped with a staff, a bunch of wool and wooden pots. They differ here and there in the rules of outward behaviour which affect their mode of touring, eating etc. The inner religious life, however, is fundamentally the same for the various schools.

The five smaller vows of a layman, namely, not to kill, not to lie, to abstain from sex-life and to renounce property, are called the Great Vows in the case of a monk who has to observe them with the maximum rigour and thoroughness. His one aim is to stop the influx of fresh *karman* and to destroy all that has already bound him. The flow of *karmas* into the *atman* or soul is caused by the activities of body, speech and mind, so it is necessary for him to keep these channels under strict control (*gupti*). The monk must be very cautious in walking, speaking, begging food, taking up and putting down things and in voiding the body (*samiti*). It is mainly due to the passion that the soul assimilates *karman*; so anger, pride, deception and greed must be counteracted by cultivating ten virtues (*dasadharma*), namely, forgiveness, humility, straightforwardness, contentment, truthfulness, restraint, austerities and renunciation.

To cultivate the necessary religious attitude he should constantly reflect on twleve religlous topics, (*anupreksa*) namely, everything is transitory, men are helpless against death etc, the circuit of existence is full of misery, the soul has to struggle all alone, the relatives and others are quite separate, the body is impure, the *karman* is constantly inflowing, the *karman* should be stopped by cultivating necessary virtues, the *karman* should be destroyed by penances, the nature of the universe, the rarity of religious knowledge, and lastly, the true nature of religion.

The last but not the least routine of a monk consists in wisely practising penances or austerities (*tapas*). He should not be tempted and stopped in the middle by acquiring miraculous powers etc.; his one aim is to reach *nirvana* or *moksa*. Penance is twofold, external referring to food and physical activities, and internal , referring to spiritual discipline, each of which is of six kinds. Meditation or contemplation (*dhyana*) is the most important spiritual exercise whereby alone the soul progresses on to higher *gunasthanas* and destroys all the *karmas*.

It is clear from the Jaina metaphysics that **there is no place in Jainism for God as a creator and distributor of prizes and punishments. By God Jainism understands a**

liberated soul as well as the *Tirthankara,* who is the highest spiritual ideal after which every soul can aspire. Jainas offer prayers to his worship both in concept and in concrete, and meditate on him. Respectful prayers are offered to the *Tirthankara,* the preceptor, preacher and monk. Such a routine keeps one vigilant about one's ideal and strengthens one's heart, warning every time that one is to depend on oneself to destroy the *karmas.* Jainism is thus the religion of self-help and can be practised by the self-reliant and brave.

6

The Doctrine of Karma: Common Factor

The doctrine of *karma* is of great antiquity in India. It gradually broke away from Vedic naturalism, mysticism and piety. All the Indian systems believe that whatever action is done by an individual, it leaves behind some sort of potency which gives him sorrow or pleasure in the future. The notion prevalent in the Samhitas is that he who commits wicked deeds suffers in another world whereas he who performs good deeds enjoys the highest material pleasure.

According to the Brahmanas, the doctrine of *karma* is combined with that of transmigration and this makes it possible to explain any apparently underserved pleasure or pain of a person by the theory that the *karma* causing them was done by him in a former existence. The Hindu view of *karma* is based upon the assumption of the existence of a soul. **The law of *karma* has been accepted in all the main systems of Indian philosophy and religion as an article of faith.** The result of *karma*, whether good or bad, cannot be obviated. It is a force, which must produce its own consequence.

According to the popular Hindu belief, *karma* is the sum total of a man's action in a previous birth, determining his unalterable future destiny. Its effect remains until it is exhausted through suffering or enjoyment. No doubt *karma* struck hard against the old belief in sacrifice, penance and repentance. This popular notion of *karma* is also found in a Buddhist *Jataka*. In the *Brihadaranyaka Upanishad* and in the teachings of Yajnavalkya we meet with a clear formulation of this doctrine, and the resemblance between this formulation and that which is found in Buddhist texts is so close that one may be perfectly justified in maintaining that this doctrine is nothing but a further elucidation of the subject in the Upanishad.

Jaratkarava Artabhaga, another Upanishadic thinker, had a discussion with Yajnavalkya about the mysterious effect of *karma*. The *Brhadaranyaka Upanishad* contains the gospel of *karma* which determines, on a man's death, the nature of his next birth. Yajnavalkya works out the view of *karma* thus: A man is of desire. As is his desire, so is his resolve. As is his resolve, so is his action. And as he acts, so he attains. In other words, a man attains with his action the object to which his mind is attached. After having enjoyed the full benefit of his deeds, he returns again from that world to this world of action. Here Yajnavalkya and Artabhaga are found to praise *karma*. They therefore state jointly that one becomes virtuous by virtuous action and vicious by vicious action.

Karma draws the soul back into a new corporeality. In the words of Yajnavalkya, 'As a caterpillar, after having reached the end of a blade of grass, and after having made an approach to another blade, draws itself together towards it, thus does his self, after having thrown off his body and dispelled all ignorance, and after making an approach to another body, draw itself together towards it. And as a goldsmith taking a piece of gold turns it into another newer and more beautiful shape, so does this self, after having thrown off this body and dispelled all ignorance, make unto itself another newer and more beautiful shape, whether it be like that of the Fathers, or of the *gandharvas* or of the gods or of Prajapati, or of Brahma, or of other beings'.

The notion of metempsychosis is nicely depicted in the *Chhandogya Upanishad* (V.10). The various stages which one has to traverse after death, according to one's *karma*, are elaborately dealt with in this particular section. Thus it is stated in this connection that those who are of good conduct will enter into superior womb, and those who are of evil conduct will be born into the womb of a dog or swine or an outcast. In support of this the following may be cited: 'One who steals away gold, one who drinks liquor, one who ascends the bed of his teacher, one who kills a Brahmin—these four are destined to sink downward. So also happens with the fifth who keeps company with them. The doctrine of *karma* has also been treated in the *Yoga Sutra* (II.12.13) and especially in its commentary.

The Buddhists could not adopt the Hindu theory in their own system without modification. Hopkins points out that the *karma* notion begins to appear in the Brahmanas but not in the *samsara* shape of transmigration. According to Kern, *karma* is the link that preserves the identity of a being through all the countless changes which it undergoes in its progress through *samsara*.

The Buddha is generally credited with the propounding of this doctrine but there is a clear statement in the *Majjhima Nikaya* (I, pp. 483ff) to show that the doctrine had not originated with the Buddha. The statement is to the effect that the doctrine was propounded before the advent of the Buddha by an Indian teacher who was a householder.

In Buddhism this doctrine reaches its climax and assumes a unique character. We also find in Buddhism two extreme views of thought bearing upon the doctrine of *Karma*: (1) all that a being suffers from or experiences in life is due to the sum total of his deeds in the past and (2) all that a being experiences in this life is only a matter of chance.

It is true that for every sin commited here punishment follows in the next existence. The Buddhists approached the problem from a purely psychological point of view. It has been pointed out that a man need not be afraid of the vast accumulation of *karma* through a long cycle of births and rebirths. The whole of such accumulation may be completely undone by a momentary action of mind. Mind in its own place and as such can make and unmake all such accumulation of *karma*. The doctrine of *karma* is emphatically formulated in the *Cula Kammavibhanga Sutta*. This Sutta addressed to Subha, a young Brahmin scholar, is substantially the same as that in the *Brihadaranyaka Upanishad*. It says: 'The beings have the *karma* as their own, they have their heritage from *karma* which determines their birth, the *karma* is their friend and ultimate refuge, and it is the *karma* that divides them relegating them either to the inferior or to the superior state to existence.' The *Devaduta Sutta* of the *Majjhima Nikaya* bases the whole discourse on the doctrine of *karma* on the current popular belief about Yama and his messengers. It represent Yama as the lord of the neither world whose business is to judge the actions of the different sinners who were brought to his court by his emissaries.

When a man dies, the *khandhas* of which he is constituted, perish, but by the force of his *karma* a new set of *khandhas* instantly starts into existence and a new being appears in another world, who though possessing different *khandhas* and a different form, is in reality identical with the man just passed away because his *karma* is the same. It has been asserted that Buddhism does not admit transmigration. When a being dies, a new being is born and inherits his *karma*. What transmigrates is not the person but his *karma*. There is no agent; there is nothing but the act and its fruits; organs, thoughts, and external things are all the fruits of acts, in the same way as pleasant and unpleasant sensations. The Buddhist doctrine of *karma* should not be misinterpreted as a sort of fatalism. It is broadbased on morality and the law of causation and it clearly explains the principal of just requital.

There are two kinds of acts, pure and impure. The acts which are free from *asravas* are pure and those accompanied by them are impure. The act with pleasant retribution is good and that with unpleasant retribution is bad. The acts performed with a view to happiness in this world are bad and those performed with a view to happiness in the world beyond are good. Acts are also distinguished as of three kinds: good, bad and indifferent. They may also be classified as meritorious, demeritorious, and fixed. The fruit of retribution of acts includes not only the sensation but also everything that determines the sensation—organs, etc. Acts may be determinate and indeterminate. They involve or do not involve a necessary retribution.

Karma came to be defined as *cetana* or volition. Volition as moral action without qualification was meant by the Buddha. Volition which is morally indeterminate is without moral result. A person cannot be morally or legally held responsible for his or her unintentional act. The Buddhist teachers therefore tried to define *karma* on a rational and practical basis. This point of view has been criticised in the Jain *Sutrakritanga*. The Abhidhamma philosophy seeks to furnish the psychological data of ethics, conduct or external behaviour of men being regarded as an outward expression of their internal character.

The celebrated Buddhist commentator of the fifth century A.D., Buddhaghosa, defines *karma* as volition expressed in action. An action is no action until the will is manifested in conduct. *Karma* also means consciousness of good and bad, merit and demerit. It is of four kinds: 1) *karma* producing result in this life, 2) producing result in the next life, 3) producing result from time to time, and 4) past *karma*.

There is another four-fold division of *karma*: (1) an act whether it is good or bad produces serious results, (2) excess of either virtue or vice which produces its respective results, (3) an act which is thought of at the time of death, and (4) an act which has been often done by one in his life-time and which in the absence of three previous *karmas* causes rebirth. We have still another classifications of *karma*: (1) determining the character of rebirth, (2) sustaining, (3) oppressive, and (4) hurting. These twelve kinds of acts and consequences are manifested in their true aspect in Buddha's knowledge of the consequences of *karma*. Those endowed with the spiritual insight are acquainted with *kammantara* and *vipakantara*. *Karma* produces consequence, retribution is born of action, action is the cause of rebirth—in this way the world continues. No action passes from the past life to the present nor from the present to the future.

As regards the relation between action and its consequence (*vipaka*), Buddhaghosa says: There is no *karma* in *vipaka* and no *vipaka* in *karma*. Each of them by itself is void, at the same time there is no *vipaka* without *karma*. Just as there is no fire in the sun, nor in the lens, nor in the dried cowdung, and likewise fire is not outside them but comes into existence on account of their requisites, in the same way *vipaka* is not seen within the *karma* nor outside it. A *karma* is void of its *vipaka* which comes through *karma*. *Vipaka* comes into existence on account of *karma*. In the past the *khandhas* which originated as the consequences of action (*volition*) ceased. In this existence other *khandhas* arise out of the consequences of part deeds. There is no condition which has come to this existence from the past, in this existence the *khandhas* which are originated on account of the consequences of *karma* are destroyed. In another existence others will be produced from this existence, not a single condition will pass on to the next existence.

Karma is ultimately reduced to the psychological factor of volition. Volition is the unique determination of will. Will-exercise has its power over its co-existent mental properties and physical qualities. All our activities, in deed, word, or thought, are due to its influence.

A careful study of the Buddhist books, especially those dealing with Heavens and Hells is enough to show that the inmates of these places are as much subject to the iron law of *karma* as are the dwellers upon this earth itself. The highest of the pleasures that the Buddhist heavens bestow is not, however, everlasting. When the fruits of good deeds are exhausted, the beings have to come down again to the earth to be buffeted by the waves of *karma*.

In Jainism, *karma* does not mean a deed or some invisible mystical force. It is nothing but a complexity of a very subtle matter which is super-sensuous and which pervades the whole world. It is the cause of its own state or modification working in and through its own nature. From *karmic* delusion comes the bondage, and desire is its sole cause.

In Hinduism we find that God awards the fruits of *karma* whereas in Jainism *karma* accumulates energy and automatically works itself out without any outside intervention. The Hindus think of *karma* as formless while the Jainas, think of it as having form. The Jainas divide *karma* according to its nature, duration, essence and content. *Karma* is intimately bound up with the soul. According to the Jainas there are eight kinds of *karma*: the first kind hides knowledge from us, the second kind prevents us from beholding the true faith, the third kind causes us to experience either the sweetness of happiness or the bitterness of misery, the fourth kind bemuses all the human faculties. It leads to delusion. It results from worldly attachments and indulgence of the passions. The fifth kind determines the length of time which a *jiva* must spend in the form with which its *karma* has endowed it. The sixth *karma* decides which of the four states of conditions (*gati*) shall be our particular *gati*. In short, it determines the name or individuality of the embodied soul. The seventh kind decides whether a living being shall be born in a high or in a low caste family. The last and the eighth kind is the *karma* which always stands as an obstacle. It prevents a person from entering the path leading to eternal bliss.

The Jaina *Sutrakritanga* speaks of various types of *Kriyavada* then current in India. Buddhism was promulgated as a form of *Kriyavada* or *Karmavada*. There are four main types of *Akriyavada* that correspond to those attributed in the Pali *Nikayas* to four leading thinkers of the time, e.g., athiesm like that of Ajita, eternalism like that of Katyayana, absolutism like that of Kasyapa and fatalism like that of Gosala. They believed that the *atman* is a living individual, a biological entity. The whole self does not outlast the destruction of the body. With the body ends life. One man admits action and another man does not admit action. Both men are alike, their case is the same because they are actuated by the same force, i.e., by fate. It is their destiny that all beings come to have a body to undergo the vicissitudes of life and to experience pleasure and pain.

The types of *Kriyavada* that do not come up to the standard of Jainism are two in number:

(1) The soul of a man who is pure will become free from bad *karma* on reaching beatitude, but in that state it will again become defiled through pleasant excitement or hatred.

(2) If a man with the intention of killing a body hurts a gourd mistaking if for a baby, he will be guilty of murder. If a man with the intention of roasting a gourd roasts a baby,

mistaking it for a gourd, he will not be guilty of murder. According to Mahavira, the painful condition of the self is brought about by one's own action and not by any other cause. Pleasure and pain are brought about by one's own action. Individually a man is born, individually he dies, individually he falls and individually he rises. His passions, consciousness, intellect, perceptions, and impressions belong to the individual exclusively.

There are four kinds of obstructive *karma* which retain the soul in mundane existence. They are as follows: (1) knowledge-obscuring *karma*, (2) faith-obscuring *karma*, (3) *karma* which obstructs the progress or success of the soul, and (4) *karma* which infatuates or deludes the soul.

In short, Mahavira's great message to mankind is that birth is nothing, caste is nothing, and *karma* is everything and on the destruction of *karma* the future happiness depends. *Karma* is the deed of the soul. It is a material forming a subtle bond of extremely refined *karmic* matter, which keeps the soul confined to its place of orgin, or the natural abode of full knowledge and everlasting peace.

7

The New Style Puranas

The Puranas consitiute important sources for the political and cultural history of India, embodying as they do particulars about every aspect of life—religious, philosophical, social, political and personal. **They were meant especially for the women and the Shudras and represented the Veda for the laity.** It is to be observed in this connection that the aims and ideals of the writers of the Puranas and the ways and means employed by them to achieve these objectives were quite distinct from those of the modern historians and writers of cultural treatise. All great events that added to the cultural content of India figure in the Puranas, and the main aim of the writers of the Puranas was to preserve for posterity the important contributions of eminent personages, to perpetuate the principles propounded by illustrious thinkers and to present the entire material so as to make them appear fresh to the readers so that they may constantly place those ideals before them.

Allegory was the device frequently resorted to by the Puranas in order to make a popular appeal and to preserve the tradition. In its wider sense allegory represents the meaning put by the reader on a piece of writing which he finds to be more or less in the need of interpretation. It may be noted that the tendency to allegorise arises from the natural desire to perpetuate some idea or truth which has come to be regarded as sacred. There are several stories or episodes in ancient literature, which are absurd if taken literally. It would certainly be unwise to reject the entire story on account of such apparent absurdities, but one should try to look deeper beyond the literal meaning to extract the wisdom of the ancients. Even today it is active because there is the need of reading a new meaning into the sacred tradition in order to protect in from the satire of critics. The conception of *Virata Purusa* is explained now in terms of social solidarity, and *Narayana-sev*a as humanitarianism. The gods and goddesses having three, four, five heads, and four, eight, sixteen hands are interpreted to be divine, immensely more powerful than man with the usual number.

The Puranic allegories may be divided into four broad headings: (1) natural phenomena, (2) origin of the castes, (3) stories of the epics, and (4) Kartavirya Arjuna and Parasurama.

Natural Phenomena: We begin with the allegories connected with natural phenomena with reference to the story of the descent of the Ganga. Bhagiratha of the solar dynasty is said to have brought down the Ganga from the Himalayas through his penance and had to propitiate Shiva. The story seems to refer to directing the course of the Ganga from the Himalayas to the eastern regions to water and fertilise the tract. It involved the efforts of four generations of the rulers of the Ayodhya dynasty, viz., Sagara, Anshuman, Dilipa and Bhagiratha. The penance of Bhagiratha at Gokarna in the Himalayas represents his efforts to turn the flow of the stream or glacier in the Himalayas in a particular direction through the valleys. Of the seven streams Bhagiratha guided one eastwards. In order to chasten the proud and elated Ganga Lord Shiva is said to have completely held her in his matted locks. This indicates the disappearance of the stream in the dense forest of Mt. Kailasa region which could not be traced.

Bhagiratha's further penance and propitiation of Shiva represent his thorough search through the thick forests and then finally the blocking of the outlet to the valleys which led to the disappearance of the stream, which resulted in the flow of the stream in the desired direction. In the further progress of the Ganga through the plains after she had negotiated the Himalayas, king Jahnu is said to have drunk the river as it overflowed his ashrama and submerged his sacrificial *mandapa*. This indicates the diversion of the stream in another direction; and this was stopped after Bhagiratha pacified Jahnu and the stream began to flow through the channel prepared by Bhagiratha who carried the stream to the eastern sea. **This magnificient achievement of Bhagiratha represents one of the greatest irrigation works in the world more than a thousand miles in length.**

As king Brihadashva prepared to go to the forest after crowning his son, Uttanka, who resided in Marubhumi in the Rajputana desert, requested him not to resort to *tapovana* without first accounting for the monster Dhundhu. Brihadashva assigned the task of killing Dhundhu to his son, Kuvalashva, who later came to be known as Dhundhumara after his achieving this feat. The description in the *Harivamsa* shows that near Uttanka's hermitage there was a sandy sea in the marshy land, and the monster Dhundhu at the interval of each year showered fire and dust all round. Kuvalashva first cleared the land of its marsh by digging deep ditches near the sea and then dug the sandy sea in order to locate the monster which was nothing else but a volcanic pit towards the west. The prince extinguished the pit by the flow of subterranean water. **This was the famous sea into which flowed the Vedic Saraswati.**

The third natural phenomenon concerns the emergence

of the Konkan (and Kerala) out of the subsequent colonisation by the Bhargava hero, Parasurama. After donating the whole earth to sage Kasyapa as sacrificial fee, Parasurama was banished by Kasyapa from the earth. In order to have some land for himself he demanded it of the sea which the latter ignored. Enraged at this insult, Parasurama shot an arrow—or his famous axe—at the ocean, and it retreated exposing the land up to the point covered by the arrow—or axe—. The land thus recovered extended from the Sahya mountains to the sea, covering the entire west coast. Parasurama colonised the land by bringing Brahmins, either from the north or other parts of India or from outside, or by reviving dead corpses. **This story shows that Parasurama was the first coloniser of the tract, and it also refers to the natural phenomenon of the land coming out of the sea due to some seismic disturbances.** So far as Kerala is concerned, it has also been confirmed by geological evidence.

Origin of the Castes: The origin of the castes through the different limbs of the Purusa, as mentioned in Purusa Sukta, has been repeated in several Puranas. This has been allegorically interpreted as implying a scheme of social stratification based on the principle to the division of labour. Thus, the Brahmins, created from the mouth, the seat of speech, enact the part of preceptors of humanity, while the Kshatriyas, produced from arms, the symbol of valour and strength, are entrusted with the protection of people through "arms." Born through thighs, the Vaishyas provide food to the people, and the Shudras, coming from feet, are servants (footmen) of the three higher Varnas. Thus the whole social organisation is symbolically represented as one cosmic being with its different limbs playing the roles of the different classes of social order.

Stories of the Epics: As the stories of *Mahabharata* and the *Ramayana* form the subject-matter of the Puranas, we may as well consider the allegorical significance of these. In the huge forest of different interpretations of the *Mahabharata* in their enthusiasm to unravel the mystery and discover its hidden meaning, most of the scholars miss the plain meaning—that the *Mahabharata* is a history (*itihasa*), as it claims to be, of the Kuru princes, of their dissentions, loss of kingdom and victory.

Now to refer to some more important interpretations of the *Mahabharata*. According to Joseph Dahlmann, the *Mahabharata*, which "was composed with the avowed and exclusive object of expounding all the different aspects of Hindu Law, in the widest sense of the term, not omitting even its historical and archaic features and oddities' welded together the pre-existing narrative and didactic elements artificially with a view to popularising Dharma Sastra among the masses. The Pandavas and Kauravas represent personifications of Dharma and Adharma and there is no authenticity for the feud between them. Ludwig, however, on the basis of nature-myth, took the *Mahabharata* to be the seasonal myth in which the Pandavas symbolised the seasons with Draupadi their common spouse, as the dark earth (Krishna) is possessed alternately by the five seasons. The Bharata War represented the struggle between the sun and the darkness of night. Lassen took the *dramatis personae* of the epic to be not ordinary human beings but rather historical conditions or circumstances. Pandu (lit. white), thus, was originally the name of the royal family of the "white" race which had migrated to India from the north and which was later known as Arjuna (lit. white). There is also a view that the Bharata War represents but the struggle for the victory of the principle of Aryo-Dravidian synthesis over orthodox Aryandom, the Pandavas standing for the former, and the Kauravas for the later, principle. Thadani takes the *Mahabharata* as the symbolisation of the six systems of Hindu philosophy which meet in the region of mind. Robert Shafer opens his *Ethnography of India* with the sentence: 'The Great Epic of India is essentially the story of native rebellion against Aryan exploitation.'

According to Dr. Sukthankar, whose posthumous publication, on the meaning of the *Mahabharata*, represents the essence of his life-long study of *Mahabharata* to the historical interpretation, is but the meaning of *Mahabharata* on the mundane plane. He dives deep into the *Mahabharata* and carries us to ethical and metaphysical planes, where the story assumes quite an important significance. The ethical plane views the Bharata War as a conflict between the principles of Dharma and Adharma, between justice and injustice, and on the metaphyical plane, the War is fought not only in Kurukshetra, but also in our mind, between the higher self and the lower self of man, symbolised by the family of cousins fighting for the sovereignty of the kingdom over the body. Here we are face to face with the deep mysteries of life. In this intepretation, Sri Krishna is the Paramatman (Super Self) while Arjuna is the Jivatman (individual self).

The case of the *Ramayana* is similar. Most of the scholars accept the historical basis for the *Ramayana* that it represents the adventure of the prince of Ayodhya though the marvellous and the miraculous have been mixed up with the nucleus to a large extent. Though Jacobi takes the *Ramayana* as the blending of two distinct elements, history and allegory, viz., (1) palace intrigue and banishment, and (2) the abduction of Sita and the killing of Ravana, it is evident that the entire *Ramayana* is a complete unit.

To refer to some of the allegorical interpretations, we find that though Lassen takes it as an allegorical representation of the Aryan conquest of the South, he accepts Dasarathi Rama as a historical personage, transported later into the rank of gods, Sita then being turned into the daughter of the earth, a deified furrow. According to Weber, the characters of the *Ramayana* are not historical persons but merely personification of certain occurances and situations. Sita represents Aryan husbandry which has to be protected by Rama, the plough-bearer (*halabhrit*) against the attacks of the predatory aborigines represented as inimical demons and giants, and friendly monkeys (who were strikingly ugly). Wheeler regards the war between Rama and Ravana as but a poetic version of the conflict between Brahminism and Buddhism. Jacobi takes Rama's conflict with Ravana as but a poetic version of the Indra-Vritra myth of the Rig Veda, and Hanumat, the chief ally of Rama, is called 'Maruti', son of the Maruts, reminiscent of Indra's association with Maruts, the storm-gods.

In idealising the hero as the paragon of virtue, his adversaries have been portrayed as embodiments of sin and vice. The *Ramayana* has thus an obvious allegorical significance and suggestiveness as indicated in the *Moha Mudgara* of *Samkaracharya*, according to which the soul (Rama) after crossing *moha* (in the form of forest) and killing *raga* (passion) and *dvesa* (hatred) symbolising the Raksasas, shines resplendently united with *shanti* (peace), in the form of Sita. It may, however, be remarked here that to stretch this idea of allegory and symbolism so far and to try to see symbolism in every character and incident in the *Ramayana* would be absurd and would also be far from the intention of Valmiki himself.

Kartavirya Arjuna and Parashurama: The story of the Bhrigu-Haihaya conflict, well known to the students of Puranas, may be interpreted in the following way:

Haihayas, scions of the Yadava family of the lunar

dynasty, were great warriors, and Bhrigus, though belonging to the priestly class, were great navigators, expert mariners and enterprising tradesmen who controlled the trade between India and the western world, acting as intermediaries between Indians and the foreigners such as the Assyrians. They had amassed great wealth by helping foreigners at the cost of indigenous population. Mahismati on the Narmada was a great trading centre which was the focus of the routes running north and south, and hence was the prize coveted by ancient rulers. Karkotaka Nagas seized it from the Haihayas, but Kartavirya recovered it. In order to secure the allegiance of the Bhrigus and to alienate them from the Nagas, Asuras etc. Kartvirya bestowed wealth on them.

Arjuna, son of Kartavirya, was a great warrior who spread the Haihaya sway for and wide. He wanted the trade and commerce of India to be under the control of Aryans, and did not like that the Bhrigus, who were the agents of the foreigners, should prosper at the cost of the common man, and this was the main reason of the Bhrgiu-Haihaya conflict. Haihayas in his time were in need of money presumably for continuing their military operations, and they demanded the return of the wealth from the Bhrigus. On their refusal, Haihayas pursued the Bhrigus and recovered the wealth buried by them. Bhrigus ran helter-skelter for safety, and one of them, Aurva (who was so named because he was brought up by his mother in secret in her thighs—*urus*—through the fear of the pursuing Haihayas) was probably brought up outside India in Ur.

This supposition receives confirmation from the names of Aurva's son, Richika, who appears to have been connected with Erech in Ur, possibly as ruler. In order to counter the attaks of the Haihayas, the Bhrigus thought of entering into marital relations with the ruling families. Richika approached Gadhi for the hand of his daughter, with a view to open new trade-routes through Sindh which formed part of Gadhi's kingdom as indicated by his appellation Saindhavayana, and successfully fulfilled the condition prescribed by Gadhi in order to test Richika's capacity for trade, of supplying a thousand horses. Richika could supply the requisite number because Ur in those days dominated over horse-producing regions. A son Jamadagni was born to him, and Parashurama was born to Jamadagni.

Meanwhile, Arjuna made alliance with the Atris, rivals of the Bhrigus, and sought the help of Dattatreya, who made him invincible in war. Datta made him Sahasrabahu, i.e., possessing thousand ships. With these ships Arjuna became Anupapati, invaded Lanka, and defeated Ravana through naval manoeuvres; Ravana was brought as captive to Mahismati and released later. Arjuna ruled righteously and his police system was so efficient that nothing was said to be lost in his kingdom, and whatever was lost was made over to the owner by the king. In order to test the efficacy of incendiary arrows, Arjuna selected a solitary spot, but as ill luck would have it, the sage Apava had his hermitage in the locality and one of the arrows discharged by Arjuna burnt that hermitage.

Parashurama, as the leader of the opposition against the Haihayas, carried a ruthless war and entirely eliminated the Haihayas from the Narmada valley. He periodically continued his operations of liquidating the population in the Narmada valley in order to blot out the traces of his ruthless wars and wipe out the memory of the popular ruler Arjuna. This is represented in the Puranas as Parashurama's killing of the Kshatriyas twenty-one times. On the ruins of the Haihaya occupations in the Narmada valley, Parashurama founded new cities and also colonised the region known as Aparanta on the west coast, where Surparaka became a great trading centre.

It is possible, as urged by Pargiter, that the account as handed down by the Puranas, is "largely Brahminical", or to put it more correctly, a version under the Bhargava influence. The fact that, barring his relations with the Bhrigus, Arjuna is uniformly praised in all accounts shows that despite the Bhargava manipulations, the greatness of Arjuna could not be effaced.

8

Indian Ethical Values

The essence of the Vedic system of life lay in practice and not in theory, in realisation and not in belief, in transformation and not in profession. In other words, instead of evolving an ecclesiastical mentality and bequeathing to posterity an organised church-religion, the Vedic seers fostered broad-based intellectual progress and set up a tradition of philosophical quest and honest effort to know oneself. **Theirs was a system not of creed-bound religion but of self-culture, leading straight on to the social ideal of mutual concord and adjustment.**

Some of the basic concepts of the system may be gathered from a study of what follows, being a pithy parable from the *Brihadaranyaka Upanishad:*

1. Three classes of Prajapati's progeny—Devas (gods), Manusyas (men) and Asuras (demons)—lived a life of discipline under their father, Prajapati, On the completion of the course, Devas said unto him, 'Be pleased to instruct.' He uttered the syllable *Da* unto them and asked, 'Have you understood?' They said, 'We have. You tell us: "Control yourselves." 'Yes', said He, 'You have understood.'
2. The Manusyas said unto Him, 'Be pleased to instruct us.' He uttered the same syllable *Da* unto them and asked, 'Have you understood?' They said,

'We have. You tell us: "Be charitable." 'Yes', said He. 'You have understood.'

3. Then Asuras said unto Him, 'Be pleased to instruct us.' He uttered the same syllable *Da* unto them and asked, 'Have you understood?' They said, 'We have. You tell us: "Be merciful." 'Yes', said He, 'You have understood.'

The three classes of the recipients of instruction represent the three orders of one and the same humanity. Neither Devas are any heavenly beings nor Asuras are any subterranean evil spirits. There are men who by the mere act of their existence press hard against their environment. Their mode of living is oppressive and their machinating mentality highly harmful. Mischief is of the very essence of their inner being and they are always after hunting others down for their personal aggrandisement. The wails and cries of their poor, unfortunate victims are of no avail; for, the more they suffer and exhibit the signs of suffering, the more they infuriate their oppressors so that they may inflict fresh wounds and injuries on them.

While addressing this class, Prajapati indicated the real use of power and prowess, It will be recognised that unless a man has acquired by dint of his laborious efforts a sufficient store of strength, there can hardly be any scope for exercising the divine virtue of mercy. When one is actually mighty, then and then alone, one is in a position to understand the right use of this newly acquired might. **So, merciful behaviour is the first upward step in the moral evolution of a man who has become entitled to a rightful and equal status among his normally functioning fellow beings.** He must need to know the due applications of his attainments with reference to those who surround him lest he should receive a setback in his onward march. He should feel that others also like himself are marching onwards and he should therefore march alongside of them and not stand in their way.

Prajapati's teaching presupposes the acquisition of a proper measure of *shakti* which denotes the capacity to depend upon one's own strength to hold one's ground. Every attractive and properly functioning object in nature is a embodiment and expression of this *shakti*. To attain its normal growth and achieve self-expression by bearing its characteristic fruit is the basic principle which every form of life in the world is pursuing and struggling hard to realise. Weakness as such is not desired by nature. Beauty, symmetry, harmony, attraction and enjoyment are the outward signs of the internal existence of *shakti*. It comes as a sweet reward to him who has continuously and successfully fought against the rigorous of heat and cold, satisfactorily exercised and trained his physical and mental potentialities, put upon himself the armour of a well-regulated diet, physical culture and balanced mind and stood firm against the onslaught of disease and decrepitude. The seedof *shakti* lies in every being, but it has to undergo a cultural process before it can shine forth as the beautiful blossom of life.

Asuras are the people who have rather become surcharged with *shakti* but lack its proper control and co-ordination. This defect is responsible for the presence in them of morbid lust and inordinate avarice. They seldom think of others, far less of their right to live in this world. They are intemperate in their social behaviour. Anything that they may be after is their god, their religion and their everything. Anybody who dares stand in their way ceases to have any right to live in the world which, according to their mode of thinking, is solely meant for their use and enjoyment. They are embodiments of selfishness, ambition, sensuality, avarice and infatuation. They require a chastening influence, may be, a purgatory process. Now that, as the parable goes, they have of their own accord resorted to Prajapati for guidance, He utilises the opportunity towards setting them right and, thereby, saving their surplus energy from being misused. And, what does he teach them? "Be merciful, my children!" says He unto them, "Live and let others live, for they have as good a right to it as yourselves." This is the bedrock of all evolutionary processes in our lives as human beings.

All individuals should have an equal right to live and live happily. The sun shines for all and the moon sheds her mellow light on all. Showers of rains make no distinction between man and man. Air accords no preferential treatment to anybody. The mother earth is the common cradle for all her children. But how sad it is that these children should always be trying to jostle one another out of the field? And, sadder still, that they should be exercising their ingenuity inventing strange arguments in defence of this foul play. As human beings, it does not behove us to arrogate to ourselves the sole right of deciding the fate of our fellow-beings who may in any respect be weaker than ourselves.

Wealth of expression and power of impression on one's surroundings are indications of the possession of *shakti*. To be strong enough to keep it unadulterated with arrogance and infatuation is the essence of true manliness. To be just toward oneself and others is the light on the path of valour. It is bitter humiliation to be cowed down by others, but it is doubly so to try unjustly to overawe others. Man is said to have been created by God, in his own image. And, what else is the image of God, if not love and law together? Look wherever you may, your attentive gaze will ever and ever inform you that love and law are responsible for the presence of all real sweetness and strength in life. It is by realising the presence of these twin virtues in every movement of every particle of this limitless universe, that one can attain supreme bliss and beatitude.

To make every honest effort to become economically independent is desirable, but there is hardly any need of amassing wealth. For it is a means to an end and not an end in itself. It is required for securing various amenities of life, and that can be done by spending it in the right way and not by hoarding or worshipping it. Mammon-worship is a worship of the worst type. It makes its votary cowardly and callous. No tender feeling, no elevating sentiment, no elevating sentiment, no high emotion ever gets a foothold in his barren heart. Day and night, he lives in wealth, counting it when awake and dreaming of it when asleep. Prajapati does not relish the sight of those who love money for its own sake. What a pity—one labouring all day long and not enjoying and ennobling one's life in any way! Earn hard and spend well is, then, the first lesson that man should learn. If misuse of wealth generates evil influences for the dread and dismay of the world, not to use it is equally responsible for cowardice, avarice, selfishness and hardness in those who possess it, and for jealousy, injustice, cruelty and lawlessness in those who do not.

So, wealth should be neither uselessly hoarded up nor mercilessly squandered away. It should be rightly used. But this use should not be confined to one's personal comforts and enjoyments alone. Old relatives and children depend upon us and so they naturally should have their proper claim on our purse. To help them and look to their comforts and satisfaction is the beginning of charity. It should, however, be remembered that by doing this much, we only reach its borderland, and do not enter its proper sphere. That we owe much to our parents and relatives is quite clear to us. If we help them, we only give them much less than what is their due. In our children are stored up our future hopes and so we have to look to their satisfaction at all costs. This aspect of charity, however, is very useful in consolidating our domestic life. For, the satisfied looks of elders and the smiling faces of young ones are due to its charming influence, and whenever it becomes absent in a family, the sting is at once felt.

Charity proper begins when we help those who are not bound to us by any ties of relationship and whom we know to be not in a position to return the good done to them. It is the never-failing antidote to poverty, disease and suffering. It cures people of wounds inflicted by sorrow and separation. It ennobles those who rightly and dutifully exercise it. It is the greatest sweetening influence in our social life. There could be no enduring fabric of society if it were absent. It produces a noble feeling of spiritual satisfaction in the hearts of those who get used to its righteous practice.

In order that charity should be a strong pillar to support the superstructure of social life, it must needs be of the right type. It is true that every individual should feel it incumbent upon himself to help the needy, it is doubly true that he should by nature be against receiving anything in charity. Dependence upon others is not a good thing. It removes the last vestige of self-assertion. So, independence should be the aim of life and only they whose unfitness, physical or otherwise, precludes the possibility of self-relief, may accept any offers of help from others. As a rule, a thing which cannot be got by self-effort, should not be worth having at all. Misplaced charity has a very poisonous effect on the donor as well as on the receiver. The donor loses his fine sense of the right use of what he earns and, also, becomes responsible for the presence of many heinous crimes and misdeeds in the world. The receiver loses his very self and ceases any more to be manly enough to scale the ladder of moral and spiritual evolution.

On the mental plane also, charitability of disposition

and goodwill constitute the basic principles of social solidarity. Co-ordination of effort and concerted action presuppose mutual confidence and fellow-feeling. Life in society is a game of 'give' and 'take' both and not of 'take' alone. Social interests demand that besides directing one's charity towards seeing to nobody suffering from material want, one should also develop the habit of being charitably disposed in adjudging things pertaining to the mind. One so disposed will always be on his guard not to say or do anything that severs man from man. Society owes its strength to the presence of men who may not be able to discourse upon the meanings of charity and charitability but who do possess these virtues in their actual conduct. In the light of the above, it is they alone who deserve to be called men. Their mercy and justice will form the foundation-stone of society and their charity and charitability will cement and consolidate it.

To gods the heavenly sound *Da* signified self-restraint and self-sacrifice. To embody these in one's life would be the culmination of the human cultural process. The demons are used to 'take' only; the men get accustomed to 'give' and 'take' both; but the **gods are those supermen, who are always busy doing good to others.** They are flowers whose fragrance gives freshness to all who approach them. They are the centre of psychic currents of love, goodwill, purity and piety, which constantly purify the whole social atmosphere. To them the sun shines forth, not as an ordinary luminary, but as a divine sacrifice who is constantly burning himself up in order that countless beings should receive life and light from him. The fire in the hearth and the lightning flash in the clouds convey the same message to them. The wind blows, now hot and now cold, not for any object of its own, but for the good of the world. The showers of rain and flowing rivers tell the same tale. The whole world is a huge altar of sacrifice and every object in nature is offering at it its personal oblation during every moment of its existence.

To sacrifice oneself and all one's worldly interests for the good of others is the great pivot on which the life divine revolves. It is always in motion and action and knows no stagnation. Its constant activity is a guarantee for its own health and its health-generating capacity for those around it. The consummation of its evolution consists in self-realisation, namely, the wrong recognition that the transitory, flitting things that are and are not, are to be used and left behind as steps in a staircase and not to be treated as our permanent abodes. It has an inexhaustible store of sympathy, good advice and helpfulness to distribute freely among the suffering and struggling mankind, but its own sufferings and personal struggles have come to an end. Free from the last vestige of personal ambition and worldly anxiety, it is far from even the dreams of exploiting others for its own glorification and praise. And this attitude itself comes quite naturally to it, unmixed with any feeling that anything is being done to oblige others.

The saintly souls that enrich themselves with this divine life are the salt of human society. It grows, evolves and prospers under their benign supervision. There can be no injustice and no vicious exploitation in their presence. Their integrity and uprightness inspire awe and respect in the minds of their fellow-men. Their spirit of service and sympathetic attention set the stream of pure love a-flowing all round. They are brotherly towards the sick and the sorrowful and fatherly towards the breadless and the shelterless. All may look to them for help, but they look to none for anything. Their heart is ever bubbling with new life, of vigour and inspiration. They are humble but know no humiliation. They live on the nectar begotten of self-control and self-sacrifice which leads them to the fountainhead of this essence of their being and it was to this end that Prajapati inculcated in them the supreme need of practising and developing the aforesaid virtues as denoted by the word, *Dama*.

In terms of this parable, the ancient seers conceived of men who would respect justice, possess a charitable turn of mind and put reasonable restraints upon themselves as representing the normal standard of humanity. Weaklings if any, must mend their mode of living so that they might attain to their full share of strength of body and character. Society would offer them facilities to raise themselves in every way. The development of the virtues of mercy and charity on the part of every individual would be a safeguard against any setback being given to those who were trying to regain what they had lost or attain to a new status in life higher than the one held by them before. These two virtues would befit individuals to form themselves into a good, cultured society. The Asuras would not be liked because they would be guilty of considered misdirection and abuse of their attainments. The Devas would be respected and adored on account of their serviceable existence, every breath of their precious life being dedicated to the good of society.

Judged from this point of view, mad, imperialistic tendencies, whether of ancient despots or of modern states, shall have to be called inhuman. National solidarity of rightful self-expression and characteristic contribution to the world culture has its own justification. As in the case of an individual, in that of communities and nations as well, to be weak and impotent should be despicable . But it must be candidly confessed that big, organised and pooled monopolisations are the bane of the world of today. They are seriously hampering humanity from scaling the due and clearly visualised social heights. Capital and labour organise themselves not in self-defence or for internal self-consolidation but for crushing each other. Leagues and pacts are, in fact, alliances of those who are in possession of power, however ill-earned, and do not want to part with it, even though not to do so may be against the dictates of right and justice. Individuals and nations clutch at anything they come across and want to usurp it. High-sounding euphemisms are invented to conceal the worst types of crimes and ill-dealings. They thwart individual progress and stand in the way of backward classes of people ever being able to come to their own.

In the world of religion also organised sectarian movements are equally unjust exploitation-grounds for the supposed benefit of the few who have the knack or the means to come in the forefront and canvass votes in their favour. The dumb masses are led by clever people who work up religious fanaticism and sectarian bigotry in their minds and use them at the time of polling for their own personal ends. Sycophancy, presumption and corruption hold the ground whereas real worth is at a discount. **Public service has become another name for majestic living, tempting declarations are seldom translated into action. The so-called religious organisations are mostly manned and controlled by persons who seldom feel called to those high offices by any spiritual indication in their own experience.** These are more often than not used as vantage grounds for the advancement of the worldly ends of certain individuals as well as groups of individuals.

Differences of worldly position and ways of living may constitute reasonable ground for classifying peoples, but the so-called religious differences should not be any justifiable basis for dividing them. Real religious life can and does evolve in the human heart everywhere and at all times a uniformity in its general aspect, even though it may vary in the degree of its intensity or outward expression.

It should under favourable circumstances function as being the greatest unifying potentiality. As regards the dogmas and doctrines, ninety-nine out of every hundred persons are mentally unfit to think rightly about them. **External rituals and ceremonial observances, mostly symbolical as they are, represent the preparatory, non-essential aspect of real religion.** But it is these that offer the fruitful soil to the exploiter to come and sow the seed of dissension and jealousy and set man against man in the very name of God Himself. Dreadful engines of destruction are in this way called into service and the learned and the foolish alike are mercilessly victimised.

If the triple ideal of mercy, charity and self-sacrifice begins to be widely and rightly understood and sincerely and consistently followed in daily practice, it should help a good deal in creating an atmosphere in which it may be possible to advance the course of social equity and equality as a step towards the realisation by every individual of his real self. For, then, the extent of an individual's service and utility from the public point of view on the one hand and limitations and restraints which he imposes upon himself on the other, should form the basis for assigning to him his proper place in society. The learned and capable alone should be sent to the legislative bodies and the system of election and voting should be thoroughly revised and overhauled towards that end. To go to a council should not be a self-sought honour but should rather be a duty imposed upon an individual who has been fairly tried and found to be public-spirited and devoted to the good of society, to serve his motherland to the best to his lights. In a word, it is the record of individual evolution and public service at one's back, which should be the deciding factor in the award and distribution of social prestige and power.

9

Vivekananda and Modern India

In order to evaluate the contribution which Swami Vivekananda has made to the evolution of New India, it is necessary to remind ourselves of the times in which he lived and worked. India was then in a state of ferment. Vivekananda was born only six years after India's first revolutionary movement of independence in 1857. The national upsurge, however, was much wider than the political struggle. The second half of the nineteenth century was marked by activities of social and religious reform. Some reformist movements like the Brahmo Samaj in Bengal laid emphasis on the unity of God and discarded idol worship; it carried on a crusade for removal of social evils and for elevating the status of women. Others like the Arya Samaj in the north sought to go back to the pristine purity of the ancient scriptures and strove to attain the ideal of an Indian Nationality. The Indian National Congress which became the spearhead of the national struggle for independence was also established during these days.

It was in these times of turmoil and unrest that Vivekananda came under the influence of Ramakrishna Paramahamsa, a poor priest in a temple near Calcutta, and became, in due course, the standard-bearer of the master's teaching. Ramakrishna had scarcely any formal education and led an intensely spiritual life in splendid isolation. He had deep faith in the inherent truth of all religions and tested his belief by performing religious exercises in accordance with the practice and usage not only of different Hindu sects, but also of Christianity and Islam. His broad catholicity, mysticism and spiritual ecstasy attracted considerable attention of the people. But he lived and died a lonely spiritual devotee, unknown except to small groups of disciples and followers.

But Vivekananda was not only a disciple, he was an exponent and interpreter. His learning, eloquence, zest and energy and his wonderful personality gathered round him a band of followers which included the rich and the poor, intellectuals and illiterate, his own countrymen and foreigners.

In Vivekananda, patriotic and religious impulses aroused a supreme desire to uplift the manhood of India with a view to restoring India to a self-respecting place in the comity of nations. He believed that India had a definite contribution to make to the peace and progress of the world, but before she could do so, she had to win recognition from other nations by raising her own status. India could co-operate for the common good by eradicating poverty, by redressing social wrongs, and by developing her inherent strength. For this purpose, the people of India had to draw their inspiration from her ancient heritage. For the first time in the modern age, he boldly proclaimed before the world the cultural tradition and the spiritual qualities of Hindu civilisation, the greatness of her past, and the aspirations for her future. Instead of being apologetic or exhibiting a sense of inferiority which marked the attitude of many Indians in those days towards Western culture and civilisation a refreshing courage and a consciousness of innate strength marked Vivekananda's utterances. This, combined with a burning patriotic zeal, made him an embodiment of the ideals of a resurgent Indian nation. He was, in the words of Sir Valentine Chirol, 'the first Hindu whose personality won demonstrative recognition abroad for India's ancient civilisation and for her newborn claim to nationhood.'

Vivekananda was not a politician. He did not fight any political battles nor did he participate in civic and legislative bodies. He was primarily a religious reformer, but he propounded the fundamentals and emphasised the verities which years later were reinforced by Mahatma Gandhi and became in many ways the beacon light of the national renaissance. As Shri Nehru has observed: 'Vivekananda was one of the great founders of the modern national movement of India, and a great number of people who took more or less active part in that movement later on drew their inspiration from him.'

It is not easy to determine the way in which Vivekananda has influenced modern India nor to detail the spheres in which his influence has been felt. Such influence as a man like Vivekananda exercised was subtle and imperceptible, for the work of a spiritual teacher is concerned with the minds and hearts of men, not with institutions and laws. The footprints which a great man leaves on the sands of time are not always visible to the naked eye. Nevertheless, Vivekananda's inspiration and work abide.

The national movement of India, particularly after Gandhiji became its leader, has been not merely national in its aims and temper, but also democratic and social in its outlook. From 1931, when the Indian National Congress in its session at Karachi laid down the broad principle on which the Constitution of India was to be framed, until its session at Avadi in Madras in 1955, the emphasis of the Indian movement has been on the building up of a welfare state through improvement in the condition of the masses and the evolution of an equalitarian society by democratic means. And here is what Vivekananda, known as the 'cyclonic Hindu', had to say on this subject on different occasions.

> 'The only hope of India is from the masses. He who sees God in the poor, in the weak, and in the diseased really worships Him. He who has served and has helped one poor man, seeing God in him, without thinking of his caste, creed or race, or anything, with him God is more pleased than He is with the man who sees Him only in temples. Do you love your fellowmen? Where should you go to seek for God—are not all the poor, the miserable, the weak, gods? Why not worship them first? I consider that the great national sin is the neglect of the masses, and that is one of the causes of our downfall. No amount of politics will be of any avail until the masses in India are once more well-fed, and well-cared for.'

Again and again, Vivekananda said that religion had to be translated into our daily life and practice, that it should remove tyrannies and privileges and barriers. He firmly believed that the noblest way to serve God was through the service of man, that temples should not become ivory towers. **The term *Daridra-narayana* (to signify the dignity of the poor) which Gandhiji popularised was Swami Vivekananda's expression; it embodied his faith in and compassion for the weak, the humble and the lowly.** The most practical form which Vedanta should take, said Vivekananda, was the uplift of the mass of people. In this he was truly the forerunner of Gandhiji. **'An empty stomach', Vivekananda once remakred, 'is no good for religion.'** It was he, too, who observed that 'God comes to the poor in the form of bread.' We should constantly remind ourselves of these words now when we are involved in conflicts of creeds and wars between rival 'isms'. We have to act up to the ideals of a true democracy; we have to rid the world of dire poverty and want; we have to bring some ray of hope and cheer in countless lives immersed in squalor and misery. And this we have to do irrespective of communism or capitalism. The world can no more be half-starving and half-overfed than it can be half-free and half-slave. To meet Vivekananda's challenge in constructive terms is the superme task of statemanship today.

India's political system and constitutional structure are squarely based on principles of secularism. The Fundamental Rights laid down in the Constitution prohibit discrimination against any citizen on grounds of religion, race, caste, sex, place of birth, and prevent the imposition of any disability or restriction on such grounds. Complete religious freedom is assured to all citizens of India. This is the corner-stone of New India. Hindu-Muslim unity was one of the ideals for which Gandhiji strove and, indeed, it was in vindicating this ideal that he sacrificed his very life. Throughout his life, Vivekananda laid stress on brotherhood and tolerance. In his famous address to the Parliament of Religions in Chicago, he said: **'Sectarianism, bigotry and its horrible descendant, fanaticism, have long possessed this beautiful earth. They have filled the earth with violence, drenched it often and often with human blood, destroyed civilisation, and sent whole nations to despair.'** Indeed, he realised that social barriers could not be sanctioned by religious tenets. **India's doom was sealed the very day the caste system was invented and stopped free communion with one another...** No man, no nation can hate others and live.' For he believed like his great master that different religions are but diverse ways leading to the same goal. As the Vedanta proclaims: 'He is one, but the sages describe Him differently.'

Although a true nationalist, Swami Vivekananda was not narrow in his outlook or parochial in his approach. It is remarkable that over sixty years ago he had what we today call an international outlook. 'Even in politics and sociology, problems that were national twenty years ago can no longer be solved on national grounds only,' he observed. 'They are assuming huge proportions, gigantic shapes. They can only be solved when looked at in the broader light of international grounds. **International organisations, international combinations, international laws are the cry of the day. There cannot be any progress without the whole world being based on Truth and Justice.** It is becoming every dray clearer that the solution of any problem can never be attained on racial, national or narrow grounds. Every idea has to become broad till it covers the whole of this world, every aspiration must go on increasing till it has engulfed the whole of humanity. I am thoroughly convinced that no individual or nation can live by holding itself apart from the community of others. Colonialism breeds exclusiveness. This is the main cause of the degradation of Man today. **All nations must get back into the world current.** Motion is the sign of life.' How true these words are today so many years after they were spoken! With Vivekananda, however, internationalism was not a slogan or an instrument of power politics, but an expression of his innate sense of human brotherhood.

It is of interest to note that long before Gandhiji, Vivekananda emphasised not only the vital importance of truthfulness and even the principle of non-aggression. When Gandhiji returned to India from South Africa in 1914, what pained him most was a lack of moral strength among people; he was oppressed by the atmosphere of cowardice and fear. Gandhiji thought this to be the worst evil of the foreign rule, worse even than economic exploitation, since it corroded the souls of men and women and robbed them of their human dignity. He, therefore, tried to instil fearlessness among his people so that they might stand erect and upright before social tyrants, oppressive landlords and arrogant rulers.

But it is not only individual fear that matters. We live today in an age of fear, the richer are more afraid than the poorer, the more powerful nations are in greater terror than the weaker ones. Measures of security seem only to increase the feeling of insecurity all round. Atomic power accentuated our apprehensions, bringing the whole world under a shadow. Fear is at the root of much of the world's troubles today and has involved us in a terrible race in production of nuclear weapons which, if we are not prudent, can only end in universal disaster. Vivekananda proclaimed; 'Be not afraid of anything...It is fear that is the great cause of misery in the world. It is fear that is the greatest of all superstitions. It is fear that is the cause of our woes, and it is fearlessness that brings heaven even in a moment'.

So, too, about non-aggression. He once said; 'There is no virtue higher than non-injury. Non-injury has to be attained by him who would be free. No one is more powerful than he who has attained perfect non-injury.' This, indeed, has been the teaching of all great religions. This conception of non-aggression was later translated by Gandhiji into the principle of non-violence, and its wise application in the international sphere is the only hope for human survival.

10

Superman: Sri Aurobindo's Experiment in Yoga

The Upanishadic seeker has a most remarkable courage and tenacity in asking for the truth of his own self and that of the universal existence. What is *atman*? What is *Brahman*? How is immortality to be attained? And what reality belongs to the world? are the questions which powerfully moved his mind. He seems to have had a clear perception of their abiding worth and would not be deterred by any rival considerations of wealth and power from insistently asking for their meanings. He had evidently a clear sense of the inadequacy of the ordinary life and its ideals and therefore sought goals which were worth realising for their own sake.

The Upanishadic seeker wants such knowledge as will light up the mystery of all existence. He wants a joy and satisfaction, which is complete and final. The modern man with his long practical preoccupation will demur at such ideology and will protestingly declare that it is all theoretical. After all, he will say, a perfect life can have reality only in the imagination of man, the actual life is too imperfect and has to be like that. But this is too unfortunate. If we refuse to see the essential possibilities of our life, we can surely have no seeking for the realisation of them.

Sri Aurobindo reaffirms in a most vivid manner the reality of the Upanishadic seeking and that is a striking contribution to our modern life. In fact, he goes beyond conventional spirituality in declaring that it is possible for man in this terrestrial life, and in this physical body, to attain to complete Divinity. **The world is not to be necessarily rejected for rising to the spiritual status. The whole world and society must be spiritualised. There is certainly nothing essentially evil about the world and the body. This is the vision of life that Sri Aurobindo sets about realising in perfect seriousness through his Integral Yoga,** which is the instrument for effecting the transformation from the present imperfect human nature to perfected Divine nature. The whole truth of a kingdom of heaven on earth is the objective and its attainability a definite possibility. **In fact, says Sri Aurobindo, that is the inevitable evolutional destiny of man.** Sri Aurobindo's own words on this subject are most heartening and elevating:

"To know, possess and be the divine being in an animal and egoistic consciousness, to convert our twilit or obscure physical mentality into the plenary supermental illumination, to build peace and a self-existent bliss where there is only a stress of transitory satisfactions besieged by physical pain and emotional suffering, to establish an infinite freedom in a world which presents itself as a group of mechanical necessities, to discover and realise the immortal life in a body subjected to death and constant mutation—this is offered to us as the manifestation of God in Matter and the goal of Nature in her terrestrial evolution."

Further "if it be true that Spirit is involved in matter and apparent Nature is secret God, then the manifestation of the divine in himself and the realisation of God within and without are the highest and most legitimate aims possible to man upon earth."

As man succeeded the animal, so will he be followed by the *superman*, who will possess and manifest the higher divine consciousness in him. The implications of a harmonised consciousness are inherent in the division and conflict of human consciousness. This higher consciousness, according to Sri Aurobindo, has to come even as a necessity of evolution, through nature's unconscious yoga, but in man the possibility of conscious yoga can greatly expedite the realisation of that ideal.

According to Sri Aurobindo, the reality of the universe is *Sat, Cit* and *Ananda* or *Saccidananda.* It is characterised by the qualities of existence, consciousness and delight. It is the Absolute which comprehends everything. It is a concrete Absolute which gives validity to every detail of happening and existence and offers the best and the completest synthesis of all apparent contradictions. This Absolute is the source and the end of all things. But while the Absolute is ever perfect, it is nevertheless dynamic. **Sri Aurobindo's Absolute is a most remarkable conception. Philosophically one could say, it is an Absolute in an absolutely absolute way. It is governed by its own logic of the Absolute, the logic of the finite and the relative being inadequate for it. The former conceptions of the Absolute in the history of philosophy have often suffered in one way or another from some taint of the relative.** Here the Absolute is a real Absolute, which is personal as well as impersonal, complete and perfect as well as dynamic and evolutionary and an infinite lot more.

The world, consisting of inanimate matter, plants, animals and man, is a dynamic expression of the Absolute. The successive stages of Matter, Life and Mind are the evolutionary stages, through which the Absolute is progressively rising to its own full self-consciousness. The very fact, assures Sri Aurobindo, that life seems to come out of matter and mind out of life, necessitates the conclusion that the last term of evolution must have been present as a potentiality from the beginning. **Mind, which is at present the highest term of evolution, already seems to point out to something higher than itself.**

The rational mind of man working by logical judgements, as it does, also seems to reveal at times intuitive cognition of direct and certain knowledge, affirms Sri Aurobindo, on the basis of both argument as well as personal yogic experience, is the essential quality of the next higher stage of evolution, which he calls 'Supermind', as rationality is of the present mind of man. The progress of evolution seems to be towards the full realisation of the Absolute Consciousness. It is the Absolute returning to its own full self-consciousness after an enriched experience of an evolutionary progress gone through. Since the last stage is the Absolute returning to its full self-consciousness it must be supposed to be present in matter itself right at the initial stage. The matter is thus the Absolute involved; Matter is Brahman, declared the Upanishad, involution and evolution are thus the complementary processes of the world drama.

But what is the motive of the whole show? The love of the thing or self-delight or *Lila*—that is the answer. A utilitarian age will find is hard to appreciate this motive as a possible goal to action at all. But a little reflection will show that the highest motive which man too realises in his moments of creativity is just joy for the thing itself. An artist's delight in artistic creation is its own motive as well as the reward. That can be the only motive conceivable for the Absolute in its activity of cosmic manifestation.

Human life is, at the moment, the highest term of the cosmic evolutionary process. Man, representing the manifestation of mind in evolution, anticipates the next higher stage, which is that of Supermind. Mind is analytical, supermind, as affirmed on the basis of concrete yogic experience and also as an inference from mind and the general character of the evolutionary process, will be intuitive, comprehending the spiritual unity of all. Our present consciousness is egoistic, that is, in the words of C.G. Jung, it is characterised by 'exclusiveness, selection and discrimination.' The next stage of Supermind will be marked by comprehensiveness, unity and identity. That gives evidently the main purpose of our life and our endeavours and aspirations will naturally draw their meanings from their relation to this evolutionary purpose of our existence. The world, the stage of human activity and the evolutionary drama of the *Sacchidananda*, is surely real. It is the artistic creation of the self-delight of the Absolute Consciousness. Life and the world have an earnest meaning in the self-expressing and self realising activity of the Ultimate Reality. The whole evolution is engaged in the labour of forging ahead to the next higher stage, the super-rational or super-human or the stage of Superman. There is an unconscious yoga or discipline working through all nature, but **in man consciousness becomes capable of being used intensively, so as to expedite the realisation of the higher stage. Sri Aurobindo's occupation with yoga has had just this object that of consciously and intensively preparing the ground and expediting through collective effort the realisation of the next higher stage on earth.**

The word 'superman' has many European associations attached to it, which will unfortunately tend to pervert Sri Aurobindo's meaning. The Superman to him is no magnification of the egoistic man, however great. It is qualitatively a new value in evolution, involving a complete supersession of the present egoistic consciousness. Supermind is intuitive, involving a perception of the spiritual unity of all reality. It is Divine consciousness itself and the superman is an angel of god. A race of such Supermen is in the making, affirms Sri Aurobindo. **The present man, ignorant and grieving, is**

going to be replaced by a higher man who will possess light, love and power. Such is the great message of hope and fulfilment which Sri Aurobindo has to offer to the world.

But the reader naturally will ask, how is this epochal transformation going to be effected? Well, yoga is the instrument of this change. Sri Aurobindo worked long at testing and improving this instrument and in his comprehensive exposition, entitled *The Synthesis of Yoga*, through a comparative investigation of the various systems of yoga he perfected a new instrument called by him the Integral Yoga. An essential psychological soundness is the principal merit of it, which, however, to be properly appreciated will require some practical experience.

Yoga is, with Sri Aurobindo, a very comprehensive term. "All life is yoga." "In the right view of both life and yoga," says he "all life is either consciously or sub-consciously a yoga. For we mean by this term a methodised effort towards self-perfection by the expression of the potentialities of the being." However, in man this effort becomes self-conscious, through which the work of self-perfection can be carried on very much more swiftly and puissantly. More directly, yoga, therefore, comes to mean this self-conscious effort at self-perfection. It is really an effort at the realisation of the spiritual possibilities of our life.

The concept 'spiritual life' carries with it usually a number of misgivings. Firstly, its contrast with worldly life is unfortunate. The separation between the two in the past has had the necessary effect of leaving worldly life relatively unspiritualised and the spiritual life devoid of proper content. Sri Aurobindo's yoga, however, contemplates spiritualisation of the entire life of man. "Our subject is", says he, "to make the spiritual life and its experiences fully active and fully utilisable in the waking state and even in the normal use of functions." **The**

spirituality here contemplated, therfore, is not for the individual's release from life though individual seekers may for a time, as needed by the circumstances of their yogic discipline, go into a relative seclusion from society. But the ultimate goal is always a complete transformation of the concrete whole life of man.

Now we shall take up the technique of yoga. Aspiration, rejection and opening oneself up to the higher consciousness constitute the triple process of Sri Aurobindo's yoga. When once it has been clearly recognised that the root of all that we think and do lies in our 'willing', then it will be easy to realise the ineffectivity of controlling life from the outside. One who continues inwardly to will a thing, but in bodily behaviour denies it, we get, what the *Gita* calls *Mithyacara,* false behaviour. The right thing to do is to aim, while controlling behaviour, primarily at the modification and transformation of the will. This transformation is to be achieved through a sincere and a whole-hearted aspiration for the right will or the higher will, which progressively seeks delights of the spirit, the calm and serener joys of life rather than the violent pleasures of the senses and the body. Man's life is a clear picture of conflict and transition.

We are animals, who have the capacity of becoming gods. And the way of our progress exactly consists in rising from the status of the animal instincts to that of the spirit, which will not reject the body and its pleasures, but transform and enhance them. To rise to that fuller status of the spirit or the soul is the aim of spiritual life and yoga. But obviously that calls for great patience and perseverance. However, that is the only way in life for which any effort put in never goes wasted. The *yogabhrasta* as says Krishna, is reborn under more favourable circumstances from where he can more easily go forward with the interrupted work of yoga.

An undying aspiration for the complete and full life of the soul-status is the main lever of the yogic transformation. Knock at the door and it shall be opened unto you, is the language of the Christian scripture, stating the same essential idea. But the idea of the original and fundamental sin we do not countenance in yoga. There are right movements and there are wrong ones in our being. The wrong ones, every time that they occur, must be readily noticed and sincerely rejected, and the right willing in place of them aspired for. Each such sincere rejection and aspiration will silently but surely perfect the change in you that you desire to produce. And you will before long begin to feel an increasing tendency to think and act in the right way spontaneously.

The third movement in the triple yogic process is opening oneself to the Higher Consciousness. The task of a complete transformation of the lower nature into higher nature is the greatest and most adventurous of all undertakings. One who achieves it is greater than one who conquers the whole world. The accomplishment of such a thing will require calling into action the Supreme Consciousness of the universe. The individual gives himself up, surrenders or invokes and calls in the working of the Divine Consciousness for the complete change. It involves essentially an attitude of adoration and love for the Superme Reality, with which a complete union and identification is sought by the human individual.

It is obvious, reality and life have fundamentally been conceived as spiritual and perfection consists in the full realisation and expression of the spiritual potentialities of life and existence. The reader will see that the same or something similar is aimed at and attempted by religion. But there is a real difference between the religious and the yogic approach to the problem of life. To religion a 'hereafter' is almost essential. 'Fear' and 'repentance' too play a very dominant part in religious life. Religion further involves rather a sharp contrast with secularism. Yoga demands of the individual, on the other hand, a dispassionate, scientific attitude towards life. Instead of sin it contemplates wrong movements in our nature, which have simply to be recongnised, acknowledged, and whole-heartedly rejected. This must be done without shrinking and worrying. Fear is a weak attitude to be necessarily eliminated. A 'hereafter' like that of religions is irrelevant. Here and now and ever hereafter, that is what yoga aims at. Besides it claims the whole life. It can brook no departmentalisation. Ceremonial is to religion, at the least, an indispensable part. To yoga it is, however, at best, a secondary means, which the individual may use for a particular purpose of transformation in his experience.

The yogic view of life and world has an immense posssibility for the future as a general instrument for human spiritual advancement and perfection. In fact, it may prove to be an all-comprehensive future religion of mankind. **It has an essential respect for the scientific attitude and does thereby assimilate the principle value of the scientific age. It secures more effectively, here and now, and in the full sphere of life, the spiritual realisation, which all religions aspire after.** Sri Aurobindo's philosophy is not just a thought-construction. It furnishes also an effective instrument of yoga for testing for oneself the realisation of experience which it presents.

11

Ashoka: The First King of Peace

Ashoka gave to his empire certain principles of administration which, in their breadth of vision and outlook, their spirit of humanity and internationalism, are an aspiration even to the modern world. **He based his empire upon the principles of non-violence, universal peace, peace between man and man and between man and every sentient creature, so that it was an empire of righteousness, an empire resting on right and not on might, and thus too far ahead of the times** to stand the ordained and ordinary historic process of a painful development from the brute to the man. **He also gave to his subject peoples of different communities, castes and creeds, certain common and cardinal ideals of thought and conduct which make him to be humanity's first teacher of universal morality and religion.** These priciples of policy and morality may be read to this day on the rocks and proclamation pillars on which they were inscribed in imperishable characters in the different provinces of his far-flung empire. These 'sermons in stone' are a sort of autobiography of the emperor, and the most important and fruitful sources of this remarkable history.

The art of government, of imperial administration, is by no means less practical than the other arts of civilised life like engineering or architecture. It calls for practical ability, insight into the needs and conditions of men, and capacity for business and organisation. The problem for governments was not an easy one for the Mauryan emperors. The area of government was too wide to be conveniently controlled from one centre by a single authority. This is apparent from the very distribution of Ashoka's inscriptions, proclaiming his authority and message from the northern frontiers to Mysore, associated with the sacred memory of his grandfather's retirement in religious life. The area was further extended by Ashoka's conquest of Kalinga, signalised by 150,000 persons carried away as captives, 100,000 wounded and many times that number succumbing to their wounds or other after-effects of war. There was also much suffering caused indirectly to the civilian population of the country related to the combatants affected in the war by blood or by other ties of friendship or dependence. This almost modern appraisement of the violence wrought by his first war made Ashoka determine that it should be his last and attached him earnestly to a more humane creed of non-violence, viz., Buddhism. Thus his empire ceased to extend at the expense of the freedom of the neighbouring states and peoples, which was henceforth to be scrupulously respected.

The government had necessarily to be multi-central. A unitary, centralised admininstration could not hope to control an empire larger than British India in those pre-mechanical ages of primitive transport. Thus the empire was split up into a number of provincial administrations and viceroyalties modelled on a common plan. The head of the government was, of course, the sovereign, whose authority was in theory, or in the legal sense, unlimited. But in practice it was limited in many ways under the established usages and customs of the Hindu state.

There was no central sovereign or legislature that legislated for the entire country. The laws of the realm were not uniform or standardised, but were various according to various local conditions. Thus castes, country, people (*janapada*), guilds and families were permitted to make their own laws, which were respected by the sovereign or the state. Along with the legislative functions, the executive and judicial functions of the sovereign were also considerably decentralised. The result was that the people were practically self-governing in the various groups and communities to which they belonged. The Hindu state, like some of the more advanced of modern democracies in the West, encouraged group-life and the vital and natural associations, and was thus autocratic only in name or theory. Its autocracy was limited from below by a vast subterranean democracy, a self-governing society moving in its own orbit, apart from the state.

Ashoka emphasised still further the moral foundations of his authority, his responsibility to his people as the guardian of their well-being. **He was fond of declaring that 'all men were his children, for whom as their father he desired every kind of prosperity and happiness both in this world and the next and that his governors were created for the welfare and happiness of the governed, who were committed to their care as a child is committed to a skilful nurse'.** And his sense of responsibility to his people made him work very hard as a public servant. In Rock Edict VI he comments on the lapses of his predecessors, and makes a public business declaration that he will be ready for public at all hours and places even while at meals or in his bedroom or in his meditations. Even while thus working, he never "felt satisfied with his exertions and despatch of business". And the spirit which sustained him in his work was that thereby he was only "obtaining his own release from the debt he owed to his fellow human beings."

The sovereign's main work in the administration was naturally that of supervision, for which he depended upon a special class of officers called the Prativedakas who would report to him on public affairs at all hours. He was also assisted by a Parishad of Ministers, Mahamatras, or the Privy Council, whose number, according to Kautilya, depended upon the needs of administration. But he depended upon himself mostly for his own work. That the master's eye might be everywhere in his dominions, he initiated the practice of travelling through them, not in search of pleasure or sport like his predecessors but for "the inspection of the country and the people."

Besides receiving reports and travelling, the emperor's work comprised the issue of notifications or edicts, in which the following matters are dealt with, in a broad sense: (1) the policy of his government; (2) the special laws passed by him for protection of life and reprieve of three days granted to convicts sentenced to death; (3) the powers and duties of his governors and his injunction to them; (4) his orders regarding periodical tours of all his officers; (5) his institutions of a new Department of Morals and the duties of its staff; (6) the sovereign's own duties and example; (7) the moral ideals prescribed for his people; (8) his public work of utility and other innovations. It is apparent that all these subjects should fall within the province of the emperor's personal administration.

Next to the emperor ranked the viceroys in charge of the larger provinces. The viceroys were generally recruited from the princes of the royal blood, called Kumaras and Aryaputras in the edicts, which mention four such viceroys, viz., those at Taxila, Ujjain, Tosali and Suvarnagiri. According to tradition, Ashoka, as prince, was viceroy at Taxila. He himself is said to have appointed Prince Kunala as his viceroy there. According to Fa-hien he appointed his son, Prince Dharma Vivardhana, as his viceroy of Gandhara. Like the king, the viceroys also had their ministers.

The smaller provinces were under officers called

Rashtriyas and Rajukas. The governor of the western province under Chandragupta was Pusyagupta, the Vaisya, and under Ashoka, Raja Tusapha, the Yavana. The Rajukas are spoken of as being "set over hundreds of thousands of souls". They were not created by Ashoka, but were invested by him with larger powers as regards award of honours and penalties. There were other provincial officers, called the Pradesikas, in charge of the executive, revenue and judicial service, while the Rajukas, as suggested by the name itself, dealt with "survey, land settlement and irrigation". There were also other officers of a similar rank, called the Purusas, spoken of as being "set over the multitude", whose duty was to exhort the Rajukas into loyal service of the king. Buhler considers them to be like the Prativedakas or the inspectorate of the government.

The heads of departments were sometimes called Mukhas. They were also called the Mahamatras. The department assigned to a Mahamatra was indicated by its name being prefixed to that of the officer. The Mahamatra, who were the Prefects of cities, were called the Nagara-Vyavaharikas, such as those at Tosali (which was under a viceroy), Isila and Samapa. Dutas or envoys are also mentioned, but they seem to have belonged to the class of officers, called Dharma-Mahamatras. The ordinary civil servants were called Yuktas and Purusas, distinguished as being of high, low, or middle rank. The clerk, scribe, *lipikara* is also mentioned.

The most important administrative innovation of Ashoka was his creation of a new department for the spread of the Dharma as defined by him, and his recognition of the principle that the first care of the state was the moral development of the people. The edicts adumbrate the growth of this idea in Ashoka's mind. In the Kalinga Rock Edict ll, he first expresses his feeling that all might not be well with the administration, and calls upon his officers to see that no man is put under imprisonment or torture without due cause. And "for this purpose, in accordance with Dharma," to prevent all injustice, he declared his resolve that he "shall send forth in rotation every five years such persons as are of mild and temperate disposition, and regardful of the sanctity of life, who, knowing this purpose, will comply with his instructions." A similar order was sent out to the princely viceroys of Ujjain and Taxila that they should at least every three years send on tour similar bodies of officials for the same purpose. Later on this intention of the emperor was developed into a standing decree, announced into his Rock Edict III by which it was ordained that "everywhere in his dominions his officers of all ranks—the Yuktas, the Rajukas and the Pradesikas—must go out on tours, each every five years, for their ordinary administrative business as for this special purpose, the inculcation of the Dharma." Next, after a year, this scheme of religious tours by his officials received a further development in the institution of a special class of officers, the Dharma-Mahamatras, charged with the duty of attending to the moral and spiritual welfare of all his subjects, irrespective of their creed or community, Brahmins, Buddhists, Jaina, Ajivikas and others, or "soldiers and their chiefs, the rich and the destitute, the old and the infirm," or members of the royal family, male and female, both in the capital and provincial towns.

Their first duty was to prevent and remedy unjust molestation, imprisonment and execution. Their more general duty was to spread and establish the Dharma and regulate the charities both of the king and of the queens and the princes for the Dharma was connected with charities. Their was also the delicate task of supervising female morals, and in that capacity they were called Striadhyaksa-mahamatras. They also seem to have been in charge of the various kinds of works of public utility in the country, such as provision of hospitals, medical aid, drinking water and rest-houses for travellers and the like. Lastly, **their work was also to organise the foreign missions which are so unique a feature of Ashoka's administration.** The missions were at work both "in the dominions of His Majesty and also among his frontagers. Among these frontagers are mentioned the Yavanas, Kambojas, Gandharas in the north-west, Rastrikas, Pitinikas, Nabhapantis, Bhojas, Andhras and Pulindas in the interior, and the Colas and Pandyas, the Satiyaputra and Keralaputra in the south. Dutas or envoys were also sent on missionary work among distant foreign states beyond the frontagers, viz., Egypt under Ptolemy Philadelphos (258-47 B.C.), Macedonia under Antigonos Gonatas (278-39 B.C.), Cyrene under Magas (285-58 B.C.), Epirus under an Alexander (272-258 B.C.), and Syria under Antiochos Theos (261-46 B.C.), all mentioned in Rock Edict XIII, and also referred to in Rock Edict II.

Now, what was the Dharma which Ashoka was at such pains in introducing and spreading both his own dominions and beyond? It comprised certain fundamental principles of thought and life, about which there can be no two opinions and which are acceptable and applicable to all mankind. In one edict they are stated to be mastery of the senses (*samyama*), purity of thought *(bhavasuddhi)*, greatfulness (*kritajnata*) and steadfastness of devotion (*dridhabhakti*); in another "little impiety, many good deeds, kindness (*daya*), charity (*dana*), truthfulness (*satya*), and purity in thoughts and deed (*sauca*); and in a third edict, *daya, dana, satya, sauca,* together with *moda*, i.e., blissfulness, and *sadhuta* or saintliness."

But the Dharma was presented not merely in the from of doctrines, but in a more concrete form, for it must be lived and not merely believed and that by the people at large, the masses, to whose average level of moral life it must adjust itself. Thus the basis of the Dharma was laid in the purity of domestic life, involving proper relations with "father and mother, kinsmen, servants and slaves, comrades, friends and supporters, seniors in age, the guru," the relations being analysed into those of service, support or of reverence. "The love that is kindled at home expands itself over the race of man." And so the next step in Ashoka's religious scheme was to include Brahmins and ascetics, homeless devotees, to whom all honour and liberality must be shown by the householders, as also lower animals depending on man.

On the basis of these practices was evolved a new ethics, which represents Ashoka's contributions in the sphere of ideals. A separate edict was issued to emphasise Toleration as the essential element of religion in a land of many faiths. It was declared that **"he who does reverence to his own sect while disparaging the sects of others wholly from attachment to his own, with intent to enhance the splendour of his own sect, in reality by such conduct inflicts the serverest injury on his own sect,"** for such a man lacks the essentials of religion, viz., respect for the essence of the matter that is in all sects, and a consequent "restraint of speech," considering that **"the sects of other people also deserve reverence for one reason or another."** Thus the emperor's special concern was that "there should be growth in the essence of the matter and the respect for all sects," and not that his own sect and faith should flourish. He was himself the best example to his people of his own precept. He declared in his edict that "the king does reverence to men of all sects by gifts and various forms of reverence." As examples of Ashoka's consideration for all sects may be mentioned his grant of cave dwellings to the Ajivikas, his enlargement of the stupa of Buddha

Konagomana on two occasions, his promotion of the interests of the Brahmins, Ajivikas, Nirgranthas and various other sects equally with the Buddhists by the employment of his special officers, and his repeated insistence in the edicts on the duty of showing liberality to Brahmins and Sramanas alike and avoiding all unseemly behaviour to them.

Lastly, along with the spheres of religion and morality. Ashoka introduced certain very high ideals in the sphere of politics too. By his high moral purpose and earnestness, he moralised and spiritualised politics. The horrors of a single war convinced him that it was an absolute wrong and evil, which should have no place in his scheme of affairs. He forthwith gave effect to his conviction by declaring that "the chiefest conquest is the conquest of right and not might." **A whole empire pledged itself to peace as an absolute good on its own initiative and inspiration without reference to its neighbouring states.** The war-drum was completely silenced; the *bherighosa* was no longer heard, but only the *dhramaghosa*. The steam-roller of Mauryan aggression, which under Chandragupta had levelled down most of the independent states of India was now brought to a halt. "Thus far and no farther" was Ashoka's command. Many a small state or people in the remaining part of India was spared its independence. **India became a happy family of nations under an international system of Liberty, Equality and Fraternity for all, great or small.**

12

Law and Justice in Ancient India

The evolution of property brought in its train the evolution of various types of institutions, e.g., family, state and government. The ancient form of government was based on the organisation of the family. Primitive society was socialistic. The family property was the joint property. Gradually there grew up a state, as a community of some kind to act in order to obtain what was good. The history of human society is the history of a development following very slowly one general law, that of the variety of forms of life—of domestic and civil institutions, which is ascribable mainly to the unequal development of the different sections of mankind.

The Vedic Aryans had a settled life. The Aryan society was looked upon as an organism which depended on the cooperation of different classes and sections. The Hindu state was more social than political like many of the states. The admixture of politics and religion everywhere marks the transition from the primitive idea of cosmology to rational explanation of the forces and factors regulating the phenomenal world. Politics came to be dominated by ritualism.

In the Vedic period *grama* (village) was the basis of social life. The sanction that lay behind villagers' insistence upon conformity and peace within the village resided objectively in the power and the willingness of the villagers to punish the offender; but there was, besides, a subjective sanction of enormous potency. Thus gradually arose the idea of justice in ancient India. Justice has been defined by Plato as 'the virtue of an individual' and sometimes as 'the virtue of a State'. In ancient India, law and justice were allied terms and the forms of government were sufficiently sanctioned by religion or tradition. State was recognised as the highest type of organisation. Law was a regulation for daily life. The administration of justice meant the determination of what is just. Village system was the most dominant. Social organisation was the most effective way of satisfying the individual needs and desires. The making of laws was in the hands of the entire population.

The Vedic political constitution consisted of (a) priestly aristocracy independent of the king and exempted from punishment for offences and taxes and tolls on land and other property, and with acknowledge claims to protection from hunger, sickness, cold or heat; (b) king and (c) state assembly consisting of priests, nobles and common people with powers to elect and banish kings, to restore banished kings and to have an authoritative voice on all political and judicial matters of the State. The punishment of criminals and a proper administration of law are the foundations on which all civilised societies are built. Law was regarded as power and nothing was higher than law. Justice was administered by family or clan and in Rigveda we find the institution of monetary compensation for offences.

The gradual crystallisation of a larger part of society into village communities favoured the growth of local particularism, strengthened the spiritual and judicial authorities of the Brahmins and as a result of that society became more complex and developed into an elaborate organism. The village headman regulated the local police and taxation. There was no differentiation of functions in the Vedic period. The absence of paramount power accounted for the permanence of popular element in ancient Indian judicial system. Centralised judicial system was in the making. The conception of law was that of a body of precepts accepted as suitable for the guidance of human action. Judicial organisation was not very elaborate. Macdonell and Keith remark: 'There is no trace of organised criminal justice vested either in the king or in the people... there was some sort of judicial procedure in vogue in the later Vedic period.' Elders of the village were appointed to decide the cases. They were not judges in the real sense of the term as they decided cases by arbitration. There was a distinction between the civil and criminal law. Punishment was rather harsh. Treachery was to be punished by death. King was the source of criminal law. Civil law was not very much developed. Some references about the plaintiff, defendant and judges are found in Vedic literature. King was the chief judge. Laws of inheritance cannot be traced before the Sutras.

The Sabha was dominated by the Brahmins and the *Maghavanas* (rich patrons). The Purohita had great influence in matters of secular importance. Legal position of the Brahmins was strong. The interpretation of the terms *Jnatra* (witness), *Pratiprasna* (arbitrator), *Pratistha* (sanctuary), *Prashna* (pleading), *Madhyamasi* (Mediator), *Jibagrah* and *Ugra* etc. may throw some more light on the judicial history of the period. Spies seem to have been largely employed not merely to ascertain validity or invalidity in the statements of parties and witness in criminal and civil cases tried by the king or state assembly, but also to gather correct and reliable information as regards movement of tribal settlement or inimical tendencies or disposition.

The judicial administration was largely the work of the village assemblies and other popular or communal bodies whether with or without the king's authority or presence. King's Purohita advised on points of laws and facts were judged by the Sabhasadas selected from the Brahmins or the elders of the towns or guilds in later Vedic and Brahminical period. The legal system arose partly due to the recognition of principles which guided the conduct of various groups of society, and partly due to the recognition of old customary laws. Later on, guild laws, evidences and procedures were also recognised.

In the Brahmanical period justice came to be administered in the name of the king. The king was the fountainhead of justice and the highest judge in criminal and civil matters. Local bodies and corporate organisations had minor jurisdictions. The administration of justice came to be regarded as one of the principle duties of the king and the Brahmanas contain sufficient material pointing to the king's exercise of the judicial functions. He was the upholder of sacred law. Divine law was prevalent during the Upanishadic period. Judicial authority of the Brahmins increased. The basis of king's authority was sought in his fulfilment of fundamental needs of the individual and society. The king was the custodian of social order.

The code of Brihaspati has been regarded as the most authoritative in ancient India. The epic distinguishes the theological and legal teachings of Brihaspati. In the epic Draupadi condemns fatalism and despondency. Both Briahspati and *Mahabharata* stress the necessity of government for security of person and property and the economic foundations of society. During the time of *Mahabharata*, administration of justice was carried on with the help of a Mantri Parishad. Ministers were men of high character. King was assisted by the Samantas (subordinate rulers), Yuvaraja, Purohita, Commander-in-chief, Chamberlain, Pradesta (Chief Justice), Dharmadhyaksa (Superintendent of Justice), Dandapala (Presiding Judge of Criminal Courts or Chief of Police), City Prefects,

Superintendent of Prisons, Warden of Fort, etc. There was a separate department of justice. Officers were instructed to detect crimes and maintain order within their jurisdiction. Each office was responsible to the next higher authority. Vyavahara laws were equally authoritative as the Dharma laws.

Brihaspati prescribes heavy fines for dishonesty and rigorous punishment for all crimes. He advocated statecraft as a means of administering justice. He divided witnesses into *krta* and *akrta* and subdivided each into six divisions. He describes four categories of judicial assemblies: (a) stationary, (b) not stationary, (c) furnished with king's signet-ring, and (d) directed by the king. Stationary courts used to sit in the town, not stationary was a movable court. King's signet-ring was supervised by the Chief Judge and the fourth court was held in the presence of the king.

Buddhism developed a moral law not merely as a veto for the immoral doer but also as a guide for the man willing to do well. Dhamma was bound up with the whole life and was to be each man's own guide. Buddhism was based on justice, charity and love. Dhamma regulated social and ritual activities. Criminal law was administered by a succession of regularly appointed officials. Justices, lawyers and rehearsers of the law maxims, the council of representatives, the general, the vice-consuls and the consul himself could acquit the accused. The council awarded the penalty according to the Book of Precedents. During the Buddhist period, criminal justice was administered by experts through the presidents and elders of the Kula Courts. According to Bhrigu, the deciding authority in a Gana was Kulika or Kula, though Kula is used in the sense of a jury by Katyayana. It was through the village headman that all government business was carried out and he had both the opportunity and power to represent the case to the higher officials.

The *Mahaparinibbana Sutta* mentions two other judicial officers among the Licchivis, the Athakulaka and the Suttadhara. In some Jatakas we find purohitas performing judicial functions. According to the Dharmasastras, the purohita seems to have associated with the king in the administration of justice and was liable to fast and penances if there was a miscarriage of justice. The Viniscayamatya was a criminal officer who combined police and judicial functions. From Jatakas we learn that cases were tried by Gramabhojakas, and appeals by purohita, the uparaja and the king. Common law also played an important part. Under the common law, the culprit was to be punished by the king and under the Dharma law he was also to be punished for the sins implied in the crime. The ideal of the right of justice, prevailing in the time of Jatakas, resulted in the fall of litigation. A reference to the administration of justice is also found in a Pali work and in this connection the famous case of Anathapindika vs. Jeta, the prince-royal, may be referred. That case was decided by the Court of Sravasti, capital of Oudh. Justice was pure and the rule of law was prevalent. The administration of justice went hand in hand with the police jurisdiction. Justice was equitable. With the emergence of Magadha as an imperial power, an estabilised judicial machinery came into vogue. During that period *grama* was the lowest unit of administration.

During the time of the Mauryas, penal laws were served and both Megasthenese and Kautilya have testified to this fact. Offenders were punished with fines. King was not the maker of laws but its guardian. The validity of laws depended on their comformity to an intrinsic standard of equality. Kautilya advocated the validity of Rajasasana and in this respect he was followed by Narada and Harita. The Mauryan age was an age of triumphant nationalism and there was a regular contact between the east and the west.

In the west king's authority was being glorified. It is possible that Kautilya might have been influenced by the western writers in adoring the authority of the king. In those days we find the exaltation of royal edict or Rajasasana above all other forms of law and convention. It is clear that the king controlled the judicial machinery. This variety of judicial system was dominated by the royal legislation and jurisdiction. It is evident that a royal law, order or regulation, if it conflicted with the other laws, was always regarded as overriding them and that the royal verdict in law-suits was final.

Kautilya planned a well-organised judiciary. In Books 3 and 4, he has dealt mainly with the administration of justice. There were two courts, viz. (a) Dharmasthiya or civil court and (b) Kantakasodhana or criminal court. Dharmasthiya was organised and directed by the Amatyas in alliance with the Dharmasthas and its main function was to dispose of such cases as arose out of the violation of the traditional rules and regulations and it could impose only nominal fines. Its scope was limited to (a) Disputes concerning the non-performance of agreements, (b) Law of marriage and women's property, (c) Law of divorce, (d) Law of inheritance and succession, (e) Laws relating to buildings and houses, (f) Law of household property and pasture lands, (g) Law of debts, deposits and slaves, (h) Law of co-operative undertaking of sale and purchase, resumption, ownership, (i) Law of crime and violence, dice-playing, etc. Prof. Rangaswami Aiyangar translates Dharmasthiya as "Common and Canon Law Courts" and Kantakasodhana as "Police and Administrative Courts." The Dharmasthiya dealt with the Vyavahara or civil litigation. Justice in that court was administered by the royal officials, advised by the learned Brahmin jurists. The Kantakasodhana was a very important court. It looked to the safety of the empire and tried such cases as arose out of the violation of the state laws and regulations. Its main functions were (a) to protect the interests of traders and artisans, (b) to find out the ways and means and to do away with the national calamity, (c) not to allow people to maintain themselves by sordid means, (d) to find out the culprit with the help of the spies, (e) to arrest one while committing crime, and (f) to keep safe the government departments. The officer of the central executive conducted these courts and here the jurists were not consulted.

Various types of cases were tried by the Kantakasodhana court. The officers of this court could get facts by torture and other means. Prof. K.A. Nilakanta Sastri observes: "The Kanatakasodhana courts were a new type introduced to meet the growing needs of an increasingly complex social economy and to implement the decisions of a highly organised bureaucracy on all matters that were being brought under their control and regulation for the first time. These courts were introduced to protect the state and the people from the baneful action of anti-social persons (*kantaka*). Kantakasodhana was a quasi-judicial department and its work had more in common with the functions of a modern police organisation than a judiciary." It was a corner-stone of the entire administrative system.

Jury system was a *de facto* instiution. The judges made up the Sabha and were the jury of the courts. Mr. P.N. Banerjee accepts the prevalence of jury system and observes: "The three or five members of the judicial assembly acted as jurors as well as judges but the final decisions rested with the Chief Judge." The Adhikarins, the Sresthins, and the Kayastha formed the jury of the court. Trial by jury was limited to criminal cases only. According to *Arthasastra,* the trial and enquiry of the case depended on Dharma or law, Vyavahara or usage and royal edicts. *Agnipurana* says, "A court should neither entertain nor leave a cross-case without first deciding the original one, nor should it take up a case or a suit dismissed or rejected by another tribunal of competent authority."

Conception of justice was very high. The judges were expected to observe the eternal law of justice and decide all cases of disputes without partiality. If the king failed to follow the accepted law of the land, he was liable to punishment by any citizens of the state. According to Upanishads, law was the king of the kings.

Law was both legal and moral. The functions of the judges were (a) to apply law to cases, (b) to interpret its technicalities, and (c) to advise the king on legal matters, morality and ethics. "A judge should be learned, sagacious, eloquent, dispassionate, impartial; he should pronounce judgment only after due deliberation and enquiry; he should be a guardian to the weak, a terror to the wicked, his heart should covet nothing, his mind be intent on nothing but equity and truth." The judges were called Dharmadhikarins, the Pradestas or Panditas. Chief Judge was called Pradivivaka. He presided over the royal Sabha, the highest court of justice. He was expected to be conversant with the eighteen titles of laws. The independence of judges was unquestioned and their terms of office depended upon their good behaviour. The judiciary was separate from the executive, generally independent in spirit. The judges were always helped by the community. Justice was always administered openly.

The king also acted as the judge. "He should learn the right law for each case from authoritative persons and in doubtful cases take the advice of learned Brahmins. He should daily repair to the hall of justice along with learned Brahmins and experienced councillors and should examine the cases of the complainants.' Council of the king, together with the king, was responsible for justice. According to Narada, the thorn of injustice may be removed only when the whole college of judges are unanimous about the decision. Gautama lays down the duty of the king to administer justice, punish the guilty and protect his subjects. "The king should conduct the enquiry of the law-suits without violating the rules of Dharmasastra and Arthasastra." Jimutavahana also holds the same view and says that the administration of justice has to be rendered in conformity with both Dharmasastra and Arthasastra. The judicial function of the king developed as a result of the patriarchical system. The royal system in ancient India did not harmonise with the spirit of the day. The villagers had a judicial system of their own at once familiar to and respected by them and the various trades and guilds had a similar system. In cases of grave crimes or when the condemned party refused to obey the judgment of the local court, the court of king was concerned with litigation.

Cases were generally heard in open court. According to Sukra, the procedure of a case was as follows: (a) petition by the complainant, (b) written statement submitted in defence by the defender, (c) defence of both sides, and (d) decision by the judges. The proceedings were written by the scribes. In cases of constitutional importance the judges used to consult Smritis and old judgments. Witnesses and oath played an important part. In order to ascertain the judges had to take into consideration the following four means: (a) visible indication *(pratyaksa)*, (b) reasoning (*yukti*), (c) inference (*anumana*), and (d) analogy (*upamana*).

Constitutionalism and the rule of Law were the characteristic features of Hindu judiciary. All were equal in the eyes of Law.

13

Varnashrama and Caste

The ancient Hindu pattern of social organisation aimed at the values of Dharma, Artha, Kama and Moksha by the individual through his physical, psychological and social evolution. This evolution was calculated to be effected through the process of the Varna-ashrama system. It was a comprehensive scheme of individual fulfilment with social purpose through concrete institutions. It has been regarded as the basic concept of Hindu culture and the pivot of Hindu social structure throughout the ages. At the same time it can not be denied that the Varna Dharma has been equally the target of vehement attack by saints and scholars alike from time to time.

We must first find out the meaning of the Varnashrama Dharma. The protagonists of this system maintain that the Varna Dharma aimed at the classification of society into four Varnas—the Brahmin, the Kshatriya, the Vaishya and the Shudra respectively in the order of precedence and on the basis of the element of *Sattva, Rajas* and *Tamas* in the nature of human beings to fulfil the multitudinous needs and purpose of the society at large. The Ashrama Dharma may be best described as the vision of normal life for the individual in his social mileau. It refers to the main stages of life through which the normal individual is expected to pass—student, householder and hermit (in two stages) in the process of evolution and fulfilment of his personality.

So far as the Ashrama Dharma is concerned, it has been appreciated by all but what is regrettable is that with the passage of time it has been observed more in breach that in practice.

Now we come to the Varna Dharma. It has been the most controversial theme since long and particularly of late. Scholars, sociologists and politicians have held diverse opinion about the origin and usefulness of this institution. Its advocates maintain that the genesis of this fourfold classification of the society is to be found in the 'Purusha Sukta' of the *Rigveda*. We also find similar references in the '*Satapatha* and the *Taittiriya Brahmana*. The Puranas and the Smrtis in particular give an elaborate account of it. The *Mahabharata* and the *Gita* are also full of references about this institution. The other school of scholars maintain that there is no mention of the four Varnas in the Vedic literature. The Veda speaks only of the Arya and Dasa Varna. The third school of scholars stress that the concept of Varna Dharma is not only eternal but also universal and it does and did exist in one form or the other in all climes, times and species. They say that the classification of society on the basis of *Guna-karma* (nature and work) exists not only in the human or animal world but also in the world of inanimate things. A peep into the ancient history of Egypt, China, Japan, Persia, Greece and Rome shows that there did exist three or four distinctive classes of the priests, the warriors or the businessmen and artisans and the agriculturists or the slaves resembling more or less the Brahmins, the Kshatriyas, the Vaishyas and Shudras of ancient India.

The next important question, although a very controversial one, that engages our attention is: What is the basis of this fourfold classification of Varnas? Whether it is *Janmana* (by birth) or *Karmana* (by work or occupation)? The Sanatana (orthodox) school of Hindu theologists regard

Janmana as the basis of the Varna classification while the scholars of the reformist school emphasise the *Karmana* aspect. Dr. Bhagwan Das propounded the *Karmana* theory. His three-volume study of Indian social organisation has been regarded as a pioneering work in the field of Hindu sociology in modern times.

The progressive school of Indian sociologists maintain that the fourfold classification of varnas was merely a poetic concept of the ancient Hindu sociologists and it did never have a practical existence. They say that it can be proved from history that the theory of the Varna Dharma remained divorced from practice. The name of Sardar K.M. Panikkar may be cited as a representative scholar of this school. His book *Hindu Society at Crossroads* deserves a careful study by the students of Hindu sociology. He has tried to prove that the Brahmins alone may be regarded as illustrations of the theory of Varna Dharma while the same thing cannot be said about the other three Varnas, i.e., the Kshatriyas, the Vaishyas and Shudras. But at the same time, Panikkar states that although the concept of four Varnas is merely an imaginary creation of ancient Hindu sociologists yet the Hindu social life is inspired and pervaded by this concept. Thousands of castes and sub-castes that comprise the Hindu society try to establish their origin from one or the other of the four Varnas. So we may say that the original concept of the four Varnas either did never find a practical form or if it ever existed in the practical world, that must have been only partially evolved. With the passage of time the original concept might have degenerated into the practical form of the castes and sub-castes that we see with all their glaring absurdities even in the present day Hindu society.

What are the cardinal principles underlying the Varna concept? The following three principles are regarded as the quintessence of the Varna Dharma:

1. Unchangeable inequality based on birth,
2. Classification of occupations and their disparity,
3. Prohibition of marriage outside one's own Varna.

The first and the third may be noted to be prevalent even today while the second has never been observed in practice. From the Vedic times upto the present day works of history and literature provide several illustrations which show that persons born in lower castes took up occupations theoretically belonging to the higher castes and vice versa. Examples of inter-Varna or inter-caste marriages are also cited from the ancient literature. A certain class of scholars maintain that the Varna is changeable but not the caste. The principle under-lying the Varna theory, according to them, is *Guna-Karma* while that of the caste is birth. So one may change one's Varna but not the caste. They cite illustrations from the old literature to prove their contention. But whatever they might believe about the practicability of the Varna concept, it has to be conceded that it played an important role in the evolution and development of Hindu social organisation.

The principle underlying the religious and secular activities of the Hindus has been spirituality. That once cardinal value is the realisation of unity in diversity. Hierarchy will exist as long as diversity remains in the world and without diversity there can be no world; but spiritual equality was regarded by the ancient seers of India as a permanent safeguard against the hierarchy breaking up into an anarchy of ego-centric individuals. Except in periods, according to an eminent thinker, when it displayed a downward curve, Indian culture has been a harmonisation of the individual and the collectivity. In the

Mahabharata it is said that if an untouchable happens to be virtuous, even the Gods would recognise him as a Brahmin. This harmonisation of the individual and the collectivity has been regarded by many as a marvel of Hindu sociology. But there are others who lay their accusing finger on the intolerant and exclusive priestcraft and petrified social hierarchy, and conclude that it has disfigured Indian history and caused the general impression of a repression of the individual under a system of hidebound orthodoxy. Prof. A.R. Wadia has taken this stand in his *Contemporary Indian Philosophy*.

A certain section of scholars maintain that the concept of fourfold Varnas was really a novel and useful device of the Hindu sociological brain to maintain the purity and solidarity of the society but later on what caused the decay and disintegration of society was not the Varna classification but its gradual degeneration into innumerable castes and sub-castes. Not only that but the caste system, despite their glaring drawbacks, did play a very significant part in maintaining the purity and solidarity of Hindu society at the time of external aggressions and alien rule. According to these scholars, which includes Dr. Suniti Kumar Chatterji, it was the caste system of Hindus that saved their culture from the onslaughts of Islam and Christianity and kept undefiled the original current.

Now we come to a very perplexing problem that poses itself before every student of Hindu sociology and that is: What is the future of the Varna and caste system after the promulgation of the present Constitution of India which does not recognise any sort of disparity or inequality on the basis of caste, colour, creed, sex or religion. The conception of the modern welfare or socialistic state with authorised powers to interfere in every sphere of human activity and to make or amend laws to fulfil its declared aims has also posed a challenge before the society which must be answered.

Sardar K.M. Panikkar's approach deserves consideration in this respect. He proves by his penetrating analysis that the various social institutions of the Hindus are not a part of religion and that they are based on laws, customs and traditions and hence they are secular. Thus he tries to establish and conclude that since these social institutions are based on laws and customs, it is desirable that the constitutions or the constituted authority should re-interpret or amend them whenever the necessity arises to do so. This he has tried to establish on the basis of the amendments and reforms made in the various Smritis from time to time.

This view is not very far from truth and carries much weight. **Varna and caste have now outlived their utility. It is time when we should recast our social structure on the basis of complete equality. History has proved that man is a highly individualistic and group-minded creature who is apt to divide and separate even where perfect unity and equality is intended. A concept or a system based on a view to divide may only aggravate the division. Man's natural separatism should not be assisted by social separatism; it should rather be fought by social equalism, at all levels and at all fronts.** Then only we can hope to acquire the minimum equality needed to harness human energies for progress, material and spiritual.

14

Pacificism Has Been the Ideal

India has never subscribed to the doctrine of militarism and war in her history. Here war was never treated as an ideal. It was only tolerated as unavoidable and inevitable, and all attempts were made to check it and bring it under control.

Inspite of the frequency of wars in ancient India, in spite of the highly developed military organisation, techniques of war and imperialism, and in spite of the open justification of war as national policy, the heart of India loved pacificism as an ideal capable of realisation. India's symbolic role was that of a peacemaker and it sincerely pinned its faith on the principle of 'live and let live.' At least philosophically, India's intelligence supported the cause of peace not only in national affairs but in international affairs also. All the great seers of the yore visualised the unity of life, permeating all beings, animate or inanimate, which ruled out killing and suicidal wars.

How far this doctrine of philosophical pacificism was practised by ancient Aryans is, no doubt, a question of controversial nature. Certainly the great Indian teachers and savants stuck to this doctrine tenaciously and in their personal life they translated it into practice and preached it to masses and even to princes of military classes. But many an aristocratic ruler born of ignoble families did not listen in their pride and vanity to the divine urge and involved themselves and their people in fratricidal wars and other pursuits of military glory.

Another culture of those times, the existence of which has been proved by the excavations of Mohanjo-daro, also enunciated the doctrine of pacificism and friendship to all. Strangely enough, the Indus Valley civilisation has revealed no fortification and very few weapons. This fact has a peculiar significance, in as much as the general prosperity of that time can only be attributable to the existence of peaceful condition and absence of wars. The Mohanjo-daro civilisation has bewildered many scholars of Indian antiquity, but their bewilderment should cease, if they take into consideration the pacific glories of that time.

Ahimsa or the doctrine of non-violence in thought, speech and action assumed a gigantic importance in the Buddhist and Jaina period. The practice of ahimsa was to eschew all kinds of injury to all beings, human and animal. By a constant practice of this virtue, man become unassailable by even wild beasts, who forgot their ferocity the moment they entered the circumference of his magnetic influence. **Gautama Buddha and Mahavira Vardhamana took up this ideal and successfully established huge monastic organisations which were veritable peace unions with the mission of disseminating the doctrine of ahimsa.** The monks and nuns of these churches were apostles of peace, who reached every nook and corner of the world and delivered the message of love to a war-weary humanity. They traversed the boundaries of far-off China, Japan, Tibet, Afghanistan and Central Asia, and taught the lesson of non-violence to fighting nations and warring peoples.

The greatest votary was the royal monk Ashoka, who in reality was responsible for transforming ahimsa as an act of personal virtue, to ahimsa as an act of national virtue.

After the war of Kalinga, he definitely renounced war as an instrument of national policy and pledged himself to a conquest by love 'which was achieved through piety only and which brought bliss in this world and in the next.' This fateful war turned Chandashoka (Ashoka the furious) into Dhammashoka (Ashoka the pious) The traditional policy of the Mauryas, of imperialism and expansion, was given a new orientation which resulted in the end of the era of political victories, and ushered in the glorious period of *dhammavijaya* or conquest by the spiritual force of non-violence. Ashoka called upon his sons and grandsons, 'as many as they may be, not to think of new conquests by sword, but to think of conquest by mildness and gentleness.' And as victories of peace are no less renowned than the victories of war, Ashoka was more successful than his imperial grandfather in expanding the boundaries of his empire.

Besides, he planted his glories in many an island, situated in far-off seas, by sending there his cultural embassies. That is why Ashoka has been reckoned 'among all the thousands of kings, emperors and majesties, great and little, as shining almost alone, a star.' Certainly, he stands at the top in the galaxy of the world's greatest kings, who established a kingdom of righteousness, after the highest ideals of theocracy. "In the history of ancient India, the figure of Ashoka stands out like some great Himalayan peak, clear against the sky, resplendent in the sun, while the lower and nearer ranges are hidden by the clouds."

Many a historian recounting the causes of the downfall of the Mauryas, hold the pacific policy of Ashoka which had eschewed the aggressive militarism of his predecessors, responsible for an early decay of the military strength of the state and its consequent disintegration, leading to the rise of Sungas, Kanvas and Andhras. But, in reality the fault lies with the weak successors of Ashoka, who could not wield the weapon of non-violence with a skill and efficiency which required the strength of a spiritual giant like Ashoka. They failed due to their subjective weakness: Pacificism itself was no cause of their failure.

Besides the foregoing philosophical and religious school of thought, even many political authorities gave their unqualified support to the cause of pacificism. They recognised the right of the rivals to exist, not mainly as enemies, but as collaborators in the building of a civilisation based on the principles of mutual toleration and co-operation. Thus, for centuries, in the pre-Mauryan India, scores of small independent republics existed and flourished without coming in clash with each other. Even in the period of the imperial Mauryas, **Arian observes in his *Indica*, "a sense of justice prevented any Indian king from attempting a conquest beyond the limits of India."**

With regard to Kautilya, the much maligned militarist and the so-called Machiavelli of India, we may reiterate our observation that in spite of his glorification of war, he also favours pacificism as an instrument of national policy. Dr. Kalidas Nag remarks the following about his attitude on war: "Though war seems inevitable to Kautilya, we notice that he seeks always to avoid or arrest war by every kind of *entente*. We also see that *entente* occupies the most important place in his system. He classifies with care in several chapters the *entente* which results either from war or peaceful combination. Again, Kautilya thinks that the object of the diplomatic war is to avoid war. On this point, he is in complete accordance with the masters of the other schools of law, who ordain that the war must be the last diplomatic means to be employed when all other expedients have failed."

The *Mahabharata* observes in this connection: "A wise man should be content with what can be obtained by the expedients of conciliation, gift and dissention." It denounces the warring world of men by comparing it to a dog-kennel. "First there comes the wagging of tails, then turning of one round the other, then the show of teeth, then the roaring and then comes the commencement of the fight. It is the same with men; there is no difference whatever." Yajnavalkya adds: 'War is the last expedient to be used when all others have failed." Kamandaka advises that as the results of war are uncertain and as it may entail loss to both the parties, it is better to effect honourable settlement of disputes by negotiation. Sukra also denounces the lust of war and admonishes kings never to get their armies butchered unnecessarily with others.

Likewise, Sri Krishna whose *Bhagvad-Gita* has been styled by some as 'a song of battle', should not be considered out and out militarist. His sermon on war to recalcitrant Arjuna was necessitated only by the force of circumstances. When all his pacific pleading with the enemies failed, then alone he was compelled to advise the Pandavas to have a recourse to war, 'the fourth expedient, as proper for those sinners.' It must be borne in mind that all possible efforts were made to avert the great war of the *Mahabharata*. When all the three expedients were exhausted, then alone the fourth was resorted to. Yudhisthira himself conveyed his message of peace to Dhritarastra through the latter's envoy, Sanjaya, in the following touching words:

> "O vanquisher of your enemies, as boys we obtained kingdom by your grace; having established us on the throne once, do not neglect us to perish. Father, united we shall live, divided we shall fall.
>
> "Great man, turn the mind of your avaricious sons away from others' property. King, there will be peace thus, and mutual love also.
>
> "Let Duryodhana give us, the five brothers, five

> villages. O illustrious scion of Bharata, with a good heart, let all of us settle down in peace."

A better case for pacificism could not be made. However, when this message of peace fell on deaf ears, Sri Krishna volunteered himself to go in person to set right the affairs that had gone wrong. He said to Yudhisthira while departing for his mission of peace: "If without spoiling the cause of the Pandavas, I am able to secure peace from the Kauravas, meritorious and highly fruitful will the part I play be, and freed, indeed, will be the world from the noose of death."

Having reached the court of the Kauravas, before the full assembly of dignitaries including Bhishma, Drona, Vidura and others, Sri Krishna delivered his message of peace in the following stirring words:

> "O scion of Bharata, I have come here to beg this, that without the ruin of warriors, there may be an amicable settlement between the Kauravas and the Pandavas.
>
> "O King, peace depends on you, as well as on me; pacify your sons, I will pacify the other party.
>
> "After giving the Pandavas their due paternal share you may enjoy along with your sons your pleasures, with your objects achieved."

To this irresistible appeal of reason and commonsense the aged king, Dhritarastra readily responded, but pleading his helplessness over his wicked sons, he said: "O mighty Krishna, Ye best of men, try to conciliate my stupid and lawless son Duryodhana. These boys who think themselves to be wise do not listen to me, though I cry hoarse. Wholesale is the ruin in battle, let us strive for peace."

Bhisma intervened and tried his best to bring round

the wicked Duryodhana to act according to Krishna's advice and not to immerse his parents in the ocean of sorrow; Dronacharya also followed suit and pleaded with Duryodhana to abide by the truthful view of Krishna and Bhisma, else he would repent. Vidura also joined the chorus of appeal. But all these appeals of reason fell on deaf ears, and Duryodhana was adamant, who repeated: "O Krishna, even that much of land as is pierced by the tip of a needle cannot be parted with to the Pandavas, without battle."

These were the circumstances which forced the hands of Sri Krishna who had no alternative left, but to advise the Pandavas to declare a war. This also explains the necessity and the apparent inconsistency of the so-called sermon on war preached in the *Bhagvad-Gita*. All possible avenues of peace such as negotiation, conciliation through conference, mediation and so on, were explored before the war was resorted to. This is what even the ultra pacifist would recommend. This proves that the heart of ancient India was sound and it longed for peace, although war also was not treated as an anathema, which was to be avoided as far as possible.

15

Greater India

The ancient history of many territories of South-East Asia is linked up with India by cultural ties. We know these lands and islands by their Sanskrit names as well. Thus, Burma, now Myanmar, was known as Suvarnabhumi, Thailand was anciently a part of Cambodia, which name is a contraction of the Sanskrit name Kambuja on Kambujadesa, Annam or Viet-Nam was called Champa, Malay Peninsula and Malay Archipelago were together designated as Suvarnadvipa, though each land and island therein must have had a proper appellation of its own, as Yavadvipa for Java. It should be noted that Suvarnabhumi is not to be confused with Suvarnadvipa.

Indonesia is a principal part of Malay Archipelago. From maps one cannot have an idea of the enormous extent of Indonesia. All told, it comprises nearly four thousand islands, of which as many as three thousand are populated. Those that are not populated also yield harvests of coconuts and the like. Five of the islands of Indonesia have all alone been in the forefront for their size and trade. The biggest of these five is Borneo, the next biggest is Sumatra, the third is Celebes, the fourth Java and the fifth Bali. Except in Bali, everywhere else in Indonesia the religion prevalent at present is Islam. Bali alone preserves Hinduism which in certain respects is of primitive type. Culturally speaking, Java has been more conspicuous by far in the whole of

Indonesia. It is divided into three main political divisions: West Java, Central Java and East Java. The capital of Indonesia is Jakarta in West Java. Like Delhi, Jakarta is a crowded and ever outstanding city.

While the earlier phases of India's contacts with the lands and islands of South-East Asia are hidden in obscurity, the later phases thereof are illumined by archaeology and epigraphy, supplemented by literature and Chinese annals. The contacts were a long and steady process extending over centuries. The possibility of the great sweeping wave of the Aryan people from Asia Minor extending to the trans-Gangetic countries like Burma, Thailand, Cambodia and so on, is not altogether precluded. According to another theory, some groups of the Dravidian people, either after their defeat at the hands of the Vedic Aryans or quite independent of such an event, penetrated to the regions of what is now commonly called Greater India. Some antiquities of the prehistoric period found at various places in Greater India are said to point to affinities between the Dravidians of India and the various original races of Greater India. These, however, have not yet resulted in any definite conclusions. Nor have the references in the *Ramayana* and later Sanskrit works to Java, etc., proved of any material help so far. The Burmese tradition, connecting the earliest royal house of Burma with the Kshatriyas of Kosala in India, is equally vague.

It is surmised that there was wave after wave of people going from various parts of India proper to various parts of Greater India. When in the third century B.C. Ashoka sent missionaries outside India for the propagation of the Buddhist teachings, two monks, Sona and Uttara, were sent also to Suvarnabhumi (Burma). This is an indication that at that early date within the historic period, some kind of communication between India and Greater India did exist.

From the side of Greater India, the earliest concrete evidence of such an intercourse is afforded by a bronze statue of the Buddha, of the school of Amaravati, discovered at a neolithic site on the west cast of the island of Celebes. This would mean that Indians from the coast of India had already by the second or third century of the Christian era penetrated so far into Greater India as Celebes.

Conversely, certain Andhra coins, discovered in the region round Amaravati in India, show the device of a two-masted ship. This again proves the existence of maritime activities of Indians during the early centuries of the Christian era.

A significant addition to this numismatic evidence was made in the shape of a Buddhist stone inscription of about the second or third century A.D., which the writer of this article happened to discover at the old site of Ghantasala (ancient Kantakasola), on the Coromandel Coast, in the Krishna District of Andhra Pradesh. This site is allied to Amaravati. The inscription is a donative tablet in the Prakrit language and Brahmi characters, recording a charity by an *upasika,* i.e., a female lay worshipper, named Siddharthamitra, who is described as the wife of a *mahanavika* named Sivaka.

For our purpose, the term *mahanavika* is very significant. It denotes 'a sea-captain' or 'a master mariner.' Kantakasola was a sea-port in olden days. Ptolemy mentions it as "the emporium Kantakossyla," immediately after the mouths of Maisolos, i.e., the river Krishna. It may be recalled that the father of Kannaki, the heroine of the Tamil classic *Silappadikaram,* assigned to about the second century A.D., is also described as a *mahanavika* (Tamil *manaikan*). These references prove that people from South India in those days used to go on sea voyages.

Another stone inscription, though of a little later date, deserves to be mentioned here. It is by a Buddhist *mahanavika* named Buddhagupta, who was an inhabitant of Raktamrittika (identified with Rangamati in Bengal). It was found as early as 1834 near a ruined Buddhist temple in the Province Wellesley of Malay Peninsula. It is of a religious character and invokes blessing for a successful voyage—*siddha-yatrah santu*! It is in Sanskrit and in the Pallava-Grantha characters of about the fifth century A.D. This is about the time, of which we have found quite a number of stone inscriptions, in chaste Sanskrit, in Champa, Java, Borneo, and other parts of Greater India. All these go to show that there was a brisk intercourse between India and those far-off lands and islands during the early centuries of the Christian era.

As to what induced these Indians to embark upon such risky and lengthy voyages, it is supposed that they did so primarily in quest of gold. When Roman gold ceased to flow into India, Indian traders turned to the east. Traders were thus perhaps the first adventurers to go to Greater India. Subsequently, scholars and priests must also have accompanied such guilds of sea-faring merchants, many of whom possibly chose to stay on in those foreign places. Glimpses of such a state of affairs are afforded by epigraphical data. Sanskrit inscriptions of King Mulavarman, discovered in Kutei on the east coast of Borneo, dating from the fourth or fifth century A.D., for instance, speaks of *viprair=ih=agataih*, 'by the Brahmins who have come here.' Such were obviously the beginnings of how cultural contacts were established and how the indigenous folk were attracted to the Indian immigrants.

These cultural contacts developed so much that in due course Greater India become a replica of India proper, so to say. As in India proper, so in Greater India, too, religion played a great part, both in the people's life and at the courts of kings. Members of the priestly caste enjoyed supreme honour everywhere. In the name of religion, people used to make rich donations, erected temples and did other meritorious deeds. The religious literature steadily increased. Many a Sanskrit work was translated or adapted into local languages.

Although ever since the time of Ashoka, Buddhism had been spreading far and wide outside India, yet according to the epigraphical evidence it was Brahminism that was first to reach the territories of Greater India. And this expressed itself there in three main forms: Saivism, Vaisnavism and the cult of Agastya. The worship of Siva in the form of linga grew as popular there as it was in India proper. The earlier Siva temple was built in Champa. It was called Bhadreshvara after the name of its builder, King Bhadravarman, according to a Sanskrit inscription of the fourth century A.D. found there. Another called Vaprakesvara sprang up in Borneo as is known from the inscriptions of King Mulavarman referred to above. A long *prasasti* engraved on a stone slab at Changal in Central Java, bearing a date in the Saka era, corresponding to A.D. 732, records the erection of a Siva temple there. Statues of Durga, Skanda, Ganesa and other deities who share popular adoration with Siva, are also found in great numbers. The worship of Visnu was equally very much in evidence, first in the form of his footprints and later also in human form, riding on his vehicle Garuda. **The temple complex of Angkor Vat in Cambodia is a marvel of architecture and sculpture for the whole world.** The cult of Agastya found a most congenial home in Greater India, especially in Java. His popularity in South India is well known, but his worship in Java is far more widespread. He is known there as Bhattara Guru, and, as such, he is supposed to be an incarnation of Siva.

Buddhism may have penetrated into Greater India about the same time as Brahminism did, if not earlier, but no epigraphy attesting to that has so far come to light. The period of which we possess some definite information regarding the existence of Buddhism in these eastern regions begins from the fifth century A.D. later on Buddhism grew rapidly and overshadowed Brahminism. In the Sailendra monarchs of Sumatra, Buddhism found the most zealous devotees and patrons. **The world-famous stupa of Barabudur in the Central Java, a worthy rival of the Visnu temple of Angkor Vat in Cambodia, was built by these very Sailendras.**

The greatest and most abiding link of India with Greater India is perhaps the Sanskrit language which permeated the hundreds of indigenous languages and dialects of those regions, greatly influencing them and vastly increasing their vocabularies. Along with Sanskrit went the Brahmi script which is the mother of all the modern scripts of Greater India. The ancient literature of Greater India, especially of Java and Bali, is very extensive. It contains original Sanskrit texts and adaptations of the *Mahabharata,* the *Ramayana,* the *Puranas,* and various Sanskrit poetical compositions of India. The best exposition of the Bharatanatya style dance is perhaps still to be found in Java.

There is a parallel, too, between India and Greater India, so far as the setback received by Hindu-Buddhist culture is concered. The introduction of Islam by the Arab traders and invaders, that of Christianity by the Portuguese, the Dutch and the French, and the exploitation practised by all these in succession, are some of the common features. Brahminical and Buddhist culture flourished in Greater India from about the second century A.D. to the beginning of the 16th century by which time Islam had established itself firmly in many parts, with the notable exception of the small island of Bali where Aryan culture still persists.

How was Greater India a Replica of India proper? This

question is perhaps best answered by saying that the two regions, so distant from each other, were living an identical life, quite independent of each other. There was no question of political dependence or allegiance on either side.

The culture of Greater India enjoyed an added glory in the spirit in which it absorbed the best of Indian culture and religion as they came in successive waves. **In India proper, Brahminism was opposed to Buddhism, but this rivalry or animosity was absent in Greater India. Nay, there were even combined shrines dedicated to Siva and the Buddha, called Siva-Buddhalayas. India proper has no such thing to her credit.** Again, in the sphere of religious art, the zeal of Greater India has, in some cases at least, outside that of India proper. To quote Professor Sylvain Levi, the famous French Indologist, **India "has produced her unsurpassed masterpieces only by the action of the foreigner or in a foreign land ...** In architecture, it is in remote Cambodia and Java that the two marvellous results of the Indian genius, Angkor and Barabudur, must be sought."

What stands out in bold relief in the whole picture is the fact that **the spread of Indian culture in the lands and islands of South-East Asia is characterized as a purely cultural and peaceful penetration. It was a case of free peoples giving and accepting free gifs.**

16

Muslims in India

The Muslims form one of the most important constituents of the national economy of India. For at least a thousand years, they have, particularly in the North, supplied one of the major forces in the shaping of India's economic, political and social history. Woven into the intricate pattern of Indian life, the Muslims have yet maintained their individuality. They have contributed to the symphony of Indian life and yet retained a distinct timbre that can be clearly recognised. **In most other countries, Muslims have assimilated the land into the main stream of Islamic culture. India is the one exception where neither has Islam been overpowered by India nor India absorbed into the Islamic world.**

In order to understand the Indian Muslim and his place in Indian history, one must remember that two factors have contributed to his mental evolution and make up. On the one hand, there has been the influence of Islam and the philosophy of life represented by it . On the other, there has been the pervasive influence of Indian culture and civilisation. If the Indian Muslim is distinct from his counterpart in other parts of the world, this is due to their interaction at many levels.

The main contributions of Islam to the mental make up of Indian Muslims have been the insistence on a militant democracy, liberal rationalism, and an uncompromising monotheism that at times verged on iconoclasm and intolerance. It is generally recognised that Islam's democratic urge was perhaps its greatest contribution to world culture. Even its worst enemies have admitted that Islam broke down the barriers of colour and birth absolutely in the formal act of worship and comparatively unimportant exceptions in daily social intercourse. Islam's attempt to break away from the domination of priestcraft and its comparative freedom from mystical speculation and superstitions are manifestations of its rationalism. Faith in an ultimate revelation through Mohammad for the spiritual uplift of the whole human race tended to intensify missionary zeal. It was perhaps natural that the religious zeal of Islam should develop into iconoclasm and beget, at times and specially among some of its new converts, narrowness and intolerance.

The traditions of pre-Islamic India represented an entirely different outlook on life. If Islam insisted on the unity of Truth, it was the diversity and manifoldness of its manifestations which had their greatest appeal to the Indian intellect. The ancient Indian genius for synthesis has rightly evoked the admiration of the entire world, but the weakness inherent in its acceptance or tolerance of everything without discrimination has not always been noticed. Caste which divided human beings into different grades is repugnant to the non-Hindu mind, but it did provide a framework for the survival of groups with different levels of culture.

The Indian Muslims were therefore subject, on the one hand, to Islam's insistence upon social homogeneity and, on the other, to the Indian tradition of rigid stratification of caste. They, however, acquired some of the habits and prejudices which characterised the rigid form of the caste system, but, because of the Islamic insistence on equality of man, evolved a type of caste based on wealth and station.

The Muslim variation of caste is seen most clearly in the institution of feudalism. Inconsistent with the spirit of Islam, it became associated especially with the Indian Muslims. Social life was disfigured by the existence of a large number of slaves both male and female in the household of kings and nobles. Indigenous converts often failed to attain the social status of those who had foreign blood in their veins and in a plutocratic regime the poor tended to form a separate class. Converts often tended to carry over their caste prejudices to their new faith.

Indian philosophy has always emphasised the wholeness of life and brought with it an attitude of toleration and forbearance. Indian Muslims were influenced by this spirit of catholicity of the traditions of ancient India. It is significant that the attempts at rapprochement between Islam and Hinduism were as strong from the Muslim side as from that of the Hindus. Just as the teachings of Chaitanya, Nanak, and Ramananda tended to narrow the distinction between Hinduism and Islam, there were also Kabir, Chishti, Dara Shikoh who attempted understanding and unification from the side of the Muslims. Nor must it be forgotton that though orthodoxy looked askance, one of the supreme architects of this movement for synthesis was Akbar the Great.

The fact that Muslim penetration into India was not a case of wholesale colonisation but of successive waves of military attack ensured that each invading group would, in its turn, be subject to the pervasive influence of Hinduism when it settled down. Small groups of men who came as military conquerors were themselves largely conquered culturally. We have also to remember that except the original invaders of Sindh, the Muslim conquerors were not Arabs, but mainly Turks, Turko-Afghans, who had themselves acquired Islamic civilisation and culture comparatively recently. **When Islam came to a country through such new converts, no cultural supremacy could be established as the conquerors were often inferior in civilisation to the people that they conquered. If the conquest of India had been undertaken by Arabs, it is probable that they would have taken over some of the elements of ancient Indian culture.** While drawing on India's past, they would at the same time have attempted the imposition of Arab culture on the Indian masses. This has been the pattern of Arab cultural conquest in other regions. It must be remembered that even the highly developed civilisations of Iran and Egypt could not withstand the impact of the Arab upsurge.

The Turko-Afghans who conquered India followed a different policy. They were at first content to preserve for themselves fragments of the Perso-Arab culture they had inherited; they sought neither to impose it on India nor enrich it by drawing upon the rich heritage of the land. One reason for this may be that they were perhaps not in a position to attempt a cultural synthesis. The Iranian-Arab culture which they flaunted was for them a comparatively new acquisition and had not entered into the texture of their life and being. They had, moreover, all the zeal of a new convert. For a long period after their advent on the Indian scene, they therefore sought to remain aloof. In course of time, however, the processes of geography and economy proved stronger than such racial exclusiveness. They were slowly woven into the Indian pattern, drawn by the tolerance and responsiveness of the Indian mind and their own capacity for absorption and imitation.

It is necessary to describe in detail the consequences which followed from centuries of common life. Throughout India, an initial clash followed by fusion and synthesis. These contacts had a profound influence on the way of life of the peoples inhabiting this land. There were far reaching changes in their dress, food, language, literature, art, painting, architecture, music and philosophy. One reason which made a fusion of Hindu and Muslim outlook not only easy, but in a sense inevitable, was the fact that large masses of the native people entered the fold of the new faith. Also, many of the invaders married Indian women and they taught their own traditions to their children.

By the time of the advent of the Muslims, Hindu society had become ossified with its rigid strata of castes. Earlier attempts to rebel against the authority of Brahmins had reached their culmination in the great movements of Buddhism and Jainism. For a time, it seemed as if Buddhism with its emphasis on equality and common humanity would permanently change the structure of Indian life. By the end of the seventh century, Buddhism had, however, spent ifself. Neo-Brahminism began to dominate India about the time of Samkara, but the triumph was not easy. The defeated Buddhists seized opportunities to express their resentment against the unwelcome domination, and, it is stated, helped Mohammed-ibn-Kasim in defeating the Brahmin king Dahir of Sindh.

In the greater part of India, Brahminical supremacy had been re-established by the seventh or eighth century. In Bengal, however, this process was not completed till about the end of ninth century. When Muslims appeared in Bengal, they found everywhere large disgruntled groups who had till recently been in opposition to, if not more powerful than the dominating religious group of the day. When one looks at the record of the struggles of this period, one is repeatedly struck by the fact that small groups of Muslims triumphed over larger indigenous armies. This cannot be explained in terms of personal valour. It is obvious that a small group of military conquerors could not for long withstand the resistance of a vast mass of local people, especially in a country like India, unless there were elements within the country itself which for some reason or other deserted the local rulers and lent their support to the invaders. This is corroborated by the record of events. In many cases the conqueror from outside had local allies who played an important role in the outcome. Local morale may at times have been affected by fear based on the military reputation and the alleged relentlessness of the invaders. The defections were however too widespread to be mere prudence or love of gain.

This also helps to explain the large proportion of Muslims in the population of Bengal, even though it was far removed from the centre of Pathan or Moghul power. The fact, however, that large masses were won over to the new faith ensured that the faith itself would be modified by the newly converts. Men can change their religion, but it is not so easy to change their ways of life. These neo-Muslims gave to Indian Islam an indigenous temper which made rapprochement between the two religions easy and natural.

The process of integration which followed profoundly changed the character of pristine Islam. Islam has always condemned a separate priesthood but there are unmistakable signs of such a growth among Indian Muslims. They also show a marked fondness for ritual and elaborate ceremony. Islam was iconoclastic, but Indian Muslims often display a veneration for saints and their tombs that reminds one of the worship of relics. Mohammed stressed the uniformity of natural law and laid hardly any store by miracles, but the Indian Muslims felt unhappy till he had built up a halo of sanctity if not divinity, round his religious heroes. Muslim practice in India thus tended to conform to Hindu religious customs. Members of the two communities also participated in one another's religious festivals.

Such influences were not, perhaps cannot be, one-sided. There are reasons for suspecting Muslim influence in some of the citadels of Hindu orthodoxy. Samkara is perhaps the greatest architect of modern Hinduism, and yet there are in his thought elements which betoken a spirit of revolt against all pluralism. His extreme monism, his repudiation of the semblance of duality, his attempt to establish this monism on the authority of revealed scripture, his tendency to regard his own activity as mere restoration of the purity of an original truth, are all elements which, barring the doctrine of *Maya,* have strange parallels in Islam. Historical factors do not bar out the possibility of Samkara's acquaintance with Islamic thought. According to Rowlandson, the first Muslim Arabs settled in the Malabar coast about the end of the seventh century. There is evidence that Arabs had regular trade connections with South India and their religious beliefs and habits may have been known to the local population. Fawcett in his notes on the people of Malabar draws attention to the growth of the Bhakti cult in the south. He suggests that this was due mainly to the influence of Islam. He quotes the tradition that the king of Kaladi where Samkara was born had been converted to Islam at the time of Samkara's birth. If this can be substantiated by means of reliable data, it would go to show that in that region at least Islam was a force. Samkara's ex-communication by the Brahmins and his performance or the last rites of his mother with the help of Nairs also suggests that Samkara was not afraid of daring innovation in practice.

One consequence of the establishment of Muslim rule was the re-establishment of internal peace throughout Northern India under one uniform administration. The break-up of the Gupta power had led to the rise of small states which were continually fighting one another. This prevented a smooth or uniform development of social life. The unitary administration — first of the Delhi Sultanate and later of the Moghul Empire — helped to re-promote the unity of Indian outlook. This was reinforced by a uniformity in social manners introduced by the Muslims. Whether in the North or in the South, the Muslims had uniformity in dress, food, customs and beliefs which could not escape the notice of their non-Muslim neighbours. The result was a growth in uniform social manners throughout the country, particularly in urban areas. Court etiquette largely influenced the conduct, irrespective of community or creed, of all who desired worldly advancement. As early as the time of Babar, this was becoming so perceptible that he described it in his autobiography as the growth of the Hindustani way of life. This process was further strengthened by the introduction of a common revenue system and the gradual spread of common method in war and peace.

The consequences of co-operative living are most manifest in the realm of art and letters. The achievements of Indo-Saracenic art were made possible by a combination of the Indian instinct for ornamentation with the Saracenic sense of form. This is exemplified not only in the wonderful architecture of the period but also in music, painting, weaving, metallurgy and garden craft. The miniatures which evoke our admiration, the shawls of inimitable workmanship, the records with their delicate inlaid work, the muslin of incomparable quality, and the wonderful gardens which the Moghuls built, all reveal a balance between form and content that is as perfect as it is rare.

Even more significant was the co-operation of the communities in the evolution of a common language wherever Muslims settled among Hindus. Urdu, Hindi or Hindustani—whatever name be given to it—was evolved out of a material derived from ancient Indian sources as well as the innovations brought in by the new settlers. Along with this growth of a common language, there was the remarkable phenomenon of the rise of literature in the different Indian languages. This efflorescence of literature was most marked where the affinity between Muslims and Hindus was greatest. The result was the achievement of a common outlook which softened the sharp formalism of Islam and simplified the elaborate rituals of Hinduism. Large-scale intermixture which followed conversion led not only to the establishment of a more or less homogeneous racial type but also to the development of a common political and cultural pattern. The Pathan rulers of Bengal identified themselves with the people of the land. As a result, a fairly homogeneous cultural group supported them in the fight against attempts at domination from Delhi. This also explains why they were such patrons of Bengali literature and opportunity for the development of indigenous poetry. With local variations, a similar process was at work in Gujarat, Malabar and the present Uttar Pradesh.

The synthesis in the field of religion has often been noticed and does not require elaborate description. It is enough to say that both from the Muslim and from the Hindu points of view, there was an attempt at rapprochement. The lives of men like Kabir, Nanak, Ramananda, Dadu and others offer unmistakable testimony of this fact. The similarities between Sufism and Vaisnavism have often been noticed and need not be stressed. Their affinity must have contributed to the popularity of Sufi saints in India.

By the end of the sixteenth century, a *modus vivendi* between the different Indian communities had already been achieved in the North. At the top, the aristocracy had attained a commonness in behaviour, mode of life and gentle outlook; regardless of differences in faith. Here, the dominant tone was that of the courts with their almost complete acceptance of the culture of Iran. At the other end of the scale, the masses also had established a kind of mutual toleration which enabled them to face their common problems and share common festive delights.

With the advent of the West, an entirely new situation developed. The two communities reacted in entirely different ways to this new force. Large elements among the Hindus could accept Western teaching without any qualms. To large groups amongst the Muslims, the very existence of European power in India was a constant reminder of their own defeat. It is not surprising that even after British power had been consolidated, the Muslims for a long time maintained an attitude of utter non-co-operation with every British. This meant not only a denial of opportunities in services and commerce but, what in the end proved even more disastrous to them, **it meant a failure to imbibe the science and knowledge of the West. The Muslims as a community went through a period of intellectual sterility, the effects of which are perceptible even to this day.**

The British attitude towards the Muslims was also a factor which kept the Muslims away from this new source of knowledge and strength. For a long time, the British did everything in their power to curb the Muslim intelligentsia and undermine their influence in every sphere of life. The British hostility towards Indian Muslims was further enhanced by the abortive struggle of 1857. Hindus and Muslims had alike taken part in the rising. Nevertheless, the fact that the Mogul Emperor was the figurehead of the revolt and that the Muslim landed classes in Bihar, Uttar Pradesh and Delhi had largely sided with the insurgents deepened the British antipathy to the community. After the rising had been quelled, the British hand was heavier on Muslim participants and on those belonging to other communities.

It was only in the last two decades of the nineteenth century that there started a shift in British policy. The rise of the Indian middle classes—mainly Hindu in their composition—led to the establishment of the Indian National Congress as the instrument for achievment of power. This evoked in the British administrators of the day an uneasy feeling that the danger from the Muslim community had perhaps disappeared but a new threat had risen from an entirely unexpected quarter. From 1886 to 1909, British policy was hesitant, divided and uncertain. After almost twenty years' hesitation, the British decided to transfer their patronage from the Hindu middle classes to their counterparts among the Muslims. The Muslim League was thus born under British patronage and devoted itself to a reestablishment of the position of the community by a dual policy of courting the favour of the rulers and challenging the position of the non-Muslims. We need not go into the troubled and sorry history of the conflicts and intrigues of the recent decades. It is enough to say that they ultimately led to a partition of the country and the emergence of two separate states.

History cannot, however, be turned back. The recreation of the past is itself influenced by all that has happened in between. India's determination to establish herself as a secular democratic state is a recognition of this fact. **The role of Indian Muslims in the new set-up is to help in this process by bringing to our common heritage the power of synthesis and assimilation which their forefathers—whether native to India or settlers from outside—exhibited throughout the days of their supremacy.**

17

Education in Aryan Times

Learning in India through the ages has been prized and pursued not for its own sake, but for the sake, and as a part, of religion. It was sought as the means of salvation or self-realisation, as the means to the highest end of life, viz., *mukti* or emancipation. It is religion that creates literature in India and wields it as an instrument for its own purpose, a vehicle of its expression. Education, according to the Indian viewpoint, must aid in self-fulfilment, and not in the acquisition of mere objective knowledge. It is more concerned with the subject than the object, the inner than the outer world. But there is a definite method about it. The theory is that it is useless to get at the knowledge of the whole through its parts, through the individual objects making up the universe. The right way is directly to seek the source of all life and knowledge, and to acquire knowledge piecemeal by the study of objects.

Individual is the chief concern and centre of this education, and education also is necessarily individual. It is an intimate relationship between teacher and the pupil. The relationship is inaugurated by a religious ceremony called *Upanayana*. It is not like the admission of a pupil to the register of a school on his payment of the prescribed fee. By *Upanayana*, the teacher, 'holding the pupil within him as in a womb, impregnates him with his spirit, and delivers him in a new birth.' The education that is thus begun is called by the significant term *Brahmacharya*, indicating that it is a mode of life, a system of practices.

The pupil must find the teacher. He must live with him as a member of his family and is treated by him as his son. It is a hermitage, beyond the distraction of urban life, functioning in solitude and silence. **The pupil is to imbibe the inward method of the teacher, the secrets of his efficiency, the spirit of his life and work. The same principle also holds in the sphere of industrial education. The apprentice must elect to live with the master craftsman to learn the secrets of his work, assimilate his spirit and method, which are not revealed in any formal manner.**

Apart from the special educative value of the teacher's home as the school, there is the factor of its environment or setting as an integral part of the scheme. The school is set in sylvan surroundings. The pupil's first daily duty is to walk to the woods, cut and collect the fuel, and fetch it home for tending the sacred fire. A profound spiritual and cultural significance attaches to this worship of *Agni* by their offering of choice objects and oblations. The ceremony of *Agnihotra* brings home to the pupil the reality of religion in the form of a sacrifice. The pupil's next duty was to tend the teacher's house and cattle. Tending the house was training the pupil in self-help, the dignity of labour, even menial service for his teacher and the student brotherhood. Tending cattle was the education through craft as a part of the highest liberal education. The school and the homestead centered round the cow whom the Indian counts as his second mother whose milk nourishes the child and is the best food even for the grown-up. The *Brihadaranyaka* tells of Rishi Yajnavalkya, who with his band of pupils, drove away home from the court of Janaka 1000 cows which the king had bestowed on him as the reward of his learning.

Another duty of the *brahmachari* was to go out on a daily round of begging. It was not begging for himself but for the support of the school. It was meant to produce in the pupil a spirit of humanity and renunciation. It is like a ritual for the cultivation of impersonal relations in the life. Isolation and intercourse thus lead to a higher synthesis of the inner and the outer, Self and the world.

The *Rigveda Samhita* reveals two stages and types of education and educational method. Its hymns are the outcome of the first, the method of the pursuit of the highest Truth on the basis of ascetic austerities and concentrated contemplation called *tapas* which marks out the *Rishi*. Then there were *Munis* who took to Yoga. When highest knowledge was built up by these seers, there were methods by which such knowledge should be conserved and transmitted to posterity. Thus every *Rishi* was a teacher who would start imparting to his son the knowledge he had personaly acquired and such texts as would be special property of his family. Each such family of Rishi was thus functioning like a Vedic school, admitting pupils for instructions in the literature in its possession.

Rigvedic education comprised the transmission of the sacred texts by the teacher to his pupil by means of regulated recitation and prescribed pronunciation. Then came contemplation and comprehension of their meaning which was considered very important. There were Brahmin Sanghas and Charanas, the assemblies or academies where the successful students flocked together for the advancement of knowledge by discussing their respective contributions to these. **The conference method for the promotion and diffusion of learning, the method of discussion in seminars and academies, was first evolved in India. The Upanishads themselves are to be regarded as the record and outcome of such disputations, the transactions, so to speak, of the philosophical societies or circles of literary celebrities of the times.**

In the Sutra period, there were six main subjects, *Shiksa* (Phonetics). *Chandas* (Prosody), *Vyakarana* (Grammar),

Nirukta (Etymology), *Kalpa* (Rituals) and *Jyotisa* (Astronomy), which were studied by students. The period of studentship consisted ordinarily of twelve years. But some students would elect to make it lifelong without any desire to marry and lead householder's life. The literature of these subjects was not stationary, but growing. In course of time the *Kalpa* alone reached large dimensions. *Vyakarana* also developed similar proportions and a scientific system of treatment as reflected in the final work of Panini. But the Angas were developing not merely in bulk but also in number. Thus Nyaya and Purva Mimamsa, the art of interpreting the rules of Veda, was added to the list of auxiliary sciences, which had to be studied in connection with the sacred texts. New special schools of science grew in response to the requirements of a growing culture. Vedic Caranas were depressed from their old position by these schools of *Kalpa, Vyakarana* and *Jyotisa* and Sacred Law. There was also progress of specialisation in other departments of knowledge not directly connected with religion. Panini refers to the school of the *Natya,* the art of drama. He mentions specialists in instrumental music, story-telling and military science.

In the time of Kautilya, the entire circle of knowledge was divided into (1) *Anviksaki,* (2) *Trayi,* (3) *Varta* and (4) *Dandaniti.* The name *Anviksaki* stands for the science derived from subjective or metaphysical speculations and as such, three systems of thought were known to him, viz., Samkhya, Yoga and Lokayata. *Trayi* was made up of the first three Vedas. *Varta* meant subjects like agriculture, cattle-rearing and trade. *Dandaniti,* the last of all, meant the science and art of government. Kautilya was primarily concerned with the education of the prince belonging to the ruling Kshatriya caste who was required to study all these subjects.

In course of time, all the six systems of orthodox

philosophy and three main systems of heterodox philosophy developed and had their separate schools in their regions of influence. The number went on increasing as their trunks bifurcated into branches and twigs. This gave the fullest scope to differences of opinion and to debate and discussion at which such differences were freely fought out, thrashed out, and solved. The method of interrogation, cross-examination, debate and discussions among fellow-seekers of Truth was, in itself, elaborated into a science, exalted into an art, and was known as Nyaya or Logic.

The Buddhist system of education centred round monasteries. The Buddhist world did not offer any educational opportunities apart from or independently of them. All education, sacred as well as secular, was in the hands of monks. The rules of Buddhist education were those of the order itself. The ceremony of initiation followed closely the lines of the Brahminical initiation. The first step was known as *Pabbajja* or 'going forth' which meant that the person admitted into the order was going out of the previous state of a layman or householder or a monk of another sect. The admission was thrown open to all the castes. Then after a period of about twelve years, his novitiate ended with the final ordination of *Upasampada,* the full status of a Bhiksu. But he could not become a *grihastha* or a householder. His outgoing was confirmed and final.

For the same reason, **these Buddhist schools were not isolated and independent units like the Brahminical schools, but were federated into larger units known as Viharas comprising thousands of teachers and students** and promoting a wider, collective, academic life with its own advantages. At the time of Buddha, Jetavana Vihara, constructed by the merchant prince Anathapindika, was very famous. Many others were built at Rajagriha, Sravasti,

Vaisali, Kapilavastu and Kausambi.

In later times, Taksasila, Nalanda and others developed into real universities, which attracted students from many parts of the world. The fame of Taksasila was due to that of its teachers. They were always spoken of as being 'world-renowned' being authorities, specialists and experts in the subjects they professed. Students went there to complete their education and not to begin it. The various centres of learning in the different parts of the country became affiliated, as it were, to the central University of Taksasila which exercised a kind of intellectual suzerainty over the wide world of letters in India.

With the rise of Mahayana Buddhism, Nalanda became famous. Hiuen Tsang mentions six monasteries built by as many kings. The whole area was marked off by a lofty enclosing wall with a gate. There were eight halls and about 300 apartments. Out of the estates endowed by the various kings, **the university provided for all its alumni free of cost their requisites of clothes, food, bedding and medicine. Out of the total of 10,000, as many as 1500 were teachers, the rest being students.** As many as one hundred chairs or pulpits were arranged every day for lectures or discourses. The courses of study were drawn from different fields of learning, Brahaminical and Buddhist, sacred and secular, philosophical and practical, sciences and arts. The huge library was situated in a special area known by the poetical name Dharmaganja (Mart of Religion), comprised three huge buildings, called Ratnasagara, Ratnodadhi and Ratnaranjaka. Ratnasagara was a nine-storoyed building and specialised in the collection of rare sacred books.

In Western India, Valabhi, the capital of Maitraka kings, was the rival of Nalanda. It specialised in the study of Hinayana. Its students after graduation used to present themselves at the courts of kings to prove their capacity, present their theories, and even demonstrate their administrative talent to be employed in government service. This shows that Valabhi provided for studies other than the purely religious, secular vidyas like Dharma, Niti, Varta or Chikitsa Sastras.

The University of Vikramasila, in northern Magadha, was also the result of royal benefactions. The Vihara was surrounded by a strong wall. At the centre was erected the temple adorned with Mahabodhi images. Fifty-three smaller temples of private character and fifty-four ordinary temples totaling 108 were also erected within the enclosure. **It had six colleges, each with a staff of 108 teachers, and a central hall called the house of science** with its six gates opening on the six colleges. The gates of the university were guarded by six most erudite scholars so that admission to it might not be cheap and its standard of scholarship lowered.

Dipamkara Srijnana or Atisa was its head when Nag-tsho was deputed by the Tibetan king for the purpose of inducing the great scholar to come to Tibet and take charge of Buddhism in that country. The following account of his arrival in Vikramasila and meeting with Atisa gives us a picture of the day-to-day life in the university:

> Nag-tsho arrived at the gate of the monastery in the evening when the gate could not be opened under its rules. He found shelter for the night at a Dharmashala at the gate. The gate was opened in the early morning when Nag-tsho was asked by a Tibetan monk to proceed to the Tibetan House of the monastery meant for the residence of its Tibetan students.
>
> At the Tibetan House Nag-tsho saw its senior monk, Gya-tson who advised him to be a resident pupil of Sthavira Ratnakara, who was also the chief of Atisa

himself, although Atisa had a higher reputation for learning and character. Gya-tson also said: We Tibetans have no influence here, but still I am well known to Atisa.

For next day was fixed a congregation of all classes of monks at Vikramasila. There was an assembly of 8,000 bhiksus. First entered Vidya Kokila who was to preside over it. The more distinguished monks were given reserved seats. The Raja Vikramasila (King of Magadha) was given an exalted seat. None of the monks, old or young, rose from their seats to mark his arrival. But all the monks, including the king, rose from their seats when the learned monk, Vira Vajra, entered. Last came Atisa from whose waist hung down a bundle of keys. He held the keys as the warden of several hostels or monasteries at Vikramasila.

In the following morning, the Tibetan messengers saw Atisa at his Vihara. Next day, he saw Atisa distributing alms and food to the poor, and how a begger boy, failing to get his share, ran after Atisa, exclaiming: "Bhala ho O Nath Atisa, Bhat-ona," (Blest be thou, O patron Atisa, Bhat-ona give me rice).

The Tibetan was much impressed by this charity, while Atisa also was very moved by the great trouble and expenses repeatedly borne by the Tibetan for his sake. Atisa now deciding to go to Tibet, told the Tibetan messengers that they would have to wait for eighteen months, which he would take to finish his work on hand before he could leave his charge of monasteries for Tibet.

Before leaving, Atisa in his usual spirit of charity and self-sacrifice, distributed the Tibetan gold brought to him as a present for his deputation.

18

Education in the Tamil Country

The ideal of universal popular education and that of all types of education being thrown open to everybody are the results of the application of the democratic idea in the field of education. Democracy as we now understand it is a new force in world history, though its feeble beginnings may be traced in the downright statement of the ancient Tamil Poet:

Yadum ure yavarum kelir
Periyorai viyattalum ilame
Siriyorai-yigaltal adaninun ilame

'All towns are one to me, all men my kindred . . . I do not fawn on the mighty, much less do I despise the lowly.'

To each according to his station, the station itself depending on the stage reached by him in the long evolution towards *mukti* lasting through several births—this was the accredited scheme of things in India in ancient times, and Tamil education was planned on this basis.

Literacy in itself is not education. It is well known that the Ashoka edicts are found engraved on the confines of Tamil country and that several short Brahmi records of about the same time or a little later are found engraved in rock-cut caves and natural caverns that must once have served as residences of monks. It has been held that the shorter inscriptions are composed in the Tamil language though written in Brahmi script. Several centuries later in the seventh and eighth centuries A.D., we have Pandya and Pallava inscriptions on stone and copper in two languages, Sanskrit and Tamil, and three scripts—Grantha, Tamil and Vatteluttu. Whatever doubts we may entertain of the capacity of the mass of the people to read and understand Brahmi and Grantha inscriptions, it seems a fair presumption to make that literacy in Tamil must have been more widespread by the time the Pandya and Pallava inscriptions came to be engraved; and the excellence of workmanship evidenced by many of these epigraphs implies that the artisans who actually carried out the work of engraving were by no means ignorant copyists of models set before them, but educated men who enjoyed their work and did not lack originality. The Chola Tamil inscriptions of Tanjore go far to strengthen this belief. The Vatteluttu, in particular, was decidedly a popular script in active use in the daily transactions of life. Rightly has it been compared to Modi and Takari by Buhler, and the script continued in use on the West Coast of South India at least to the end of the seventeenth century if not later. At one time it must have been common over the whole Tamil country, with the possible exception of its northernmost parts.

Tiruvalluvar in his *Kural*, the storehouse of early Tamil wisdom, counts writing and arithmetic as the two eyes of the soul, the means of perfecting man's insight into the nature of things. This ancient author was by no means oblivious of the role of the ear in the education; with characteristic terseness he states that of all the forms of wealth open to man, that gained by the ear is the best,—a statement calculated to emphasise both the part of the teacher in scholastic education and the possibility of another type of education for the illiterate. It has been suggested on good authority that in Akbar we have one of the most remarkable man in human history, who could not sign his name. Tiruvalluvar lays stress on the true aim of a good education and its influence on practical life. 'One should learn accurately whatever one learns (from books), and should then regulate his conduct accordingly.' The object of education then was not to pass examinations or win degrees, not even to qualify for professions or earn recognition, but to lead the good life.

We may now take leave of Tiruvalluvar with one final citation from his saying bearing on the value of a true education: "The penury of the learned is better than the affluence of the ignorant; a truly learned man does not lose his soul on account of poverty, whereas wealth controlled by an uncultured person may result in much social evil."

The commentary on the *Iraiyanar Ahapporul*, which passes under the name of Nakkirar, a Sangam poet, betrays signs of an evidently later date, and may for good reasons be assigned to the eighth century A.D. A short paragraph in the opening section of this work shows that already there had come into existence much speculation on what we should now call the theory of education. The author tells us *en passant* that for fear of prolixity he is not entering into a detailed discussion of subjects like the qualifications of the teacher, the methods of teaching, the nature of the pupil and manner of his study, and that such discussion may be found in other works specially devoted to them. But as no such early work on these topics seems to have come down to us, we are thrown on a work of relatively later date which contains the earliest discussion of such topics now accessible to us. That work is *Nannul* (The Good Book), a treatise on Tamil grammar, composed by Jaina author Pavanandi (Bhavanandi), who flourished at the court of the Ganga prince Amarabharanan Siya-Gangan, a feudatory of the Chola Emperor Kulottunga III (A.D. 1178-1216). We have every reason to presume that, speaking generally, Pavanandi was only restating positions reached by long ages of discussion centring round the topics considered by him. And his statements on educational subjects often surprise us alike by their shrewd good sense and by the possible range of their application to times and conditions other than his own.

Who is fit for the position of a teacher? The teacher, answers Pavanandi, must be a man of good birth, gentle and godly by nature and of a generous outlook. He must be deeply learned in booklore and capable of expounding his knowledge with directness and simplicity. He must also combine common sense (*ulagiyal arivu*) with these high qualities. There is perhaps nothing remarkable in these generic requirements, except the emphasis on birth and the implicit faith in the hereditary transmission of culture. But the functional differential of the teacher as such are stated by Pavanandi in a manner that tickles us by its quaintness, but was quite natural to mediaeval scholastic thought all over India. He says: 'The teacher must unite in himself the characteristic features of the earth, mountain, weighing-rod and flower'.

Obviously we need some explanation here before we can be sure of the author's meaning, and he does not omit to give us that. The earth, we learn, signifies four qualities: first, extent or vastness of size, so great that you could not take it all in at a glance from any one point; secondly, strength not to yield under the stress of great weight; thirdly, patience even towards those who dig into it and otherwise cause hurt and damage; and lastly, capacity to yield fruits commensurate to the timeliness and intensity of effort on the part of the cultivator.

The teacher, in other words, should be a man of vast

learning, not living from hand to mouth so to say, being only a little in advance of his pupils with the subject-matter of his lectures. His learning again should be thoroughly well organised and capable of sustaining positions taken up by him through the stress of the most strenuous debate—a requirement which shows incidentally the place held by public disputation in the educational system of ancient India. How many are not the occasions when pupils fall below the proper standard of diligence, rectitude or loyalty, or to take to flighty or evil courses! On such occasions the teacher should have the strength and patience to keep his temper, the better to be in a position to study the particular case, and follow the plan suited to it. To discover talent and encourage its growth, and to grade individual teaching according to the capacity of each pupil, so to arrange the work that the indifferent pupils do not hamper the better class of them was an essential feature of a sound system of education. 'To each according to his deserts' should be the motto of the teacher. Such are some of the implications of the apparently puerile statement that the teacher should be like the earth, mountain etc; and let us remember that these implications have been drawn out for us by the author himself.

Having thus defined who the good teacher is, Pavanandi proceeds to complete his account by pointing out who is not a good teacher and can never hope to make one. He says: 'Those who are not conspicuous for some noble quality or other, who are by nature mean-minded and disposed to be jealous, greedy, deceitful and cowardly cannot make good as teachers.' The peculiar demerits of the bad teacher are brought out by our author by a series of analogies. The bad teacher is first of all like a jar of Molucca-beans. The idea is this: when a jar of Molucca-beans is implied the beans rush out in any order; so also, a bad teacher expounds his points in a chaotic and disorderly manner, with no reference to their proper logical order, and is too fast and confused for his pupils to make anything out of his lessons.

We are all familiar with this type of the totally unimpressive yet undoubtedly learned teacher. There is another type who learns with difficulty himself, and has still greater difficulty in imparting his learning to others, the teacher whose intellectual powers are not adequate to his task. For an analogy to this type, Pavanandi turns to the practice of preserving carded cotton in coconut and other shells, the shells being slowly stuffed with cotton through a small hole, the only opening in the shell; the cotton is of course taken out with even greater difficulty than it was put in. The defects pointed to by these two analogies are intellectual; two others are employed to stress the moral defects of the bad teacher.

A variety of the palm has its stem covered all over with pinnate leaves carried on branches with sharp edges; its fruit can be gathered only when the tree sheds it, and not otherwise, as no one can climb the tree to get at the fruit. In the same way, one type of bad teacher refuses to do anything for the pupil who wants his aid systematically; the pupil has to wait on his whims. Another type is said to resemble a coconut tree, which though watered by one man yields its fruits to another, because its stem is bent over across the fence. The fault in the teacher is, of course, not his teaching a pupil who pays him nothing or serves him in no other way, but his neglecting the pupils who do these things.

Pavanandi then turns to a consideration of the conditions of a successful lesson. The teacher and pupil should meet in a suitable place and at a proper time of the day. The teacher should occupy a seat higher than the pupil's and begin with a prayer to his particular god. He should then concentrate his attention on the subject of the lesson, and begin to expound it, not too fast, nor impatiently, but with a loving heart, a pleasant face and a graceful mind; he should study the pupil's capacity for assimilation and regulate the weight of the lesson accordingly.

Who may be accepted as pupils? One's own son, the son of one's teacher, the king's son, one who pays well, one who does service to the teacher, and lastly, one who has the capacity to profit by the teaching — all these may become pupils. The order in this list is noteworthy. We should also note that ability is itself a passport to the realm of knowledge; if the teacher knows that a young man is likely to profit by a course, then it is his duty to admit him to the course, that is, even if he cannot afford to pay for his education.

Judged by the standard of ability, pupils are said to fall into three classes — the best resembling the *hamsa* and the cow, the middling the earth and parrot, and the last grade evincing the qualities of a leaky jar, sheep, buffalo, and filter. Here Pavanandi leaves us to guess the meaning he seeks to convey by these analogies as best we may, for he does not elaborate them. The *hamsa* in Indian literary convention can separate milk from water and leave the water behind after drinking off the milk; likewise the best student fastens on the essential points of the lesson and gains permanent hold on them, not wasting his attention on inconsequential details. When it comes across a rich pasture, the cow grazes with avidity and then reminates at leisure; this typifies what a good student seeks to do when he is thrown in the company of some great scholars. The earth yields produce commensurate to the efforts of the cultivator, and the parrot just repeats what it is taught; likewise the pupil of medium grade evinces a grasp of the subject strictly limited by the nature and intensity of the lesson to which he is treated, he has very little capacity for assimilating knowledge, much less for reflection and initiative in its acquisition.

Lastly, the worst type of pupil quickly forgets his lessons and resembles the jar with a big hole in its bottom which can never be filled with water; the sheep wanders from one tree or shrub to another and never manages to get its full feed anywhere, so too the bad pupil goes on changing his teachers and never gets the full benefit of the instruction of any single teacher; just as a buffalo muddles the water in the pond before it starts drinking it, this class of pupil causes a lot of mental anguish to the teacher before deriving any good from him; the filter lets through the essential parts of the liquids like ghee or honey, and retains the impurities, so also the bad pupil misses the essentials of a lesson and fastens on the minor and relatively useless parts of it.

The question is how far these text-book maxims were observed in practice; we have no direct evidence here, such as the description of an eye-witness, indigenous or foreign, or anything corresponding to the periodical reports of modern educational associations. Epigraphy and literature furnish sufficient data to warrant the assumption that the conditions under which education was carried on in those days were quite favourable to the attainment of tolerable good results. Large classes were unknown and the proportion of the number of teachers to that of pupils in organised centres of higher education like Ennayiram and Tribhuvani compares very favourably with what it is in many colleges today. Distractions were few, and learning was as much respected as it was more or less exclusive. The schools generally centred round temples and *mathas* even in relatively later times; the inscriptions tell us more of Sanskrit schools and colleges, even in the Tamil country, than of the other type of school devoted to the cultivation of Tamil which must have existed side by side. Education in the arts and crafts was largely a matter of caste and family tradition and training; but even to such training, the instructive analysis of Pavanandi was not altogether inapplicable.

19

Rigvedic Poetic Spirit

It is generally held that with Bharata the theory of *Rasa* as the soul of poetry came into existence or at least into vogue. Anandavardhana is modest enough to declare that the *Dhvani* theory had a great antiquity and that he was only attempting a reorientation of that thought. For the first time in the history of Indian Aesthetics Jagannatha suggestively left the idea that the Upanishadic passage, *Raso vai sah*, refers to the *Rasa* theory in that *Kavya Rasa* is the same as *bhagnavarana cit*.

The Upanishads speak of Brahman as *sat, cit* and *ananda*. One can understand how *sat* and *cit* find a place in a philosophic interpretation of universe. But the concept of *ananda* belongs to the realm of beauty, of Aesthetics. This evidently shows that to the Upanishadic mind, the Absolute is revealed in fine arts, religion and philosophy. Consequently, when Upanishads speak of Brahman as *Rasa* it resembles an experience of aesthetic bliss. This is said to be *Rasa* giving *ananda*, for it flows; it is natural or spontaneous, it is a dynamic state of existence. The transport one has in aesthetic contemplation is transcendental; and, hence, it is both bliss and knowledge. Hence it is that Abhinavagupta made a systematic analysis of the aesthetic experience or *rasanubhuti* only to bring it again on a par with religion and philosophy.

To begin with-there is *Sringara* or the sentiment of love. In the Rigveda we have some lyrics, ballad and dramatic fragments that develop this sentiment.

The sentiment of *Sringara* requires primarily an *alambana vibhava* and an *uddipana vibhava*. A lover and a beloved are absolutely essential. They should be human beings, or they should at least portray the human affections. The ballads of Juhu, Ghosa and Apala reveal how the sentiment for its fulfilment or consummation requires a lover of an equal status, so that there can be no *ratyabhasa*. As Ghosa observes: "Youth should rest within the chambers of the bride and, hence, she should marry and beget children." That is, *Sringara* is to be conceived of not as conductive to *preyas*, but only to *sreyas*. Love is to be, in other words, spiritualised. But this can arise only out of the concept of beauty. Hence Brihaspati had to discard his ugly lady, Ghosa requested beauty from the Asvins, and Indra made Apala beautiful. Chyavana was restored to youth by the Asvins. Consequently, we find that youth and beauty are absolutely essential for the development of *Sringara*, and that *Sringara* finds its value and destiny only in its being spiritualised.

The ballad of Mudgalani brings before us the importance of an *alambana vibhava* and an *uddipana vibhava*. As long as she did not bear any children, she was discarded by her husband and consequently considered an eunuch. The love of Mudgalani, therefore, tends to *rasabhasa* since it is one-sided. But she gained his love by helping him in winning back the cattle. Here we find that it is not only beauty of form that can generate love, but also beauty of skill, of adventure. It is, as Agastya said, the unification of *tapas* and *kama* that constitutes true beauty that can engender spiritual love.

Coming to the actual conception of *Sringara Rasa* in

Rigveda, we have to note the dialogues of Yama-Yami, Agastya-Lopamudra, and Urvasi-Pururava. Yami approaches her brother Yama and it is carnal lust that prevails here. The ethical and the spiritual aspects are ignored by her, though Yama invokes them. Consequently, he shuns her away. This is not only a pure case of *rasabhasa*, but also an exposition of the physical aspect of love; love that is carnal or sensuous is no true *Sringara*. Yami takes her stand on her conscience too. But the vital chord of love can be touched only with the ethical and the spiritual fervour. And yet Yami, though in a misdirected way, reveals that true love implies the abject surrender of the person to the object he or she loves intensely.

Lopamudra approaches her lord, Agastya, with the sentiments of love. She realises that her husband is engaged in penances. At the same time she feels that her beauty is wasted away. Surprisingly enough does she understand that love and duty or penance do not come into conflict with one another, for they have their respective spheres of activity. Hence it is that the ancient seers, who were the legislators of human will and action, begot progeny; and yet they did not violate their vow of continence. Agastya too at last realises that *tapas* or duty has its significance only when it is united in a synthetic way with love.

In the third dialogue, it is Pururavas that acts the part of Yami and Lopamudra. The woman he loved eluded him for she represents the stage where love is idealised and transformed into beauty, spirit, and immortality. Though Pururavas seems to be infatuated by her appearance, he longs for intellectual companionship. His consort should stay and wait in earnest so that they might converse; for their past reveals that they were happy only when they conversed. Like Shelley's skylark, he loved and 'never knew love's sad satiety', for she is like the first of the dawns and like the wind but coldly did she receive his caresses since he desired only to be the lord of her body.

It is this carnal element that made the nymphs fly from him 'like scared snakes and like chariot horses'. 'Like swans they show the beauty of their bodies, and like horses in play they bite and nibble.' At last he begins to realise that true love is something spiritual, and that its fruition lies in the child who alone can bring to view this spiritual factor.

The second sentiment is humour or *Hasya*. One poet observes: "Wake up the generous donors; let misers sleep unawakened." The same thought occurs again in another song to the dawns, where the poet observes: " The wealthy dawns urge the liberal donors to present their riches; let the misers sleep unawakened in the midst of the unlighted depths of darkness." In the songs addressed exclusively to Daksina a similar idea is noticeable. This type of humour is frivolous and highly sarcastic. There is a touch of bitterness.

In the famous dialogue between Visvamitra and the rivers, we observe that the seer requests the rivers to stay a while so that he can converse and cross the waters. But they inform him that they cannot tarry as they are commanded by Indra and Savitar. The saga had an intuitive realisation of Savitar and he, therefore, catches the clue and begins to praise Indra. This makes the rivers yield to his request. Here we find how a situation is exploited simply because the seer had a better psychological understanding.

Vrisakapi is eager to offer a sacrifice to Indra consisting of a slain wild ass, which he has found somewhere, a dresser, a knife, a pan, and wagon-load of wood. Here humour is based on incongruity and impropriety. The selling of Indra, in another context, for ten cows, brings out humour based on the contrast between the shrewd seller and needy buyer.

Vasistha's song to the frogs is a classic by itself in the

realm of poetic humour. Just like the Brahmins who begin to utter the sacred texts after keeping silence for a long time as a vow, so do the frogs after being inspired by Parjanya. Their music comes forth in concert like bellowings of cows. One repeats the other's language, as the master and the pupil do the sacred text. As they converse their limbs expand in direct proportion to the degree of this oratory. The frogs sitting around the pool are like the priests around the vessel in *atiratra*. Here the humour does not so much lie as in comparing the priests unfavourably, but only in elevating the frogs to a lofty place in the aesthetic universe.

The sentiment of *Karuna* is evidently the development of *soka* or pathos. In the conversation between Agastya, Indra and the Maruts, we find this sentiment being evoked in the character of the Maruts who are at first denied a place by Indra. The character of Yami turns out to be pathetic, but it fails to evoke this sentiment, as there is neither a proper cause for indignation, nor a similarity with the proper love. Vrisakapi becomes pathetic as he is ejected by his stepmother and left uncared for by his father who had to bow down to the wishes of Indrani. The penitent gambler becomes pathetic and he, therefore, touches the vital chords of the human hearts. Pururavas leads himself into a pathetic situation as he has not only lost his beloved, but his beloved is even cold and indifferent towards him. He is on the verge of committing suicide, and in a fit of desperation he prefers to become a pray to the ravenous wolves.

There is a striking case of pathos in one of the songs addressed to Ushas. Ushas has stayed long over the eastern skies, and it is time for the sun to appear. The sun will not simply displace her. The sun, who is conceived poetically as her son, brother, and lover, will torture her with his rays, just as one punishes a thief. So the poet adds: "Let not the sun with fervent heat consume thee like a thief." He cannot afford to see such a glorious and lovely beauty eclipsed by the sun. Here we find an interesting case of pathos in the sympathetic understanding of, or insight into things.

There are three interrelated sentiments called *Raudra*, *Bhayanaka* and *Bibhatsa*. Of these *Raudra* is based on anger. The sentiment of *Bhayanaka* is based on fear. This fear might arise out of the sentiment of *Raudra* met in the opponent. *Raudra* and *Bhayanaka* generally give rise to certain undesirable and unpalatable consequences. These are conveniently called *Bibhatsa*, which is based on *jugupsa*. This exists when a thing is to be detested.

The Rigvedic poet had very little to fear. Though he was at times moved to fear before Rudra and Varuna, yet even here he chose the path of love and friendship. He systematically eschewed the problem of sin and suffering. And hence, *Bhayanaka* and *Bibhatsa* are absent. To a certain extent, *Bhayanaka* is traceable to Agni when he fled from duty and hid himself in the waters. So did the Panis have this sentiment as they saw Sarama approaching. Indra declares that after the fight his enemies will be more or less, women; for, a man, a hero, should either die on the battlefield or come out victorious. This is a case of *Bibhatsa*. The Rigvedic poet confined *Bhayanaka* and *Bibhatsa* only to the vanquished or to the guilty.

Vira is the next important sentiment found in Rigveda. The sentiment of valour is based on *utsaha* or enthusiasm. This is the essential quality of a hero in any plot. In Rigveda we hear many a time the request for heroes, and in Rigvedic terminology *Vira* and son are convertible terms.

The text of Rigveda is full to the brim with this lofty

sentiment; for it narrates many a time the heroic exploits of Indra, the Maruts, the Asvins, Brihaspati and other deities, besides those of the human beings. The hero in Rigveda is something like a superman who is venerated and respected, and whose example is consciously emulated. Even the women took part in these heroic enterprises. We hear Indrani declaring:

" Utaham asmi virinindrapatni marut sakha"

She is Virini not only because she has heroes as her sons, but also because she herself is full of the heroic sentiment.

The martial ballads that treat of the preparations for battle and of the celebrations of victory form a rich compendium breathing this sentiment. The trilogy of Sudasas celebrates the success of the king as he was aided by Vasistha. The sage "poured forth his prayers desiring to milk Indra like a cow in goodly pasture". And "as the skilled priest clips grass within the chamber, so has Indra wrought the downfall of the enemies." Again we are told that "the armies of Sudasas worked to have in the battlefield, like thirsty men." The last four Rks of 10.103 provided a sort of exhortation to the troops on the eve of the battle. These are comparable to King Henry's famous speech in Shakespeare to his troops on the eve of Agincourt.

Adbhuta is based on *vismaya* or surprise, wonder. All the miracles brought by Indra, Agni, Brihaspati, the Maruts and the Asvins are fine examples of this sublimity. The loftiest place of Vishnu is laid up as it were in heaven; his station is most sublime, and the ever vigilant singers, lovers of holy song, light it up. The immortal and the deathless place to which Soma transports the individual is another case of the sublime. There is sublimity in Vasistha's description of the place of Varuna, and in the birth of Vasistha himself, Rudra, the cosmic fire, invokes this sublimity many a time.

The ballad of Apala is woven entirely round this sentiment. She came to the stream to carry a pitcherfull of water. But she was surprised to see the Soma plant nearby; and as she had no pressing stones with her, she pressed the leaf with her teeth, and invoked Indra who appeared before her in an instant, for he was in love with her. Similar exploits are found in the episodes of Vyamsa, Ghosa and Juhu. A jubilant tone of surprise and joy was expressed by Indrani who was to employ the herbs to control her husband. No hymn can surpass the sublimity of Hiranyagarbha whose glory is revealed even in the Himalayas.

Finally, there is the *Santa Rasa*. It arises from true knowledge and from an apprehension of the real nature of objects. It manifests itself in discipline, in spiritual training, and in sympathetic and intuitive apprehension of the universe. The philosophical hymns of Rigveda are the glowing illustrations of this aspect of *Santa*. The mystical raptures of the seers and their transcendental experience speak of *Santa* as the fundamental and ultimate sentiment. Its very nature is a sort of effulgence (*jyoti*), which the seers attributed to the highest divinity, and which they longed to obtain.

But Bharata informs us that *Santa* is the chief *Rasa* out of which the other *Rasas* sprang. *Santa* is the basis, the spring of action, the culmination or fulfilment of the other sentiments. And unless other sentiments lead to the experience of *Santa*, they have no reality and no value. The Rigvedic poets too had the same theory.

20

Sanskrit Literature

Sanskrit has been the language of India's religion, philosophy and culture, the source of inspiration for her intellectual and aesthetic achievements and the great instrument of establishing unity throughout the land. The history of Sanskrit literature generally falls into two main periods, the Vedic and the Classical. The former perhaps begins as early as 1500 B.C. and extends at the latest about 200 B.C. The Classical period concurrent with the final stages of Vedic literature, strictly speaking, close with the Muslim invasion. But owing to the continued literary use of Sanskrit this period may be regarded as coming down to the present day.

The second period came to be called Sanskrit, the 'refined' as against Prakrit, the 'unrefined' dialect. From the second century onwards, probably Sanskrit was the spoken language in the whole of Aryavarta between the Himalayas and Vindhya range. Dramas show that even those who did not speak Sanskrit understood it. From the sixth century onwards Sanskrit almost prevails in inscriptions and by the time of the Muslim invasion, it was perhaps the only written language of India.

As regards the form, the classical period contrasts with the Vedic period. While prose was employed in the Yajurveda and Brahmanas and developed to a certain degree, it disappears almost in classical Sanskrit. For,

nearly every branch of the literature, excepting perhaps grammar and philosophy, is composed in verse, literary prose being found only in fables, fairy tales, romances and partially in the dramas.

The general contents of the classical literature embrace secular subjects. The period touches perfection in many branches of literature; in Puranas, in court epics or Mahakavyas, in prose romances, in drama, in fairy tales and fables and finally in commentaries.

Sanskrit epic poetry falls into two main classes, *Itihasa* or legend, which comprises old stories, and Kavya or artificial epic. While the *Mahabharata* is the chief and oldest representative of the former group, the *Ramayana* represents the latter division. Both these great epics are composed in the *shloka* metre, which prevails in the classical period.

The *Mahabharata* in its present form consists of over 100,000 shlokas and is perhaps the longest poem in literary history. Consisting of eighteen books called Parvans, with a nineteenth, the *Harivamsa,* forming a supplement, the work is a conglomerate of the epic and didactic matter. The number of verses in each parvan varies. All the eighteen books excepting the eighth and the last three are divided into subordinate parvans which are divided into several chapters. The epic kernel of the *Mahabharata* describes the eighteen days' fight between the Kauravas and the Pandavas ending in the destruction of the former. The victors after some more years go to Himalayas leaving Parikshit, the grandson of Arjuna, to rule over Hastinapura. Within this narrative framework there are numerous legends of gods and kings and sages, accounts of cosmogony and theogony, and disquisitions on philosophy, religion and ethics. *Bhagvadgita,* the philosophical poem consisting of eighteen cantos, is included in it. The *Harivamsa*, containing 16,000 verses and divided into three sections, narrates the family history of Krishna. Sage Vyasa, the son of Parasara, is the compiler of the *Mahabharata* as is mentioned in the work itself. The exact date of the compilation remains anybody's guess.

Ramayana in the present form consists of about 24,000 verses and is divided into seven books called Kandas. Composed by sage Valmiki, the work shows excellence in plan and execution. It describes in detail Rama's exile, the theft of his wife Sita by Ravana, his effort to find and regain her and his final victory over Ravana. The second part on Uttarakanda describes the banishment of Sita, whom Valmiki takes to his hermitage where she delivers Kusa and Lava, whom the sage himself brings up. The story ends with Rama's meeting of his sons, his wife having been swallowed by the mother earth.

The Puranas constitute an important branch of Sanskrit literature and are often designated as the fifth Veda. The name Purana signifies 'old traditional story.' Composed chiefly in shloka metre with occasional passages in prose, the Puranas deal with a vast range of subject. They are eighteen in number and are said to have been composed by the ancient sage Vyasa.

The Puranas often aim at exalting one of the three gods of the Trinity. Thus the eighteen Puranas are classified according to the deity who is exalted. Thus *Brahma, Brahmanda, Brahmavaivarta, Markandeya, Bhavisya* and *Vamana Puranas* are related to Brahma, the creator. Another group namely *Vishnu, Bhagavata, Naradiya, Garuda, Padma* and *Varaha Puranas* are Vaisnava Puranas. The Puranas that glorify Siva are *Siva, Linga, Skanda, Agni, Matsya* and *Kurma.*

Besides these there are eighteen Upa-Puranas. Generally Puranas do not belong to one particular period. While some of them are very ancient, others are very recent.

It is not easy to trace the beginnings of Kavyas in Sanskrit literature. They must certainly belong to a much earlier period. For we have the important literary evidence of the references in Patanjali's *Mahabhasya* which show that Kavyas flourished in his day.

Asvaghosa's *Buddhacharita* and *Saundarananda* are two earlier Kavyas. According to the Buddhistic tradition, he was a contemporary of King Kaniska of the first century A.D. and himself a Buddhist. The two most important Kavyas are *Raghuvamsa* and *Kumarasambhava* of Kalidasa, whose date is a subject of dispute. According to Macdonell, he lived in the beginning of the fifth century A.D. His *Raghuvamsa,* the line of Raghu, in nineteen cantos, describes the story of Rama together with his forefathers and successors. Beginning with Dilipa, the story ends with the death of Agnivarna. *Kumarasambhava* consist of seventeen cantos. Beginning with the courtship of Siva and Parvati, the story ends with an account of destruction of the demon Taraka by Kumara, the son of the couple.

Bhattikavya, ascribed to Bhartrhari, is a work consisting of twenty-two cantos, which describe the story of Rama illustrating the forms of Sanskrit grammar. The *Kiratarjuniya* of Bharavi, who is mentioned in an inscription of 634 A.D. along with Kalidasa, is a Kavya abounding in richness of meaning. In eighteen cantos it describes the battle between Arjuna and Siva disguised as a Kirata. *Sisupalavadha* of Magha is a Kavya of extraordinary merit. It is famous for its three qualities, i.e., similies, richness of meaning and simplicity of diction. In twenty cantos the work describes the killing of Sisupala, the King of Chedi, by Krishna. The work is also known by the name *Magha-Kavya* having been composed by Magha. *Naisadhiyacharita* of Sri Harsa, in twenty-two cantos, deals with the story of Nala, the king of Nisadha, and Damayanti, the daughter of King Bhima. The episode is taken from the *Mahabharata* and the author belongs to the 12th century.

Among the historical Kavyas Kalhana's *Rajatarangini* stands foremost. *Navasahasankacharita* of Padmagupta also deserves mention.

The abundant use of lengthy compounds, vivid description of Nature and long strings of similies and metaphors often teeming with puns are some of the most important characteristics of classical prose. The narrative portions are almost meagre. The high standards prescribed for prose writing render it difficult and only men of the calibre of Bana and Dandin could lay hands on it. There are two types of romances, the Akhyayika and Katha, the theme of the former type being historical while Katha is purely imaginative.

Subandhu's *Vasavadatta* is an interesting but fictitious story. In style it comes up to the prescribed standard. Bana's *Harsacharita* and *Kadambari* are two important works in this field. The former is an example of Akhyayika while the latter is model for Katha. *Harsacharita* in eight chapters describes the story of King Harsa only partially. The first three chapters contain a short biography of the poet. *Kadambari* is an imaginative story comprehending several generations. Both these works are composed in ornate prose.

Dasakumaracharita of Dandin contains the story of common life and reflects a cross section of corrupt society. The work reveals the ability of the author in writing beautiful prose.

Owing to the higher standard prescribed for prose, works in this branch of literature are comparatively less in number. There is, however, a species of writing called Champu where prose and poetry are mingled together. Works like *Bharat Champu* and *Ramayana Champu* are excellent treatises in this field.

Generally lyrics in Sanskrit are short poems. The merit of every lyric poem consists in its description of dynamic feeling expressed in simple, direct and impassioned language, which would thrill and captivate the hearts of the readers.

Kalidasa's *Meghaduta* or 'Cloud Messenger' is a lyric gem which won the admiration of critics as the most wonderful love poem in any language. It consists of 115 stanzas composed in Mandakranta meter and is divided into two parts. The theme is a love message sent by a Yaksa, an exile living in Ramagiri, by a cloud to his wife dwelling far away in Alaka at the top of Himalayas. The work formed a model and many a similar work was produced in this field. His *Ritusamhara* of 144 stanzas divided into six cantos and composed in various meters gives a vivid and highly poetical description of the six seasons into which the classical Sanskrit poets divide the year.

The *Chaurapancasika* of Kashmiri Bilhana is a poem in fifty stanzas describing the poet's experience of the joys of love. Another short lyric is *Ghatakarparakavya* in twenty-two stanzas. The *Sringarasataka* of Bhartrihari deals with erotic sentiment and reveals the deep insight of the poet in the arts of love. However, the most important work which deals with the erotic sentiment is *Amarusataka* of Amaru, where the author exhibits his skill in painting lovers in all their moods. *Gitagovinda* of Jayadeva, a native of Bengal, is a notable work in this field in that it deals with the divine love and that it indirectly hints at the relation of the Supreme Deity to the human soul.

Sage Bharata is the mythical inventor of the Nataka. The chief characteristics of the drama are: (i) Vira or Sringara should be the predominant sentiment, the others being subordinated to it. The last act should contain the sentiment of wonder. (ii) The hero should be one of the four types, viz.- Dhirodatta, Dhiroddhata, Dhiralalita and Dhirasanta. (iii) The plot must be either famous or imaginative, preference being given to the former. (iv) There should be five to ten acts in a play. Besides the Nataka there are several other forms of representations such as Prakarana, Bhana, Prahasana, etc.

The earliest forms of dramatic literature may be found in the Rigvedic dialogues such as those of Sarama and Panis, Yama and Yami, Pururavas and Urvasi. But the earliest reference to the acted dramas may be found in *Mahabhasya* where *Kamsavadha* and *Balibandha* are mentioned.

Bhasa is an earlier dramatist mentioned by Kalidasa. Thirteen plays are ascribed to him, the chief of which are *Svapnavasavadatta, Madhyamavyayoga,* etc. Many scholars question his authorship of the dramas. But Kalidasa is perhaps the greatest dramatist. Three of his plays have come down to us. His *Vikramorvasiya* is a play in five acts describing the love of king Pururavas and Urvasi, a celestial nymph. *Malavikagnimitra* in five acts describes the love between King Agnimitra and Malavika, a princess. *Sakuntala* is the greatest of his dramas both length and in merit. In seven acts the drama describes the love of King Dusyanta for Sakuntala, the daughter of Menaka.

Mricchakatika of Sudraka in ten acts is distinct from others in its dramatic qualities of vigour of life and action and its humour. The heroine of the play is a courtesan. Sri Harsa is the author of three dramas. They are *Ratnavali*, describing the love of Udayana and Sagarika, *Nagananda*, a play with a Buddhistic colouring, and *Priyadarsika*. Another important dramatist is Bhavabhuti with three dramas to his credit. His *Malatimadhava* is a Prakarana in ten acts, and his *Mahaviracharita* derives its plot from the *Ramayana* and consists of seven acts. *Uttarararamacharita* is perhaps the greatest of his plays. The description of the love of Rama for Sita, purified by sorrow, is perhaps unique in Indian drama. Critics say that it is a dramatic poem rather than pure drama.

Visakhadatta's *Mudraraksasa* is a unique play since it contains political intrigues. The hero is Chandragupta, the founder of Gupta Dynasty. Bhattanarayana's *Venisamhara* is a drama of considerable merit based on the *Mahabharata*. Among other dramatists Rajasekhara deserves mention. Four of his plays *Viddhasalabhanjika, Karpuramanjari, Bala Ramayana* and *Bala Bharata* have survived.

Among allegorical plays *Prabodhachandrodaya* of Krishna Misra in six acts is important. Abstract notions such as religion, reason, knowledge, etc., are personified as characters in the play. There are numerous dramas with varying merit produced in Sanskrit down to the modern times.

Fairy tales and fables in classical Sanskrit literature are noteworthy for their didactical value. Ethical reflections and proverbial philosophy are the characteristics of the fables. It is often difficult to follow the main thread of the story for there are numerous stories inserted within the framework of the main story.

Panchatantra is perhaps the greatest didactical fable and it has been translated into almost every language in the world. Probably the work was written for instructing some prince in moral values. The author is believed to have been a Brahmin. Through these stories various human vices are exposed. *Hitopadesa* is an old fable of doubtful authorship. It contains instructions in domestic and foreign policies. *Nitisara* is a similar work dealing with the principles of polity.

Among various collections of fairy tales *Vetala Panchavimsati* of Jambhaladatta, where a Vetala narrates twenty-five quizzical stories to King Vikramaditya is interesting. *Simhasanadvatrimsika* is a collection of thirty-two stories narrated to the king by the throne. Another collection is *Sukasaptati*, where a parrot narrates seventy stories to a wife in separation in order to dissuade her from running after other men.

The greatest of them all is *Kathasaritsagara* of the Kashmiri Somadeva consisting of 124 tarangas divided into 18 chapters. The work is based on Gunadhya's *Brihatkatha* supposed to have been written in Paisachi language. *Brihatkatha* itself is not available and is known only through references of Bana and Dandin. Another important work based on *Brihatkatha* is the *Brihatkathamanjari* of Kshemendra.

Commentaries on various books form a good division of our literature. The greatest commentator is perhaps Mallinatha, a Brahmin scholar, who besides writing other commentaries has commented on all the five Mahakavyas. **The growth of this branch is evident from the fact that *Kumarasambhava* has more than twenty-two commentaries and there is a similar number on *Meghaduta* and *Raghuvamsa*.** This branch continues down to the present day.

21

Literatures of India: A General Survey

Like the Indian languages, the history of Indian literature may conveniently be divided into two main stages or phases, the old and modern. The old is also capable of being sub-divided into ancient and medieval, and the lower limit of this old period has been put down roughly at 1,000 A.D. This is a period when the Indian people experienced some of the greatest transformations in its political and cultural set-up. It was about this time the Northern Indian Aryan languages as they are current at the present day took definite forms, evolving out of the earlier Apabhramsas and Prakrits, and these in there turn represent the second phase of the Aryan speech in India, the earlier phase being indicated by Vedic and Classical Sanskrit.

Round about 1,000 A.D. in the different parts of North India and the Deccan, the Modern Indo-Aryan language took shape—languages like Bengali, Assamese and Oriya, Maithili, Magahi and Bhojpuri, Kosali (Eastern Hindi), Brajbhasha and other connected dialects belonging to the "Western Hindi" speech; the Pahari or Himalayan dialects; and dialects of Rajasthan and Malwa with Gujarati; Marathi and Konkani; the speeches of Eastern Punjab, Western Punjab and Sindh; and Kashmiri—all these first came into being about this time. Although the language changed its character by entering a new phase, which differed in its grammatical development from the earlier one, there was no break in the tradition of literary composition, which was current in India before 1,000 B.C.

The scholarly and scientific literature of India continued to be written in Sanskrit even after the development of the Prakrit or middle Indo-Aryan dialects and the Bhasa or Modern Indo-Aryan speeches. The older literary tradition was partly religious and partly secular, such as we find in both Sanskrit and the Prakrits. The religious literature consisted of philosophical disquisition and narrative poems describing the legends and stories of the ancient heroes as preserved in the great epics and the Puranas, and in the case of Jainas, in the stories of religious edification on the lives of the Jaina saints. The atmosphere of Brahminism, Buddhism and Jainism was carried over from Middle Indo-Aryan to New Indo-Aryan.

On the secular side, the literature consisted of little lyrics of love and life, and the habit of composing long narrative poems on romantic legends, which obtained in Sanskrit also, received a new form in the New Indo-Aryan languages. Modern Indian literature thus started with inheritances from Prakrit and its later phase the Apabhramsa, and from Sanskrit, in Northern India; and in South India, in the case of Dravidian languages, there was a profound influence of Sanskrit all through. Although certain types of literature appeared to have developed independently in various Dravidian languages, particularly Tamil, the Sanskrit influence became predominant. With a general Brahminical revival throughout the whole of India just about the time when the North Indian Aryan Modern languages were taking shape and the Dravidian languages of the South were also being modified to something like their present forms from earlier stages in their development, there was a revival of the Sanskrit language all over India, as a concomitant to this Brahminical revival.

The Turki conquest of North India started during the second half of the 11th century, and it took two centuries for the Turki Muslim power to be established from Western Punjab to West Bengal; and further extension of the Turki rule or conflict with the Turks and their clients, the Indian Muslims, in other and more distant parts of India, took place in the second half of the 13th and early part of the 14th centuries. This Turki conquest was the direct cause of a Brahminical revival and this revival also found its fullest expressions in the literatures in Modern Indian languages, both Aryan and Dravidian in their earlier phases.

Apart from a slender stream of secular literature, the inherited religious of literature the Modern Indian languages presents a common factor for all the Indian languages of the present day. The great Sanskrit epics, the *Mahabharata* and *Ramayana*, the story of Krishna as in the *Bhagvata Purana*, and other Puranic stories, were like the Bible and the Golden Legends of the Saints in Medieval Christian Europe, in supplying the basic material for literature in Modern Indian languages. This forms the great link for the whole of India, and its importance as forming the background of modern Indian thought and literature can never be over-estimated. Over and above this common ancient Indian inheritance, there were a number of local cults and legends in different parts of the country which were going quite strong, although as submerged forms of pre-Aryan or extra-scriptural religion; and these, too, were rapidly becoming Brahminised. The Modern Indian languages in the earlier phase of their literatures also treated these cults and legends as subject- matter for popular work.

Cross divisions cannot be avoided in considering both

subject-matters and their literary treatment. About Early modern Indian literature we may say that on the side of story-telling–romance and narrative poetry—there were, to start with, two distinct matters or cycles in almost every language: (1) the matter or cycle of ancient India as preserved primarily in Sanskrit, and (2) the matter or cycle of the province or linguistic area concerned—what may be called the matter of medieval India—which sometimes was found treated not in one language but in many and which were thus inter-provincial or even Pan-Indian. Some of the most distinctive or characteristic literary creations in the different Modern Indian literatures belong to this matter of medieval India. Then, from the 16th century onwards, and particularly from the 17th century, some of the North Indian languages like Hindustani or Hindi, Bengali, Punjabi and Sindhi, under Mohammedan inspiration developed a new matter or cycle, viz. (3) the matter or cycle of the Islamic world—Persia and Arabia. In the Urdu form of the Hindi speech and in the earlier Dakhni, this matter of the Islamic world became most prominent naturally, and in Bengal from 17th century onwards, we have respectable literature of this type treating Muslim religious, mythological, legendary and romantic themes. A thin stream of it is noticeable in other literatures, also wherever there are Muslims, whether in the Tamil country or in the North Bihar, in Maratha country or in the Rajasthan.

The matter of ancient India in Early Modern Indian literature consisting as it does of adaptations or translations, which most languages show in verse, of the *Ramayana* and the *Mahabharata*, the *Bhagavata* and other *Puranas*, need not detain us. The movement to translate or adapt in the languages of the people the *Ramayana* and the *Mahabharata*, the Puranas and other texts of Brahminical Hinduism, which we note all over India, was accompanied also by a resuscitation or renaissance of Sanskrit studies which was specially noticeable from the 15th century and was operative in full force in the 16th and 17th.

Akbar the Great consciously fell in line with this movement and he made Persian-knowing scholars in his court adapt the *Mahabharata* and a few other great Sanskrit works into Persian, to bring it all before his Muslim nobility of Turki and Iranian origin and to propagate its study among Muslim scholars whether in India or outside India. He made his best artists illustrate them on a magnificent scale and their pictures show quite a revival of Hindu tradition through art. Emperor Jahangir patronised Hindu astrologers and Shah Jahan supported Sanskrit scholars. Shah Jahan's son Dara Shikoh is well known for his Hindu sympathies and for his study of Sanskrit philosophy—he caused Upanishads to be translated into Persian. Those Hindus who acquired a Persian culture were indirectly strengthened by all this in their own religion and culture, e.g., we have the case of a Brahmin from the Punjab, Chandra Bhan of Lahore (c.1650), who was a finished poet in Persian, testifying to his unabated adherence to the faith and ways of his fathers, and through his affiliation to Vedanta and to Sufism he also declared his faith in Universalism.

The matter of medieval India in Modern Indian literature consists of different cycles of romantic or heroic stories which had their origin from the time of the rise of the New Indo-Aryan languages and later. Thus in Bengal we have the cycle of stories relating to the hero Lau Sen and his adventures (as in the *Dharma-Mangala* romances), to the young merchant prince Lakshmidhara and his devoted wife Bihula and the snake goddess Manasa (as in the *Manasa-Mangala* and *Padma-Purana* poems) and to the merchant Dhanapati, his wives Khullana and Lahana and his son

Srimanta as well as to the stories of huntsman Kalaketu and his wife Phullara (in the *Chandi-Mangala* poems); in Orrisa, we have stories about the kings of Orissa, paticularly the highly romantic story of kind Purushottamadeva and princess Padmavati; in the Awadhi or Kosali areas, we have a number of romantic tales which were treated largely by the early Muslim writers of Awadhi—and one such story, that of Padmini of Chittor, was treated in a novel way by the Sufi poet Malik Muhammad Jayasi in 1540; in Rajasthan and the North Indian Rajput world, we have a number of noble stories of Rajput romance and chivalry which were treated in poems in early Rajasthani and Brajbhasha as well as in the Bundeli forms of Western Hindi (e.g., the romance Alha and Udal). Punjab had also its romantic stories (e.g. those relating to Raja Risalu and Bharthari); and the Maratha country has its ballads (*powadas*) relating to the Maratha heroes from Shivaji onwards (17th to the 19th centuries). A number of exquisite romantic ballads were also written in Bengal from the 17th century and these have been published.

The matter of the Islamic world as in Early Bengali, in Dakhni, in Urdu, and in Punjabi consists of stories relating to what may be called Muslim myth and legend (of both Arab and Persian origin)—the story of the Prophet with all miraculous embellishments, or the heroes of ancient Arabia (including those of the period of "Ignorance", with contacts with Islam) and of ancient Persia (as in the *Shahnama* which has always been looked upon in India as a Muslim classic); the legends of Sikandar or Alexander the Great and of other Greek personages as they came through the Arabic and Persian; old Arab and Persian tales; the stories of the *Arabian Nights*; and above all, the story of tragic fight at Kerbala leading to the death of the Prophet Mohammad's grandson at the hands of the army of the godless Arab Omayyad Emperor Yazid.

These together with works on the doctrine, the theology, the legal institutions and social prescriptions of Islam, from the mass of literature for Indian Muslims to draw from. Sufi philosophy and the spiritual culture also form part of it. As a part of the matter of the Islamic World, the ideas and the philosophy of Sufism came to India through both Persian literature and the Indian languages, and were received with open arms by some Hindu religious groups and thus Sufism became a common platform where liberal Muslims and Hindus freely met in India from the 13th century onwards.

Certain literary genres were well–established in the North Indian languages. One is the Barah-Masiya poems. Poems describing in a series of pictures, so to say, for the 12 months of the year, the suffering of lovers pining through separation of their joys in union. Another is the *Chautisa* or poems with initials of the lines consisting of the 34 consonants successively in the Indian alphabet, similarly describing the pangs of separation or praise of the Divinity (where the Persian alphabet became established, as among the Sufis in the Panjab, the Indian *Chautisa* became the Persian *Si-harfi* or the '30-letters'). The description of the seasons, of fights, of love-making, of woman's beauty, etc., were mostly stereotyped lines borrowed from Sanskrit.

Prose was very rarely cultivated in most of the Modern Indian languages in their early periods. Exceptions are Early Assamese which developed a prose style in its histories of Sino-Tibetan (*Ahom*) inspiration, the Buranji literature, from the 17th century; Brajbhasha which from the 17th century also developed a Vaisnava hagiographical and biographical literature; and early Gujarati, in which the Jainas created a rich and varied narrative literature. In early Punjabi also (in Hindi or West Punjabi, and then in East Punjabi) we have a Sikh biographical literature in prose. Prose was used but it was confined to letters and to legal and other documents. Bengali prose (apart from what we see in epistolary compositions going to the 16th century) started from the 18th century and that too largely under Portuguese missionary auspices.

The range of Early Modern Indian literature, however, was rather limited, if we compare it with that of Early Modern European literature, particularly from after the Renaissance. The real Renaissance in India came through the contact with English literature and European culture from the early part of the 19th century, and from this time we have a new orientation and a totally new development of Modern Indian literatures. English literature itself and the literatures of ancient Greece and Rome, of Italy, France and Germany, and later on of Russia and Scandinavia (from the 20th century) which were brought to the door of the English-knowing Indian, revolutionised the attitude of literature and inaugurated the current or modern phase in Indian literature.

This contact with the European mind first began in Bengal and by the middle of the 19th century, the emancipation or modernisation of Bengali literature had already begun. European methods of literary approach were early adopted. The essay, the drama, the novel and the short story were born; prose flourished and gradually an expressive and nervous Bengali prose style became established during the sixties of the 19th century. The European type of blank verse and verse forms like the Italian sonnet were introduced. We have an astonishing *floraison* of literature of Bengali at first and then gradually in the other languages as European education through the colleges and the universities began to shape the mind of the intelligentsia; and India became linked up with the modern world as much in the sciences as in literature and Rabindranath Tagore, who won the Nobel Prize for literature in 1913, became the symbol of this new spirit in Indian literature. All the present-day Indian literatures in the different languages whether Urdu or Telugu, Hindi or Kannada, Marathi or Punjabi, Tamil or Oriya and the rest have acquired the modern attitude of enquiry, of criticism, of realism, and have thus become worthy of India as a modern nation.

It has also to be noted that in the Indian cultural renaissance through contact with the West, India's past had to play an equally great part. Sanskrit has been a great heritage which India never lost, and the European spirit through English literature and the profundity of Indian thought as well as the cultured mentality that is behind the Indian way of life became complimentary forces in India's self-expression in the modern age. The study and appreciation of Sanskrit and Indian thought and then Indian letters and Indian art by the advanced peoples of the West put heart in Indians; and the attitude of the best thought-leaders of the present age in India who are also responsible for a great deal of India's modern creative literature, is to effect for the benefit of India as well as humanity, a compromise of the best elements in both Indian and European civilisations.

22

Ancient Tamil Literature

Tamil literature reaches back into the legendary land of Lemuria — that huge plateau which is said to have connected Africa, Australia and South America when the Himalayas lay under the sea. Our earliest stories are full of reminiscences concerning an early flood and the shifting of the population north. It is common knowledge that **the original inhabitants of India before the Aryans came from Central Asia were the ancestors of the Tamil-speaking people whom the historians call the Dravidians. Lemuria is said to have been their ancient home,** and the story goes that, when parts of that continent began to subside under the seas, they moved northward to occupy what is now the subcontinent of India. The Aryans, sweeping down from the northwest in perhaps the third millennium before Christ, drove the Dravidians south again. But by that time there was no Lemuria for them to take refuge in, and so the two peoples intermingled and mixing of strains took place. The fusion was so complete that in southern India today, except the linguistic differences, there is no possibility of distinguishing the Aryans from Dravidians.

The Dravidians were great explorers, colonisers, merchants and seafarers. The famous three kingdoms of the

Tamils—the Chera, the Chola and the Pandya—flourished contemporaneously for nearly fifteen hundred years (500 B.C. – 1000 A.D.). In the present, the Tamils occupy the eastern part of South India between Madras City and Cape Kumari, where the Bay of Bengal, the Arabian Sea and the Indian Ocean all mingle. The Tamil language, by common consent, is honoured as the oldest and the purest of the Dravidians tongues; it has flourished for twenty centuries more or less as it is today. It still keeps its individuality and distinction from the Aryan Sanskrit tongue.

The earliest extant Tamil book is known as *Tolkappiam* (The Old Book), but this work speaks of many other even older books and quotes from them. A grammar of a peculiar kind which is not only interested in the different forms of literature, it is also a textbook of sociology and discusses extensively the subject matter of literature. The whole text takes the form of mnemonic *sutras*, short, easily memorised stanzas, pithy and epigrammatic.

While there is every reason to believe that older and contemporary textbooks on the metrics, on rhetoric, on the dance, on the drama and on many other arts and sciences existed at the time of *Tolkappiam*, none of them have survived except in stray snatches and quotations. At a conservative estimate, *Tolkappiam* is not perhaps later than the third century B.C; when Aryan Sanskritic influences had already come in, albeit in a small way, and had moulded the language to its present state of fluidity and polish. In the text of *Tolkappiam* itself is to be found sufficient evidence that the Tamils had daily contact with the rest of India.

As depicted in *Tolkappiam*, the life of the Tamils is quite sophisticated. In life, as in letters, certain well-developed conventions are defined; indeed, it is within rigid rules that both life and letters flow. **Love predominates as the**

theme of letters, while war and charity come a close second and third. Almost modern analytical psychology, we discover, has been defined as a methodological approach to art and letters. For more than twenty centuries now, the poetic conventions of the Tamils have been those laid down by the Old Book. Even today one may hear scholars quoting extensively and rhythmically the sutras from *Tolkappiam* to prove their points. One discovers, too, sometimes with much surprise, that the classifications and contents of even present-day poetry are styled from the Old Book.

Scholars are not agreed among themselves on what happened after *Tolkappiam*. There appears to have been fairly large amount of creative activity of every sort in the Tamil country. A few centuries after *Tolkappiam* **the quantity of verse output seems to have been so great that a learned body called the Sangam had to sit in judgement and sift out the poetry most worthy of attention for future generations.** Traditionally this work of selection and the persons associated with it have been placed far back in time, but it is probable that this work was done at a time not later than the third century. In any case, the Sangam classification still rules Tamil poetry, and what was not passed by that body of learned men has not survived at all. According to length and subject all the extant poetry was divided and classified.

Apart from occasional verse of great merit, there were consistent longer works, and these are also usually, though loosely, referred to Sangam works. It is evident that these longer pieces too date back to that age, if not to an older era. **The Tamils of that time were especially active colonisers, empire-builders and merchants, and seem, to have had contact with the known parts of the world. This life of activity and splendour and riches and prosperity is reflected in ample measure in their letters.**

The precise limits of this period are not ascertainable with certainty, but the so-called five epics of the Tamils belong to the Sangam period. Of the five, only three are still extant, the other two being lost in their entirety, except for references in other texts—a few snatches of story and song. Though not the first in time, the first in importance of three epics available is *Silappadhikaram* (The Story of the Anklet), which tells a purely Tamil tale, well–loved even today:

> Kovalan, a merchant of the city of Puhar, the capital of the Chola King, is enamoured of Madhavi, a dancer, and spends his time and wealth on her, neglecting his wife Kannagi. Madhavi loves him, but owing to a misunderstanding, Kovalan, having lost all his wealth, thinks she does not. He leaves her and goes back to his wife who then accompanies him to Madhurai, capital of the Pandya King, in the hope that they may recoup his fortunes. Kovalan, trying to sell his wife's anklets in Madhurai, is suspected of having stolen it from the queen of the land and is executed as a thief. When she hears of her lord's fate, Kannagi takes her other anklet, goes to the Pandya King, proves her dead husband's innocence and calls down divine vengeance on the city. The Pandya King dies on knowing the injustice he has been the cause of. The city of Madhurai is burned to ashes, and people begin to worship Kannagi as a Goddess. The Chera King, hearing of these events, undertakes a pilgrimage of conquest north, brings stones from the Himalayas and water from the river Ganges and builds a temple for Kannagi.

It is the Chera King's brother, Ilango, who sings this

epic. In the emotional stasis it achieves this epic is very modern in spirit and can rank as one of the best long poems of the world, along with Homer and Dante.

The second epic, *Manimekhalai*, is somewhat of a sequel to *Silappadhikaram* and talks of the life and deeds of Manimekhalai, the daughter of Kovalan and the dancer Madhavi — how she turns a *sanyasin* or ascetic and attains deep wisdom. This epic reveals in some detail the religious life of the Tamils of that age. *Jivaka Chintamani*, the third epic of this set, is a mass of competent verse dealing with the marital adventures of its hero and sketching a well-defined social picture of that age.

Along with the epics and the other Sangam works should be named the great ethical text, Tiruvalluvar's *Tirukkural*, which can fall under no recognised classification. It is a text that is at least twenty centuries old, but it is still current in the daily life of the Tamils today. In artificial chapters of ten verses each, *Tirukkural* touches on all aspects of the life of man — as lover, as householder, as king, as minister, as soldier, as teacher, as learner, as a member of society. Terse and epigrammatic, in two lines each verse of *Tirukkural* searches human life and beyond, and, by a curious technique of condensation, achieves often highly lyrical notes.

The next great in Tamil can be called the Bhakti phase. In parts of *Silappadhikaram*, we find evidence of a lyric ecstasy, which in the Bhakti phase was duly developed to great heights. *Manimekhalai* reveals the ascendancy of Jaina and Buddhist doctrines among the Tamils, and it was perhaps to offset this trend that the Vaisnava and Saiva saints began to sing their songs of pure devotional ecstasy.

Bhakti, to the Tamil, is not devotion simply as the other understand it, but devotion which is at once a way of life and a passionate philosophy. The religious concept

of Bhakti is a pure Tamil contribution to Indian culture. It emerged, no doubt, as a reaction to the severe and exacting discipline of Jaina and Buddhist doctrines: men rose and became poets. From the second or third century A.D. to the eleventh or the twelfth century—roughly for eight hundred years—the country of the Tamils seems to have been alive with wandering saints and singers, travelling from shrine to shrine with the simplest of stringed instruments in their hands, rousing an unsophisticated people to heights of religious ecstasy.

The Vaisnava lyrics reveal quality, range, vision and a great poetic sensibility. *The Four Thousand Divine Songs* have deep meaning in the lives of the Vaisnavas even today. The Saivas attempted something loftier, but failed to capture the intensity of the Vaisnava lyric ecstasy—except in the case of Manikkavacakar, by common consent one of the oldest of the Tamil Bhakti poets, whose verse is collected under the title *Tiruvacakam*. Among the Bhakti poets, two deserving special mention, Andal and Karaikkal Ammayar, were women. Andal is mundane and sensuous in her poetry, while the other is metaphysical and other-worldly in hers. The codifications of the Vaisanava and Saiva poems were undertaken some time after the eleventh century, but unlike the Sangam classification, there was no process of selection, all the poems being collected by royal edict, and as a result much bad poetry was preserved as good Bhakti.

Before the Bhakti period ended in Tamil letters, that is, some time before the twelfth or thirteenth century, Kamban wrote his *Ramayanam* in Tamil verse, a work that is epic in sweep, dramatic in its situations and lyric in the quality of its verse. It is an epic different in quality from the earlier epic *Silappadhikaram* and is comparable to the works of Shakespeare. There are controversies today over the genuineness of particular words and verses, and there are never-ending debates on interpretations of Kamban's verse, but modern Tamils reveal their deep appreciation of the poet by celebrating fairs and festivals in Kamban's name.

Proper history and precise chronology do not exist in Tamil, but I am inclined to place the end to the Bhakti age, along with many unlearned ones, somewhere in the thirteenth or fourteenth century. **Ever since the days of *Tolkappiam,* Sanskrit has been in background as always a major influence, and the interaction of north and south in India is worth further study.** To date, no digested material is available on the subject, and it would be no easy task to disentangle the Sanskrit and the pure Tamil elements that are so closely intertwined.

For more than six centuries Tamil genius was dormant, and there was no major figure or movement comparable to those gone before. The three ancient kingdoms were breaking up into smaller principalities—independent and semi-independent—under their own petty rulers, or their elements were being absorbed into new and vital waves from the middle and north of India. Unsettled, the Tamils forgot even their past glories and former vitality of their life and letters was being stifled by attitudes that were academic and, in the long run, sterile. Cleverness and artifice in form were replacing the older, more enduring poetic values. The point was reached where kings and their favourites demanded poems, and lo! overnight there were poems, and poets, by the dozen. The meretorious and the false and the artificial were applauded, and all that was good was condemned as unfashionable and not pleasing. As a class the poets were a menace, going about from place to place, singing this man's praise or that man's downfall for favour and money. Poetry had left the common soil and the common man, and in turn the common man despised the poets.

During these years the poets built round themselves a host of ridiculous legends such as the one in which Saraswati, the Goddess of learning, was said to visit each one in turn under cover of night. Yet even in this dull and barren period there are a few names that stand out; Kalamegham, who despite hundred of mediocre poems, reached heights with a handful; Pattinathar, who distilled out of pornography a refreshingly ascetic philosophy; the Auvaiyar of this age (Every age of Tamil history has had its Auvaiyar—literally, old woman—who wrote poems that were clear, telling and cynical); the Saint Thayumanavar, who mingled Sanskrit with his Tamil to effect sonorous sequences; Arunagirinathar, whose experiments in verse form suggest some of the experiments of modern versifiers in France and England; and lastly, not the least of them, Jothi Ramalingam, who, in the middle of the nineteenth century, purified Tamil hearts and Tamil poetry of much that was alien.

These centuries saw other important developments in Tamil poetry: a non-academic, popular literature; the heroic poems or dramas celebrating the victories of local heroes and chieftains; the poems of all–knowledge and the temple plays—all rose in this period. The popular poems, only a few of which have survived, were largely anonymous. Dating between the fifteenth and the eighteenth centuries, they celebrate in a readable, racy ballad form events in the lives of the *Mahabharata* heroes and heroines, and many of the themes are exquisitely handled. There is practically no historical evidence to indicate when plays were first danced and enacted in the temples. Certainly the most beautiful of all the temple plays in Tamil, the *Kuttalakkuravanchi* (the Gypsy Girl of Kuttalam) is not older than the seventeenth century. In any case, to stock characters and everyday situations the poet had managed to bring a beauty and timelessness that are artistic.

23

Sciences in India

All Sciences and Arts of ancient India trace their origin to the Vedas, which contain the roots thereof in however condensed and sometimes mystic form. While the principal Vedas contain more of metaphysical and ritual knowledge, the fourth Veda, Atharva, gives us an insight into the scientific knowledge of Vedic times. **The necessity of laying out the *Yajnasala* or the sacrificial place accurately and in accordance with measurements given in the instructions, evolved in very early times a simple system of Geometry. But in the sphere of exact sciences, it is probably Mathematics and Astronomy wherein there was phenomenal development in later times** especially in the Gupta Period and reached a stage far in advance of the ancient nations. The Indian mathematician had a clear conception of the abstract number as distinguished from numeral quantity or spacial extension. **With the aid of simple numeral notation, India devised a rudimentary Algebra which allowed more complicated processes than known to the Greeks.**

The value of Sunya or Zero was a fundamental contribution made by India even before Aryabhatta (A.D. 449). The Arabs and the Romans seem to have got this knowledge from India; the former calling mathematics as the ' Indian Art' (*Al-Hindsa*). There is no doubt that the decimal notation, with the other mathematical lore, was learnt by the Muslim world through early commercial contacts with India. Medieval Indian mathematicians such as Brahmagupta (7th century), Mahavira (9th century) and Bhaskara (12th century) made several discoveries which were not known to Europe till the Renaissance or later. **They understood the import of positive and negative quantities and developed methods of extracting square and cube roots and of solving quadratic and other indeterminate equations.** It is Bhaskara who finally proved that value of Zero or Sunya was infinity.

Alberuni, the learned Arab traveller, who spent a decade in India during the period of Mahmud of Ghazni in the beginning of 11th century A.D., freely admits the greatness of Hindu mathematicians and astronomers, though he does not spare any criticism of Hindus in matters of religious and social practices. **He has also praised their capability in engineering, specially their capacity to build water-reservoirs.** His work is a remarkable attempt of an ancient Arab scholar endowed with a rational and scientific spirit to examine and assess the religious, philosophic and scientific thought of India within the limits of the knowledge vouchsafed to him during a period of 12 years' sojourn in India. He has elaborately discussed the metaphysical, cosmological, mathematical, astronomical and other scientific theories then known to the Hindus. It is inconceivable that he was entirely uninfluenced by this knowledge in the presentation of his magnum opus a decade later.

Medical and physiological lore is to be found in the Vedas in its primitive form, especially in the *Atharvaveda*, which contains references to diseases and their treatment through Mantras and medicines. Ayurveda, the science of Indian medicine, and the science of Astronomy (including Astrology) form part of the six *angas* of the Vedas included in Vedic studies. But the basic texts of Ayurveda which are extant are ascribed **to Charaka and Susruta and they are the products of fully evolved systems resembling those of Hippocrates and Galen in many respects and much more advanced in some other respects.** This stage of development of Ayurveda could have been attained only after a long period of gradual evolution both during the pre-Buddhist and pre-Christian eras before these masters. **Surgery was not at all unknown, as over 125 surgical instruments have been mentioned in these texts of Susruta who mainly dealt with surgery. The Indian *materia medica* is considered to be the most comprehensive in the world,** and still constitutes in the modern and scientifically developed form the mainstay of Allopathic and other systems of medicine.

Both physiology and medicine developed early enough through the phenomena of Yoga practices, and through Buddhism. The Buddhist monk like the Christian missionary served the sick and not being content with the medical magic and *mantras*, developed a rational attitude. It is inconceivable that a medical science so developed as Ayurveda in those days could have been the result of mere empirical knowledge. On the other hand, the systematic manner in which the Indian sciences of Medicine, Physics, Chemistry, Metallurgy, Engineering and Architecture and others were gradually developed, clearly shows that they followed the same scientific methodology of observation and experiments and logical processes of thought which led scientists of today to the discovery of truth. It may be that the early Indian mind laid stress on the intuitive perception of these truths and rendered them more liable to be branded as empirical, but **the principles of *Tarka-Sastra* or Logic as understood and propounded by Indian logicians have not been improved upon so far,** and it would be clearly untenable to suppose that those principles were not followed by them in the development of their scientific thought. The remains of old Buddhist *viharas* and universities clearly indicate the existence of laboratories for experimenting in positive sciences.

The development of medicine seems to have been stimulated by contact with Hellenic physicians. The resemblance between the Greek and Indian systems suggests mutual borrowing. The Unani system of medicine came to India through Arabs who improved upon it and passed on to the West again in medieval times, for further development. The similarity of the Ayurvedic and Unani systems in their fundamentals like the humoral theory of the origin of diseases and the methodology of treatment is significant. In the Middle East, the Arab system continued to be called as Unani (Greek) Tibb and was patronised by the Eastern Caliphs like Haroon-al-Rashed. During his period many learned Indian scholars including scientists and medical men enjoyed his patronage and the latter exercised considerable influence on the Unani system. **It is well known that Vagbhata's work *Astanga Hridaya* was translated during the Caliph's time. The Bermacides, a line of the Vazirs of the Caliph's, seemed to trace their lineage from India.** The universities of Baghdad and Cordova were great centres of scientific and philosophic synthesis.

Thus the Ayurveda from its hoary beginnings in the Vedic times assumed a very developed form and continued to grow till the 16th century A.D. when Bhavamisra wrote his *Bhavaprakasa*, the last of the original works on Ayurveda which contains descriptions of new venereal diseases and new prescriptions and drugs of other countries. This shows clearly that the ancient Hindus were not averse to adopting new theories and ideas and were in the habit of including foreign medicines in their pharmacopoeia.

Apart from the Ayurvedic and Unani systems of medicine, the old Siddha system prevalent in South India is directly responsible for the growth of Chemistry, which probably originated as a necessary branch of medicine, but later transcended that sphere. The origin of this Siddha system seems to be traceable to the Siva cult of Mohenjo-daro. The word 'Siddhar' is prevalent in the south and flourished in Tamil Nadu. **It is said that there are more than 500 Siddha medical works containing over 3,000 valuable formulas composed of 5 lakhs of poems or stanzas. This system seems to have developed Chemistry and Alchemy to a high degree of perfection.** These Siddhars knew the processes of calcination, preparation essence, extraction from minerals and the preparation of what is known as *muppu*, the chemical agent used in making animated mercury pills or *kattu* with high potency capable of transmuting metals and rejuvenating the human system. Mercury was the special subject of their study and experimentation. The high degree of development which had attained in Chemistry and Alchemy during the pre-Buddhist periods in India can be known from the number of valuable works on Rasa Sastra which have been discovered and some of which have been translated into English. It would appear therefore that they had followed a scientific method and had a highly developed Applied Logic of the Sciences 'which was more comprehensive and rigorous than that of J.S. Mill'.

It is apparent that the ancient Saivite Tantras prevalent both in the North and North-West of India and in the South, and their later counterparts of the Buddhist Tantras, stimulated the scientific spirit of enquiry into the physical properties of various forms of matter, apart from their esoteric or mystic aspects which are to be found in them. The renowned Nagarjuna who was born and brought up in the Brahminic faith but was afterwards converted to Buddhism was not only the originator of the Madhyamika philosophy of the Mahayana school but a great adept in magic, conjuration and above all a celebrated Alchemist. He seems to have been contemporary of Satavahana, if the *Rasa Ratnakara*, the Buddhist Tantric work ascribed to him on Alchemy, is to be believed.

From the 5th to the 11th century A.D., the Buddhist universities of Pataliputra, Nalanda, Vikramasila, and Udantapura and probably Vijayapuri (at Nagarjunakonda) were seats of learning where Alchemy was included in the curricula of studies. This spread to Tibet and the Deccan through the monks who fled from the universities after their destruction.

The knowledge of chemistry reflected in the later *Tantras* is considered by some eminent orientalists as having been derived by the intercourse with Arabs. In fact not only in the matter of medicine and chemistry (including Alchemy) but also in Astronomy, there seems to have been considerable lending and borrowing between the Greeks, the Arabs and the Romans on the one hand and the Indians on the other. Though all the sciences which the Indians developed had an indigenous origin and developed on their own lines, they seem to have never hesitated to derive knowledge from Mleccha sources, the term being generically applied indiscriminately to Sakas, Yavanas (Greeks or Bactrians), the Chinas (Chinese) and others. In fact Varahamihira expresses his admiration for the Mlecchas and Yavanas for their great proficiency in Astronomy. *Romaka Siddhanta*, an important work on Astronomy, is an ample proof of Roman influence.

The mechanical, physical and chemical theories of the ancient Hindus make an interesting study. **The Samkhya system accounts for the universe on principles of cosmic**

evolution while the Vaisesika-Nyaya system lays down the scientific methodology and elaborates the concepts of mechanics, physics and chemistry. The Vedanta, the Mimamsa, the Bauddha, the Jaina and the Charvaka systems, all make incidental contributions of special interest. Their conception of the universe as Prakrit, which is conceived as formless and undifferentiated, limitless and indestructible, without beginning and without end, led them to the differentiation of three famous gunas of Sattva, Rajas and Tamas. The creation according to them is the result of the disturbances in the equilibrium in these *gunas* caused by the Purusa. On this was based their formula of evolution and creation.

They had a conception of the atomic theory of matter and worked it out in surprising detail both in the pre-Buddhist and Buddhist periods. We find a gradual evolution of theories of matter into Paramanuvada of the Nyaya-Vaisesika system of thought. **The properties of mass and of sound and all other kinds of matter were well known to them,** and if a detailed study of these theories is made, it will be found that in the course of the millennial evolution of scientific knowledge in the ancient days, there has been enough of lending and borrowing from their contemporaries. Sciences and arts are international and universal in their essence. In this realm of human activity, there has always been lending and borrowing, thus making for the advancement of the sum total of human knowledge.

24

Buddhist Art

Art has no lessons to teach; it can only sharpen human sensibilities, and by doing so make man more and more conscious of the realities of life and nature. Nor is there any art that can, strictly speaking, be called "Buddhist" art. Yet one readily recognises that this is a most convenient phrase to denote the art that was, for centuries, pressed to the service of Buddhism, and to bring out in visual form some of the specific contents of Buddhist spiritual ideology and way of life.

The Buddhist art of India as much as that of China, Japan and Central Asia, of Nepal and Tibet, of Ceylon, Burma and Thailand, of Java, Sumatra and Cambodia, is that chapter of each cultural region which deals with Buddhist themes. In form and technique, Buddhist art conforms to the general principles of contemporary art of the respective cultural regions, but in certain phases and periods, specific Buddhist contents of ideas and conceptions called for and conditioned correspondingly specific language of form. It is only such phases and periods of art that can legitimately be called Buddhist.

All forms of art, according to the teachings of the Master, the Lord Buddha, are expressions of and lead to desire and nostalgia; they are instruments of pleasures of the moment and are, therefore, to be shunned by one who aspires after *nirvana*. In its attitude to art, orthodox

Buddhism is thus very close to Jainism, the Sankarite Vedanta and Islam.

Yet, paradoxically, as within the folds of the last three faiths mentioned, so **within that of Buddhism, art did play a role, a great and significant role, one might say, not only in extending the physical boundaries of the religion but also in expressing the subtlest and the most sublime ideas and thoughts of the faith and in the concretisation of most elusive, abstract and subjective visions.** To prove this statement, one has only to refer to the Buddha and Bodhisattva figures of Sarnath, Mathura and Sanchi of the 6th and 7th centuries, some of the segments of the wide stretches of painted walls of Bagh and Ajanta, a number of Vajrayana and Tantrayana cult images in stone and metal of Eastern India of the ninth through to the eleventh century A.D. Needless to say, the list is not exhaustive nor does it include examples from outside India. Indeed, the achievements of art in Buddhism and the services it rendered to the faith are eloquent of the creative potentialities of the faith, its depth and refinement, its appeal and strength.

Early Buddhist sculpture in India is fundamentally narrative in character; its main purpose is to tell in continuous narration, edifying tales, simply and attractively, against the background of contemporary life, tales that were supposed to underline the main principles of the faith and its important historical episodes. Architecturally, the art consisted of solid massive *stupas* with elaborate gateways and railing, all richly carved in relief, and rock-cut caves—*viharas* and *chaityas*—with or without sun-windowed doorways and pillared halls. A somewhat primitive solidity and massiveness belonged as much to the spirit of the age as to the rock itself that was their receptacle.

But already by about the 2nd century A.D. certain fundamental changes in attitude seem to have taken place, changes that were ultimately responsible for a definite shift in the form and content of Buddhist art. Buddhism was no longer a simple way of life that the Lord Buddha spoke of, nor the Lord himself simply the mundane historical being that trod the dust of Rajagriha, Bodh-Gaya and dozens of other cities and villages and ceaselessly strove his way to supreme wisdom. The message of the Master was no longer confined within the borders of India nor to sons of the soil. It had come into intimate contact with other peoples, places, cultures and religions including Judaism and Christianity.

Within Buddhism itself and out of its own seeds had grown up powerful sects, each with their own specific emphasis and way of life. The Sangha itself and its hold on the rich agricultural and commercial communities, sometimes also on the royalty and nobility, had increased in extension. Even from earlier times the Sangha had been drawing its material sustenance from the rich banking and trading communities, and the relatively more substantial agricultural householders. As years rolled on, the Sangha came more and more to learn on these segments of society, and in the second and third centuries of the Christian era, one of its main sources of material sustenance, the werewithal of the elaborate monastic establishments, was the rich Indo-Roman trade of the times.

All this could not but have its inevitable impact on the contemporary Buddhist art of India, and nowhere is impact so clearly marked than at Mathura and throughout the lower valleys of the Krishna and the Godavari, in the rich and elaborate monastic establishments of the two places—the *viharas* and *caityas*—and the still more elaborately carved railing and gateways, a fraction only of which has yielded to the excavator's spade. This is true, to an extent at any rate, of the contemporary Buddhist establishments of

Western India as well.

With the creation of a real bourgeois society a change in the social taste and also in the attitude towards life was but inevitable. What this change was like is writ large on the sculptures of Mathura of the 1st and 2nd centuries A.D., but more on the marbles of Amaravati and Nagarjunakonda, Goti and other places of the Krishna-Godavari valley, and belonging to the first three centuries of the Christian era.

In the meanwhile, the image of the Buddha had come to stay, the Buddha as understood either in terms of superhuman physical form and temporal power and dignity, or in the terms of Hellenistic iconography, or in those of both. The inner meaning of the term 'Buddha', the Illumined One, in whom shone the effulgence of the light of supreme wisdom, whose body had shed all its earthly weight and had become like melting butter with compassion, also aglow with spiritual light and energy, was yet to make itself felt in visual art.

Frankly this was a matter of spiritual realisation, and that realisation becoming a common property of the people including the artists. But the story of India's inner life during the 3rd and 4th centuries is not sufficiently known. Many things happened during these two centuries, and we can only somewhat vaguely feel that a tremendous inner turmoil and searching of hearts had been going on inside all the Indian religions and philosophies, Buddhism and Buddhist thought not excepted, as much as within the various cadres and orders of social and economic life.

Out of the seeds of these two hundred years emerges such names as those of Vatsyayana and Kalidasa, of Udyotakara and Dinnaga, of Asanga and Vasubandhu, and such facts as the final redaction of India's two great epics, of the Puranas and perhaps also a large section of Pali Buddhist literature, as new Buddhist logic and a new Buddhist ideology.

The last this Buddhist thought and ideology was crystallised into is known as *Yogachara*, very closely related to the evolved yoga system of contemporary Hinduism and Jainism. The fluid and luminous ideology of the Yogachara coupled with the Mahayanist ideal of compassion, imparted to the age-old Theravada and Sarvastivada ideologies a new vision and a new meaning brought out fully what was latent in the teachings and practices of the Lord Buddha himself. Indeed, the full connotation of the term Buddha, the great conqueror of the body and the mind, the supremely illumined being, yet at the same time soft, tender and melting in compassion for all sentient beings, emerged at last and slowly but surely took shape and form under the hammer and chisel of the sculptor, and the brush and colour of the painter.

And **thus was born the supremely refined and sensitive and profoundly spiritual Gupta Buddhist sculptures of the Ganga-Yamuna valley, particularly of Sarnath, of Bengal and Bihar, of Sanchi, and the paintings of Bagh, Ajanta and Sigiriya** (Ceylon) all belonging to the fifth, sixth and seventh centuries.

This is, indeed the peak period of Buddhist art in India as anywhere in the world, and once and for all set the standard of vision and imagination, of form and technique, of conceptions of volume and plasticity, of later Buddhist art in India, of contemporary and later Buddhist art of Central Asia, China and Japan, of Nepal and Tibet, of Ceylon, Burma and Thailand, of Java, Sumatra and Cambodia.

All these local schools and periods drew their sustenance from this golden period of Buddhist art in India and sought to work on their specific local tastes, ideologies and atmospheres in terms of standards of achievement of these few centuries. Indeed the measure of the aesthetic and spiritual value and significance of all later schools and periods of Buddhist art in India and outside is the measure of the extent they reached towards the attainment of this ideal.

The first of these high peaks of Buddhist art is the human figure which is the receptacle of an inner dynamism lying latent almost in a state of rest and yet imparting to the body, its limbs and face, to its fingers and its gestures a form that is vibrant with life and a meaning that suggest calm and contemplative joy. This is true not only of the Buddha figure but of those of the Boddhisattvas and of ordinary human beings, and in an extended manner, of plants and animals as well. Stories from the old life of the Master and sometimes from the *Jatakas*, continued to be sculptured and painted, but they had all but lost their narrative character, except in the paintings of Ajanta, and the emphasis centred more and more round the figures of the Buddhas and Bodhisattvas.

The story of later Buddhist sculpture in Bengal, Bihar, Orissa, as much as in Nepal and Tibet where Buddhism came practically to be confined during the eighth and the following centuries, is the story of the consolidation of the values learnt and imbibed during the 6th and 7th centuries but with slow but sure lessening of the understanding of inner dynamism of the essential life-process as well as of the specific Buddhist content of inner spiritual illumination. This led inevitably to a hardening of the plasticity of volume, and increasing petrifiaction of what was once fluid and luminous.

This somewhat stagnating process was, however, relieved to a great extent by the increasingly varied and complex pantheon reared up by the highly esoteric Vajrayana and other later forms of Buddhism. These later schools and sects of Buddhism, all, saturated by Tantric ideas and ideologies, had a vigour and vitality of their own which imparted a quality of dynamic naturalism, of a somewhat sensuous character, to the complexity of the vigorous compositional structure. **In the expression of sheer vitality and strength, of external dynamism, and in craftsmanship, some of the Vajrayana-Tantrayana images in stone and bronze, also in manuscript painting, reach the high tide of medieval art in India,** and did largely influence the contemporary Buddhist art of South-East Asia.

Even in a short survey the paintings of Bagh and Ajanta deserve more than a passing notice, not merely for the high, noble and dignified quality of the painter's art that Ajanta and Bagh record for a continuous five or six centuries, a fact which has found recognition all the world over, but for the picture they afford of the specific Buddhist way of life as understood and lived by the contemporary Buddhist Sangha.

Here is no negation but only fullest acceptance of life in its variegated hues, in its mundane pains and pleasures as much as in its spiritual joys and bliss, all in the midst of a fresh and abundant nature, but of life understood and lived in a chaste, elegant and contemplative atmosphere and accepted in calm and dignified repose. From out of this reposeful and contemplative life emerge the chaste and dignified, the luminously fluid and compassionate figures of Padmapani and Avalokitesvara, the personifications, as it were, of the quintessence of Mahayana Buddhism.

Buddhist architecture in India after the 3rd century has not much to show except in the sphere of structural *viharas* or monasteries, and in one or two instances of *chaityas* and temples.

But contemporary Buddhism made the most significant contribution to Indian and Eastern architecture, in the sphere of *vihara* or monastic establishments. **From primitive**

rock-cut *viharas* to the elaborate structural *viharas* built of brick and intended for residence, whose worship, study and congregation, it is a long story of gradual evolution from simple and rudimentary to complex and elaborate establishments in different segments and in several pyramidically receding storey.

The ruins of the long and elaborate rows of *viharas* of the university city of Nalanda of early medieval times, the ruins of similar *viharas* at Paharpur and Lauriya-Nandangarh, provide sufficient evidence of what these elaborate monastic establishments were like and what architectural grandeur and magnificence they had reached. They are the great pride of Buddhist architecture in India, these structural *viharas*, and served presumably as models of the storeyed temples of Pagan in Burma and of the group of Brahminical tamples of Parambanam in Java.

25

Hindu Temples

Travellers in India are struck by a number and variety of temples that are sometimes vast sacred domains containing whole religious cities, and sometimes humble village chapels just big enough to contain a statuette and place for offerings. Several evolutionary trends can be distinguished in this vast variety: pre-Aryan cults, Aryan cults, social or family cults, to which must be added foreign influences—generally Muslim or Christian—and the reactions opposing them. All that goes to make a life—for the Indian religion is essentially a living thing—in which three principal styles, Nagara (Indo-Aryan), Vesara (Chalukya) and Dravida dominate, accompanied by three minor styles, those of Bengal, Himalayas and Thiruvanantapuram.

The ancient Aryans did not build temples and had only sacrificial altars, built in the open air, on a piece of consecrated ground, carefully oriented and measured. We find no allusion to the representation of gods in the form of statues or paintings in the Vedas.

For an idea of what the first temples were like, we must come down to Ashoka, the fervent Buddhist emperor. He sent ambassadors to Greece, Egypt, and Syria and above all to Persia. Persia's civilisation, like that of India, is Aryan. At that time the country still showed the vigorous remains of a marvelous tradition to which Greece, no doubt, owed much of the progress she was making. Her stone sculptors were extremely skilful and Ashoka brought several of them to his states. There they sculptured smooth columns surmounted by symbolic animals, lions, elephants, bulls, and horses, supporting the wheel representing the Law of the Buddha.

This imperial initiative had an immense success. It is possible that the first stone statues were carved, and certain that the first artificial caves were hollowed out at this period. The cave of Sudama, at Barabar near Gaya, bears an inscription from the twelfth year of Ashoka's reign. It is not known whether this cave served as a temple but there are good reasons for supposing so. Until comparatively recent times, that is, until the 14th or 16th centuries, the gods alone lived in stone dwellings and out of hundreds of caves known to us, not one can be said with certainty to be a lay monument, while the majority are incontestably of religious origin. We may thus suppose that this was the case from the beginning and notable for the cave of Sudama.

The fashion for caves spread fairly quickly and they were excavated in Northern India from the beginning of the Christian era till the 5th and even 6th centuries, whereas we find no trace of temples constructed in masonry at this period, although one might suppose they would have been much easier to build. Ferguson remarked some time ago that this is a mistake and that it takes less work to hollow out a building of a given size than to cut, transport and assemble together the stones to build it. We might add that the use of heavy blocks of stone raises technical problems concerning building timber and the resistance of materials that do not exist when hollowing directly into the rock. The only building that can be attributed with any likelihood to this period (in and around the 4th century) are three or four Hindu temples in the South, the most famous of which are in the State of Hyderabad, at Ter and Chezarla. All are of the "elephant back" type (*hastipitha*). They are made of brick, wood or mortar.

In the North, it was in the Gupta period, perhaps a century earlier, that the first Hindu temples in stone masonry made their appearance. They consist of a rectangular sanctuary, generally square, two or three metres high and wide, the only opening being the door that is generally surrounded by sculptured friezes and bands, sometimes preceded by a porch supported on columns. The roof is flat or slightly sloping to the front in order to let the water run off into a moulded drip-stone. The Gupta temples are often admirably sculptured and the statues found in them are among the most perfect examples of all Indian art. This type of flat-roofed sanctuary has been built continually ever since, but without sculpture and reduced to its geometrical scheme, it has become the poor chapel we find in the smaller villages. There can be no doubt as to its origin; it is to be found once more in the simple farmer's cottage. Rich and profuse ornamentation can be seen on other types of buildings that have grown up out of a veritable architectural revolution.

This revolution took place, without any known external cause, at the height of the Gupta period. The material used and the method of construction remained the same as before. The innovation consisted of a roof in the form of a pyramid raised above the sanctuary. One of the earliest examples is to be found in the famous temple of Durga at Aihole where this new type of roof rises over an apsidal temple with, exceptionally, a flat roof. It soon became general and was adopted for all important temples and innumerable chapels. This custom did not correspond with any technical discovery or any sudden manifestation of some material necessity. This remained true over a long period. During the two thousand years that preceded the arrival of the Europeans in India, with their machines and their cement, the temples were built in the same way with the same materials.

The sanctuary roof shows a remarkable unity of structure, both in the North and the South. It is composed of a number of small-superimposed chapels, or little sanctuaries, resembling the main sanctuary in form. The curved, unbroken arises of the Northern temples have often been compared with the rectangular arises, with their series of clearly visible storeys that are found in the temples of the South. This is merely a matter of appearance. The North not only possesses monuments in which the storeys of the roof are as clearly marked as those in the South—at Sheohar (Tirhut), for example—but all the pyramids of the Northern temples are formed of separate storeys composed of joined pavilions. As each of these had the same individual form as the general ensemble, it was fairly easy to integrate its profile into the main line, in spite of the fact that each pavilion—or rather, chapel, since there are no lay monuments in this style—terminates at its summit in a torus with vertical sides—the *amalaka*—so that one can discover the number of storeys by counting them up the arise or the façade.

The temple of Rajarani at Bhubaneshwar, for instance, has seven storeys, and the temple of Lingaraja, ten. It was only after the 11th century that the storeys disappeared and the superimposed roofs of the pavilions merged into a vertical moulding along the façade.

There is no example in Hindu architecture prior to the 18th century of a religious monument formed by a pyramid of sanctuaries, so the roofs we are speaking of cannot be a more or less adapted reproduction of a building. They are composed, on the contrary, on the model of a single element. One realises this when one notices that each storey is an enlarged reproduction of the storey surmounting it. The successive storeys diminish in size and become simplified as they rise higher, so we may consider that the summit must be the original element and that which contains the meaning expressed by the ensemble of the roof. This last storey is a square enclosure, each of the four walls of which is formed by a chapel, while the centre is occupied by a small building easily recognisable as sanctuary.

Even today, this rectangle of chapels surrounding a sanctuary is a common monument throughout India, but it seems to become increasingly prevalent as one traces the temples back through the centuries. Examples are found in the temples of the Kailasa of Ellora, of the Kailasanatha of Vaikunta-perumal, at Kanchipuram, all of which appear to be more or less contemporary. Sometimes the peripheric chapels were found to be too cumbersome and were reduced to the roofs only, so that these formed a decoration on the summit of the walls, such as can be seen on the temple on the shore of Mahabalipuram, which also dates from the 8th century.

Temples of this kind probably existed long before those we have chosen as our point of departure and the model shows us the real difference between the Aryan and Dravidian styles, in which the pavilion element is not the same. In the North, it preserves the "cannon-ball profile" which is considered to be a derivation of the light architecture built of curved bamboo that used to support a roof over the statues of gods when they were carried in procession. In the South, the roof is a square dome, with curved facades surmounting a curved drip-stone. Sculptured examples can be seen at Mahabalipuram and at Undavalli. These small monuments greatly resemble huts with thatched roofs.

Let us now return to the starting point of this evolution,

to the cave of Sudama that obviously represents a hut and the enclosure preceding it, and that we may reasonably suppose to figure a temple. If the Sudama cave were to be enlarged, without changing its plan, and some changes made in minor details of its internal arrangement, it could be taken for a Buddhist *chaitya* or one of the old Saivite sanctuaries of Ter and Chezarla, and could thus be the forerunner of the apsidal temple. The form, however, is not the essential thing about the temple; it is conceived as a divine dwelling and thus resembles the houses most usually found in the region. In the flatroofed Gupta temples we see the little house with its four cob walls supporting a ceiling of woven branches carrying the roof of earth and straw. The Dravidian chapel has the round or pyramid-shaped thatched roof, which is to be found on the peasant huts in the region.

As the house is built for such an exceptional inhabitant, it must have a special or symbolic meaning, to be understood only through meditation, in addition to the obvious, exterior meaning. The gods are not of our world; they come down from a snowy Kailasa or an ethereal Vaikuntha to fulfil their duties, but their residence is elsewhere. The temple, where something of themselves lives in the consecrated image, is thus the meeting-place of Heaven and Earth.

The fact that the great majority of Hindu sanctuaries are square is not due to a chance nor to a convention. It is due to a conscious or unconscious psychological link that the Hindu mind normally perceives between the square shape and the meaning it attributes to the sanctuary. The union of the circle and the square—and by derivation, of the oval and the rectangle—in holy buildings, is far too general to be due to mere chance. It does not, indeed correspond to any formal doctrine in the Western manner, but the fact that it is so widely chosen and accepted, reveals its significance and psychological value. The circle is the image of the movement of the stars and the visible form of the sun and thus an almost universal symbol of Heaven; while the Earth, oriented by the cardinal points, is represented by a square. Their union in the temples is thus merely a direct expression of the fact that these buildings are the place where Heaven and Earth meet together.

The application of this idea is especially clear in the apsidal form: the god is enclosed in the circular sanctuary, while the faithful remain in the square part. The priest passes from one to the other, so that, all through the sacred rites, he is expressing his role of an intermediary creating a bridge between the two worlds. This union can be expressed vertically as well as on the horizontal level. In this case, Heaven—the circle—is superimposed on the square, just as Heaven is above Earth. This explains the tendency to raise some circular object over a square sanctuary.

It is thus that, in the North as in the South, the square pyramid of the Hindu temple terminates in a circular object. In the North, this is the *amalaka* surmounted by a cone supporting a vase destined to receive the celestial ambrosia and bearing the trident of Siva or the double triangle of Visnu. In the South, the terminal cupola itself is often round, especially since the 10th century, but even when it is octagonal or square, it bears on its summit the same vase we see in the northern temples. This a vase is nearly always round and is surmounted by a slender cone.

The *lingam* itself is an example of the same symbolism. It represents to universal creative power of the three divine aspects. These are centred on an axis (Siva) that links the vessel for libations (Visnu) with the base representing Brahma. The central axis, circular on top, is often octagonal in the middle and nearly always square at the base. This base goes right through the pillar and penetrates into a square hole in the earth. Until the 7th century, the vessel of libations was also square and in this case it also formed the pillar supporting the whole; the lingam thus represented the creative union of Heaven and Earth, of spirit and matter, instead of divine creative energy.

Nature herself has given us, in the mountain, a symbol of that which links Heaven and Earth, and it is true that the mountain has a special place in Hindu traditions. It is Meru, the axis of the world, the Kailasa, home of the gods. The same meaning is applied to rocks and these, when they are of suitable form and location, form a special category of *lingams* known as *Svaymbhu-lingams*, or *lingams* engendered by themselves. These rocks are sometimes comparatively small and low, reshaped into desired form, like those in certain minor sanctuaries of Bhubaneswar or sometimes extremely wide (that of the temple of Lingaraja is nearly five metres in diameter and only one metre high); while in the other case, huge rocks dominate the whole temple, forming one of the walls of the sanctuary, as at Tiruvadikonam, near Dalavanur. The pyramidal roof of the sanctuary confirms this idea of a mountain-home of the gods and their various dwellings are figured there in the form of a series of pavilions.

For the Dravidian architect, this roof, with the storeyed pavilions, is the holy Kailasa on which stand the homes of gods, and he named them accordingly: Meru, Mandara or Kailasa. Even today, the 60-metre high sanctuary tower of Brihadesvara at Tanjore is known as the Meru of the South. Havell has remarked that the profile of Mount Kailasa in Tibet, which is a pyramid, supported on a wide base jutting out at one side, greatly resembles that of the famous monolithic temple of Ellora, which bears its name. The same can be said of all temples, both in the North and South, built before the 14th century, since, their sanctuaries have high roofs preceded by a lower porch, then by one or more *mandapams*, and all present the same general aspect.

The sanctuary—whose name has never ceased to recall the first home of all (*garbhagriha*, womb)—thus becomes a mountain cave. It is the dark, secret place from which proceed the rays of the divine influence, the womb from which the spirit is born. On the outside walls of the sanctuary there are chapels or mere alcoves that shelter holy images. Each of them figures the encounter of some aspect of the central symbol with the external world, its projection in a given direction, an oriented view of the fundamental abstraction. It is thus that the divinity of the *lingam* reveals itself on the walls of the Saivite sanctuary as Visnu to the South, Siva to the West, Brahma to the North and to the East, where the door is placed, as the priest, the faithful, the innumerable multiplicity of the world. When the ante-chamber is decorated with sculptured figures, we find (except in the 8th century) Daksinamurti looking to the South and Durga facing the North. In front of the entrance stands the bull, Nandi—symbol of the world as a vehicle for the gods.

The dark cave of the sanctuary thus appears as the centre of divine radiance glowing out on the world, and the believer who makes the ritual circuit round the walls can thus contemplate the variety of divine manifestations before uniting them in a meditation on the central symbol.

This qualification of the species by divine influence does not stop at the sanctuary walls but fills all the consecrated space around the Holy of Holies. In Northern India, this action is expressed by a series of chambers running from the door by which the believer enters from the exterior world, to the sanctuary itself. Each chamber represents a different category of offerings, a form of sacrifice, a stage in the spiritual ascent. In the Dravidian country, the same symbol is represented by successive enclosures containing the *mandapams*. In each of them is pierced a door and to pass through it is an act corresponding to an initiation or the conquest of a new stage. The thickness and height of the door corresponds to its importance. In the 8th century these doors were surmounted by a simple house-roof, in the form of a ship's hull with two poop-rails (example: the temple on the banks of the Mahabalipuram) but from the 12th century onwards, this original door multiplied and repeated itself, developing, in the same way as the simple chapel that became the pyramid of the great sanctuaries, into the high rectangular pyramids of *gopurams* in which each storey has its doors, clearly visible on the principal facade. The door of the first enclosure, figuring the passage from the profane to the sacred world, is the highest of all. The size of the others diminishes as one approach the sanctuary covered by a modest pyramid, of the same size as the small, isolated sanctuaries.

Here, then, is yet another change in the symbolic meaning of the temple: the sanctuary is no longer the mountain rising out of the earth towards the sky and preserving the inestimable precious seed that has descended into it: it has become the centre of Divine domain, the heart of the country of the gods, the symbolic image of the world of its epitome: man .

The sanctuary of the famous temple of Chidambaram is constructed, according to local Brahmins, in such a way that its openings recall those of the heart of a man. Each enclosure corresponds to one of the 'envelopes' that constitute a human being and the *mandapams* figure the centres animated by the subtle forces of his life and his mind. This new symbolic conception and the corresponding creation of *gopurams* is a contribution of the Dravidian country to the evolution of the Hindu temple, and illustrates its special genius.

The first images of the gods had only two arms and a single face and were similar in every way, except in their power and glory, to the human beings who worshipped them. Later on, when the god, no longer a being like ourselves, came down from Heaven, and became a mediator, a representative of the Light in our world and an essentially supernatural being, his sanctuary became the symbolic grotto in which the world is fecundated. The simple humanity of the gods then disappeared in the symbol. They were figured then with two more hands, behind the original ones, in which they held the symbols of their special nature: flame and drum, conch shell and magic wheel. These hands were attached to two forearms, growing from the elbow, while the upper part of the arm remained single. Still later, some of the gods had four, six or ten complete arms and numerous faces.

Then the Dravidian land began to return to its long–past Vedic aspiration and once more the accent was laid on that symbolic world, limited by the sacred enclosure, of which the meaning and order depends, in spite of the profusion of *mandapams* and chapels, *gopurams* and vast corridors, on the humble central chapel. This return had its innovations but it remained in spirit perfectly faithful to the immemorial tradition. The centre of all architecture was still the secret sanctuary, the divine symbol, wood, bronze, flame, earthern pot, pool or empty space in which radiates Existence, Mind, Conscience and the Beatitude of the supreme Reality, as the geometric centre of a boundless spiritual sphere.

26

Indian Painting

When one contemplates the brilliant and rich mosaic of Indian art as a whole, one becomes aware that what we can clearly define and what strikes us most are the highlights, the efflorescence and upsurges stimulated by a variety and multitude of influences and circumstances, some extraneous and some local or both. But underlying these upsurges there flows and always flowed uninterrupted in one form or another the vast river of Indian creative expression, feeding at the recurrent tributaries, but constituting the undying tradition and expression of the Indian creative genius and cumulative artistic experience.

Painting in India must have existed in one form or another long before the so called Ajanta cycle and judging by the examples of sculpture and other objects of art as well as from the texts that have come down to us, must have reached a considerable plane of development at a very early date. Drawing, painting, design and sculpture usually lost, especially in countries with extreme climatic conditions.

The beautiful objects of art of the so called Indus Valley civilisation bespeak of an advanced level of design, if we can judge from the many objects found and especially the beautiful seals which show an integrated and distinct style and a sense of design of considerable technical excellence. The type of painting which might have been practised then must remain a conjecture and we must turn to surviving examples to begin any scientific study of Indian painting as it has come down to our days.

Briefly and in a general way **we can classify the known styles and schools into about half a dozen major groups** with a large number of interrelated ramifications all leading up to the modern Indian schools of painting.

1. The styles of painting which survived in the cave temples as frescoes of which the most famous are the Ajanta and Ellora cave sequences. Beginning about the 1st century B.C. they go up to about the 7th century in the case of Ajanta and right up to the close of the first millennium at Ellora. Other examples of the school, which must have spread throughout India, are to be found at Bagh, Sittanavassal and in Ceylon. These cave sequences especially Ajanta preserve for us a priceless record of the development of painting in India over a period of many centuries and the standards it had reached during this golden age. Reaching its zenith about the 5th or 6th century it gradually began to change and the evolution of the style and treatment became especially noticeable in the latter Jaina style at Ellora. These changes were conformant to the rapidly changing pattern of life, both political and otherwise.

2. The illuminated Buddhist palm leaf manuscripts and the Jaina texts which range from about the 10th to the 12th or 13th centuries in the case of Buddhist manuscripts and extend to considerably later dates with the Jaina manuscripts. They were in direct line of evolution from the great tradition as we have found it in the cave temple paintings and the beautiful palm leaf illumination from Bengal, Bihar and Nepal often exhibit striking similarity in technique and treatment, to the murals at Ajanta. The Jaina miniatures are likewise a continuation of this great

tradition, but exhibit the specific angular, less wiry, linear technique with flat colour surfaces which become such a distinct feature of Jaina art. This art reached its greatest development in Gujarat and Western India and in turn influenced other schools.

3. The complex art pattern which grew up in the South and the Deccan fed by the great earlier traditions and extended as far as the Eastern coast. Important examples of this school can be seen in the 11th century murals of the Brihadesvara temple at Tanjore. It reached a sort of culmination in Vijayanagar and though Vijayanagar is often considered as an already decadent expression, yet such murals as in the Virabhadra temple at Lepaksi bespeak of a well integrated tradition highly decorative and distinct in the general approach. The emergence of what is often referred to as the Deccan school was brought about by the advent of powerful Muslim influences which were apparently quite formed by the end of the15th and beginning of the 16th centuries, as we can see from the few examples which have recently come to light. These new influences fused with the remnants of the Southern styles and formed the so-called Bijapur and other schools in the Deccan by the last half of the 16th century.

4. The Mughal School, which was a great revival, a vital blend of Indo-Persian and European influence, began with the advent of Mughal rule. The initial impluse may have come, as it has often happened in the past, from outside, in this case from the great Persian artists of the school of Behzad and the patronage of the Mughal Court, but the Indian creative genius very soon blended and transmuted those new influences and absorbing new lessons gained from European arts, which in increasing numbers was brought to India, developed a new and vital form of expression. The Mughal School is characterised by splendid drawing, a new decorative and striking realism,

perspective, receding planes, atmosphere as well as a great sense of observation. Series of large paintings were executed, as well as books illuminated. Miniatures depicting court life were most popular and exquisite studies of flowers and animals appeared during the time of Jahangir. Artists were given a new status and miniatures were signed by the artists. The school reached its zenith under Akbar and Jahangir and gradually lost its vitality and standards with the last Mughal rulers.

5. The Rajput School of art, which must have existed even at an earlier date than the examples which we now possess indicate, covers a large geographic area. The school in its initial stages displayed extraordinary vigour, blended with an advanced sense of the decorative, as well as a great knowledge of the elements of pure composition and formal treatment. These primitives are mural in their general treatment and often gems of decorative splendour. The themes used were usually illustrations to musical modes, Ragamalas, popular poems and epic romances; the Krishna legend acquired a dominant place. The earliest known examples go back to the 16th century and this school continued through 17th and even 18th century gradually losing its originality and vitality. Udaipur in Mewar and Malwa with its Deccan influences, were great centres of this art.

A later mixed Rajput-Mughal school which absorbed many elements of the Mughal tradition flourished at the courts of the numerous Rajput rulers and elsewhere in India during the 17th and 18th centuries and is responsible for a large number of paintings.

6. The Himalayan or Kangra School which comprises all the known hill schools beginning with the more primitive Basohli and Pahari schools and culminating in the well known later Kangra style. These schools have been developed during the end of the 17th and 18th centuries

when the growing lack of the patronage and disturbed conditions made many artists from down plains migrate to the hills attracted by the new patronage and growing importance of the hills states.

The beginning of this most important school cannot, at present, be factually traced beyond the end of the 17th century, though, personally, I am inclined to believe that some form of painting must have been practised in the Himalayan hill tracts from very early periods and some traditional schools, and ateliers probably connected with the temples must have been locally at work throughout. We know that Kashmir had some excellent artists who in the 11th and 12th centuries were invited to paint frescoes in the Western Tibetan kingdom of Guge at Tsaparang and must have also contributed to the frescoes in the temples of Spiti. These artists have also worked in the areas lying between Western Tibet and Kashmir. Some of the landscape depicted in these frescoes bear a strange similitude to the landscape treatment found in the Basohli paintings. The Kangra or Himalayan School of art with its numerous branches and ramifications through Kangra proper, Nurpur, Guler, Chamba, Mandi, Suket, Kulu, Sirmoor, Garhwal and other states has left to us a priceless record of a great tradition. This infinitely tender, decorative, fully integrated art, which in its best examples must rank with some of the great treasures of the art world is indeed worthy of the beautiful legends they depicted and the unique scenery and life which inspired them. The Kangra School came to an end by the middle of the19th century though a few traditional artists survived even at later dates.

The Sikh School is very closely allied to the Kangra School, and undoubtedly many of the latter artists worked for the Sikh rulers.

Before the emergence of what we may call the Modern

Indian School of painting, there was a general decline. Through the efforts of E.B. Havell and Abanindranath Tagore a new impulse was given to the study of the great classical tradition. A new school began to form and this revival was often referred to as the Bengal Renaissance. This movement opened the way to a new appreciation of the vast artistic heritage of India and awakened the new artistic life of the century.

The modern trends in Indian art are necessarily very complex. It is but natural that Modern European art should have had a marked influence on Modern Indian paintings, yet some artists have also very successfully turned to folk art and themes. Large numbers of excellent and serious artists are now working towards new pictorial expression and already exhibit highly individual approaches and consummate mastery of their mediums. Such excellent names as Nandalal Bose, Jamini Roy, Manishi Dey, Bhabesh Sanyal, Bendre, Hebbar, Gujral, Chavda, Raval, Ara, Hussain, Palsikar, Samant and many others are all working towards new conquests, new achievements and are significantly contributing towards India's new expression and enriching the treasure house of world culture.

27

Classical Music

The origin and inspiration of music in India, like all other classic arts, are attributed to Divinity. Lord Siva is considered to have created sound, rhythm (i.e. music) as well as the dance. Of the six ancient *Ragas,* five came out of the mouth of Siva and one of his divine consort, Parvati. Sarasvati is worshipped as the Goddess of Music, Culture and Learning. Her instrument is the Vina, the most classic instrument in India, the creation of which is attributed to Rishi Narada. To Narada is also attributed the authorship of *Narada Siksha* (of uncertain date) which is a great treatise on music and is referred to by scholars to this day.

It is interesting to note here that two musical instruments that have been deified in India from time immemorial are the flute and the drum—Krishna's Murali, and Siva's Damaru. The universe is said to rotate and revolve around the woven music and rhythm of these two instruments. Even today, of all musical instruments, the flute and the drum are the ones most used amongst the common people. In remote villages, in work, play or feast, these are the two instruments that predominate. In the classical field, the flute has given place to the voice—hence the saying 'her voice resembles that of a flute'—the drums have remained, as the chief accompanying instruments.

Also forming part of the Hindu musical mythology are

the heavenly musicians and dancers of Indra's courts, the Gandharvas, Apsaras, Kinnaras, and Naras. The Gandharvas are united in matrimony with the Apsaras. The Kinnaras and Nagas were also heavenly musicians. These supernatural dancers and singers had at their command a musical art of the highest perfection. By the charm of their art they could even distract the yogic trance of a great *muni.* It was Apsara Menaka who distracted Visvamitra's meditation with her dance and out of their union was born Shakuntala.

From the supernatural we come to the real. Great *rishis* and *munis* were considered masters of the musical art. Bharata-muni was the first to draw up the laws of music, dance and drama elaborately and in great accuracy in his *Natya-Sastra* (the date is sometimes given as 500 A.D., but very likely it is much older). Tumburu (no date available) is considered to be the first singer and many legends exist regarding his great art in vocal music.

In the Sama Veda where the Divinity is worshipped through chants we find mention and trace of a scale of seven notes. It is also found that Vaira and Kafi That were prevalent in most of the SamaVeda chants. Opinion is however divided, among experts regarding the Shuddha (pure) scale during this period. Some hold that it was the Kafi That, while others believe that Vaira That was the Shuddha That at that time.

During the classic period, the Shuddha That was the Kafi That. It was also during this period that the theories of Grama (scales), Muracchana (modes) and Jati (species) came into existence. All Sanskrit musical treatises, (Bharata's) *Natya-Sastra*, Saranga Deva's *Sangita-Ratnakara,* etc., were based on these theories. The music of the period itself was based and developed on these theories.

In *Rikpratisakhya* (400 B.C.) we find mentioned the three

Gramas and the seven notes of the scale. In Panini's Grammar (4th century B.C.) comments on dancing and music are found. In the *Jatakas*, we find that the art of music had already reached a complexity and perfection very high. The Vina or Saptatantri (seven-stringed) then in use was decidedly neither a primitive nor a simple instrument, and it follows logically that the music which was composed for it was not simple either. In the treatise of Manu (200 A.D.) also we find significant references to music and dancing. In his *Artha-Sastra* Chanakya recommends 'song, instrumental music, recitation, dancing, acting, writing, playing on the Vina, flute (Venu), and drum (Mridanga), knowing the mind of others, making scents and garlands, shampooing, employing alluring words—those who know all these and can teach them to courtesans and actors should be provided with a livelihood by the state.' In *Brihaddesi* of Matanga Muni (between the 4th and 7th cent.), explanations of Ragas, as understood by the later schools of music, are found.

And perhaps the most interesting analysis of the musical art of the period can be found in the *Panchatantra* (5th century) in the story of the jackal and the ass. The ass, eager to sing and to prove his knowledge of the art, says to the jackal: 'There are seven notes (Svaras), three voice-registers (Mandra, Madhya and Tara), three layas (Vilambita, Madhya, Druta), six ways of singing and nine emotions (Rasa).'

As a result of the Moghul invasion of India, after 1,000 A.D., music in India divided into North Indian or Hindustani Music and South Indian or Karnatic Music. In North India, the Raga-Ragini theory developed and held sway till the 19th century, when the That theory of Bhatkhande was introduced. In the Raga-Ragini theory, the entire Raga world derived from six Raga and thirty-six

Raginis. These original six Ragas are considered to be of divine origin. They each have six 'wives' or feminine Ragas (Raginis) and these in turn have *Putras* or sons.

Poet Jayadeva, a native of Kunduli in Bengal (1100 A.D.), is amongst the first of the Indian musicians about whom definite facts are available and whose life and activities are not shrouded in legend. Jayadeva, author of *Gita-Govinda,* assigned to each of his poems a Raga and a Tala (rhythm). Though no musical notation was then in use and his melodies have come down to us by tradition, it is to be believed that his original melodies, as those of today, were exquisitely sensitive as were the subjects of his songs. Music at that time was not the prerogative or passion of poets and musicians only. King Nanyadeva (1096-137 A.D.) in his *Sarasvata-Hridayalankara* included many new Desi Ragas such as Daksini, Saurastri, Gurjari, etc.

In the 13th century was produced the most monumental work on Raga-Ragini: Sarangadeva's (1210-1247 A.D.) *Sangita-Ratnakara.* It is considered as one of the greatest landmarks in the musical history of the country. Many other important treatises on music were written during this period. To quote a few, *Sangita-Samayasara* of Parasvadeva (13th century), *Ragarnava* (1300 A.D.), Lochana's *Raga-Tarangini,* Ahobal's *Sangita-Parijata,* etc. These were all considered authoritative sources of reference.

The Moghul emperor **Akbar was a great patron of the arts as well as a musician himself. He was an able player on the Naqqarah (a drum used in pairs) and had composed about two hundred melodies.** Perhaps his name in relation to the musical history of the land would not have been remembered if he had not played such a vital role in the life of India's greatest musician of the time, Tansen. Akbar invited Tansen from the court of Raja Ram of Baghelkhand, to be his own court-musician. In *Ain-i-Akbari* one reads 'a singer like him has not been in India for the last thousand years'. He created many new Ragas: Darbari Todi, Mian-ki-Mallar, Mian-ki-Sarang, etc. His art was a perfect fusion between the ancient art and music of India and the arts of Arabia and Persia with which he came in contact later. The result of this fusion has left a style, an art and an imprint on North Indian music which is living still today and is at once recognisable and identifiable. He also created the instrument Rabab. Both the children of Tansen, son Bilash Khan and daughter Saraswati, were excellent musicians. Bilash Khan and his descendants adopted the Rabab and became founders of the Rabab School while Saraswati and her husband, Misri Singh—an excellent Vina-player—took up as their family instrument, the Vina, and their descendants became known as the 'Vinkars'. Both branches carried on his traditions and founded the two most important North Indian schools of music.

The disruption of the Moghul empire led to the dispersal of the descendants and followers of the Tansen school of music. They flocked to the courts of Ayodhya, Bettia, Rewa, Banaras and other princely states. Rampur was their last stronghold. The late Nawab of Rampur was a devoted patron of music and both the schools—Rababi and Vinkar—flourished in his court. Muhammad Ali Khan was the last of the great Rababiya of Mian Tansen school and Muhammad Wazir Khan, the last of the great Vinkars. This tradition surived in Ustad Dabir Khan and his uncle, Ustad Sagir Khan of Bengal.

Some of the Ragas created during the Moghul period and under their influence were Turuska (Turkish), Todi, Hijaj, Harakh, Yaman, etc. Amir Khusro, poet, musician and statesman of the court of Alauddin, created many important innovations in Indian music. He created Ragas Hafi, Iman, etc., invented the Sitar—a modification of the

Vina—and introduced the Qawwali style of singing.

Some other important treatises on music were written during the 19th century–Muhammad Reza's *Nagmat-Asharphi* (1813), Krishnananda Vyasa's *Sangita-Ragakalpadruma,* S.M. Tagore's *Universal History of Music,* Pandit Bhatkhande's treatise, etc. The latter brought the entire Raga world under ten That's or scales.

The South, owing to its geographical position, lived and developed more in isolation. Moreover, it was never completely conquered by the Moghuls. As a result, Hindu art survived and retained its purity and ancient traditions in the South. During the time of Bharata, Natya or drama was the meeting point of Gita (song), Vadya (instrumental music), and Nritya (dancing). This tradition has remained in the South. All South Indian songs can be adapted as accompaniments to a dance. Temple dancers (Devadasis) continued their art in the South while they ceased to exist in the North under the Moghul rule, as a result of which, in North India, women of respectable families were debarred from dancing which came to be looked down upon as a profane art. Consequently, vocal and instrumental music in the North developed independently of each other and of the dance. In South India, the pure scale continued to be Kafi while in the North, the Bilawal That became the pure That. In the South, approximately about the 14th century, the Mel theory developed and the entire Raga world of the South Indian music was brought under seventy-two Mels (groups). Like Tansen in the North, Thyagaraja was a great musician of the South as was also Govinda Marar. The important treatises on South Indian music are *Paripadal* (100-200 A.D.), *Svaramela-Kalanidhi* of Ramamatya (1550 A.D.) etc.

In modern times music in India has ceased to create or grow further. There is lack of inspiration, daring and venture necessary for the creation and continuance of art. Music in

India today has lost its dynamic quality. Rabindranath Tagore has given a certain impetus with his music, which has come to be identified with him as Ravindra Sangita. He wrote more than two thousand songs, all delightfully musical and poetically superb. But Tagore's music has not revolutionised music in India. He only founded another school of music and singing which has continued to live independently but happily in the parental home.

The first indication of the Indian scale is found in the Sama Veda. The names of the notes then known were however different to those of the Sanskrit or later period. I give below a table with the names of the scale as known during the Vedic period and the Sanskrit period, and as they are known today together with their corresponding equivalents of the European scale:

Vedic Period: Udatta, Anudatta, Svarita, Atisarga, Krusta, Pracaya, Atisargiya.

Sanskrit Period: Swaraj, Risav, Gandhar, Madhyam, Panchama, Dhaivat, Nisadha.

Modern Names: Sa, Re, Ga, Ma, Pa, Dha, Ni.

European Scale: Do, Re, Mi, Fa, Sol, La, Si.

As already explained there is a difference of opinion among experts regarding the pure scale in use during the Vedic period. Some believe that it was the Bhairav That, whereas others believe that it was the Kafi That. However, during the Sanskrit period (it is now definitely accepted), Kafi That was the pure That. It was also during the Sanskrit period that the theories of Grama (scale), Murcchana (modes) and Jati (species) were developed.

I shall now briefly explain these terms. Grama literally means a 'village' and therefore implies the orderly arrangement of the notes of a scale. Originally there were three Gramas, Sa Grama, Ma Grama and Ga Grama, but the last one has been long obsolete. Sa Grama Ragas included Ragas with Shuddha or pure Re while Ma Grama Ragas included effects with Komal Re or Reb. Now there are seventy-two scales in Indian Music and each scale has more than twenty Ragas derived from it. So there are really thousands of ragas.

Murcchana or mode means the rise and fall from and to a particular note of a specific scale. There are three types of Murcchanas: (1) Sampurna (complete), with all the seven notes of the octave, (2) Kharab, with six notes of the octave, and (3) Orab, with five notes of the octave. Thus there are twenty-one Murcchanas, as each of the seven notes of the octave can have three types of Murcchanas. Now each of the two Gramas have seven Murcchanas each, i.e., fourteen in all. But only seven of these fourteen are in practical use and are known as Jatis.

The Indian scale has twenty-two Srutis or microtonal intervals in the octave. Each of them has a name and specific attributions of divine qualities are implied to each of them. It is important to note that these divisions are not always equal.

There are also three pitches in Indian music: the lower or Mandra, the middle or Madhya, and the higher or Tara.

Raga—According to Bharata Muni a Raga is what 'colours and pleases the hearts of all'. Ragas are based either on definite human sentiments or manifestations of nature. The root meaning of Raga is 'passion'. Ragas are broadly divided into three classes—Shuddha, when there is one Raga only, Chhayalaga or Salanka when two Ragas are mixed, and Sankirna, when there are more than two Ragas in the composition.

The origin of Ragas is considered to have three sources:

(1) Marga Raga or Ragas having supernatural and heavenly origin, (2) Desi Raga or Ragas composed by musical seers and sung by expert musicians, and (3) Loka-Sangita or Ragas based on popular folk music. The original six Ragas and thirty six Raginis are of Marga origin. These are:

(1) Raga Bhairav. Raginis—Ramkali, Gumkeli, Asa, Prabhati, Lotila, Todi.

(2) Raga Malkos. Raginis—Bhairavi, Bagesri, Bhimpalasi, Ahiri, Khambati, Lankeswari.

(3) Raga Hindol. Raginis—Kalyani, Puria, Marwa, Vasanti, Panchami, Bibhasa.

(4) Raga Megh. Raginis—Suha, Mallari, Saindhabi, Madamati, Saurati, Adana.

(5) Raga Sri. Raginis—Jayesri, Malasri, Dhanesri, Barari, Purba, Gouri.

(6) Raga Dipak. Raginis—Bilavali, Bihangara, Sankara, Kedara, Kakubha, Natika.

In a Raga there are three important notes, Graha—the note on which the Raga begins, Nyasa—the note on which it ends, and Amsa—the predominant note or Badi of a Raga. The Amsa is the soul of the Raga. It is the note on which the life of the composition rests.

A Raga is introduced by Alap—a slow ever-unfolding exposition of the Raga which prepares the ground for further elaboration of the melodies in the succeeding movements. In Alap, the notes of the Raga are sung in a loose kind of rhythm, not to words but to syllables—A-NA-TA-RA-NA-RI-RE-NUM. In the North Indian Alap there are four Varnas of 'colouring stages'—Asthai, Antara, Sancari and Abhog. All the characteristics of the Raga are found in the Murcchanas (modes), Gamaks (graces) and Tans. A single melody may be sung in many different variations by introducing new Tans built up on the basic melody. In Indian music it is here really that the virtuosity of the musician is put to test. The richer and more varied the Tans and Gamaks, the greater the improvisational power of the musician. In this connection, it must be mentioned that all Ragas and Raginis have definite fixed hours for their performance and this rule is never broken by the musicians.

From very ancient times each Raga has been associated with a particular emotion of passion, or different manifestations of nature. Bhairava is the Raga of devotion, peace, godliness; Malkosa is the Raga of spring, joy, love; Megh that of rain, ecstatical joy; Sri that of prayer, relaxation, aspiration; Dipak that of fire, courage, enthusiasm; and Nat is the Raga of fighting.

The That theory—Prof. Bhatkhande in the 19th century divided the Raga world in Thats and thus gave rise to the That theory. He brought all existing Ragas and Raginis as deriving from ten principal Thats or scales. These were:

1. *Kalyan That*—Fourth augmented. 2. *Bilaval That*—Ordinary major scale. 3. *Kafi That*—Third minor and seventh minor. 4. *Khambaj That*—Seventh minor. 5. *Marava That*—Second minor, fourth augmented. 6. *Purbi That*—Second minor, fourth augmented, sixth minor. 7. *Todi That*— Second minor, third minor, fourth augmented, sixth minor. 8. *Bhairavi That*—Second minor, third minor, sixth minor, seventh minor. 9. *Asavari That*—Third minor, sixth minor, seventh minor. 10. *Bhairav That*—Second minor, sixth minor.

All remaining Ragas, Raginis and Putras derived their origin from one of these Thats according to the notes found in their make up.

Alap—Alap may be said to be the introduction to Raga.

It is expounded slowly and gradually with or without a fixed rhythm. Originally the term Anant Hari-Narayana was sung in the vocal Alap but during the Moghul period, for its obvious reference to the Hindu deity Visnu, the term was substituted for A Na Ta Ra Na Ri Re Num in North Indian vocal Alap. There are no fixed rules or formulas as to how these syllables should be sung. They are used by the singer in the way best suited to the notes and the rhythm of the Raga and to the individual musical of the performer.

Alap has three broad divisions regarding tempi: 1. Bilambit or slow tempo, 2. Madh or middle tempo, and 3. Drut or fast tempo. This applics generally to vocal Alap, for instrumental Alap has furthur sub-divisions which are explained later.

The Bilambit or slow movement itself has four divisions: (a) Asthai—This is considered the face of the Raga-alap. This implies that every Raga has a form and Asthai is its 'face'. This part of the Alap is played in the *mandra* (lower) and *madhya* (middle) octaves. (b) Antara—This is considered the 'heart' of the Raga-alap. The range of its execution lies between the middle octave (Mudara) and a few notes of the higher octave (Tara). (c) Sanchari or the 'navel' of the Raga—Its range lies between the middle and the lower octave. (d) Abhog or the foot of the Raga—The range of this section of the Alap lies between the middle of Mudara, high up into Tara and returning to the Mudara octave.

After the four parts of the Bilambit Alap, Madh or middle tempo comes in and this part to the Alap has no restriction regarding the three octaves. After Madh, or Madh Jord as it is also known, Drut of fast tempo follows. Here too there is no restriction regarding the octaves. In Bilambit Alap, the syllables A Na Ta Ra Na Ri Re Num are sung. In Madh and Drut these are also used. At the end of the Drut, the 'Sargam' or the notes of the scale themselves may be sung as is the use in South India.

Instrumental Alap—The Vina and the Rabab are considered the ideal instruments for playing instrumental Alap. As in the vocal Alap the instrumental Alap is also divided into three broad divisions—slow, middle and quick tempi. But, as already mentioned, these three main divisions are further sub-divided, e.g., instrumental Bilambit Alap begins slow but increases speed in the second stage of Antara. Further, the middle tempo or Madh is sub-divided into four part according to the difference in tempi and the strokes used. The Drut or fast tempo has ten divisions according to the strokes and the tempi. It is in the Drut movement the fixed rhythm or Tala comes in.

Based on the classic instruments Vina and Rabab, many other instruments have been created and there are Sursingar, Surbahar, Sarod and Sitar. In North India, in recent times it is the Sarod and the Sitar which are in great vogue and so Alap is played on these two instruments also.

Tana—The development and combination of notes is known as Tana in Indian music. There are two kinds of Tana—Shuddha (simple) and Kuta (complex). Shuddha Tana uses the notes in ascent and descent in a straight and consecutive order, e.g., Sa Re Ga Ma Ma Ga Re Sa, etc. Kuta Tana is formed by combining the notes in an irregular and wayward fashion, e.g., S G R—R G S etc. There are ten varieties of Shuddha Tana and forty nine varieties of Kuta Tana. But in *Sangita-Ratnakara* 5740 varieties are illustrated as a result of permutation and combination of notes.

Tala—The Indian Tala or time measure in music is a direct development from the metres of poetry. The beat of the time or Tala is given by the clapping of hands. Unlike the theories of Raga there is more similarity in the theory of Tala as found in the North and South. The nomenclature however varies.

Tala is based on matras or note-lengths. The normal duration of a matra is a second. Generally six main note-lengths are cited, based on their relative duration values to a matra. These are: (1) Anudruta—1/4 matras, (2) Druta—1/2 matras, (3) Laghu—1 matras, (4) Guru—2 matras, (5) Pluta—3 matras, (6) Kakpad—4 matras. The Tansen school, however, propounds an elaborate exposition of note-lengths.

The time-units or note-lengths in the various combinations make different Talas. Each section of a Tala is sub-divided into several sub-sections. That section of Tala which forms the principal beat is the most important and is known as Soma. The unaccented portion of a section of a Tala is known as Phank and is shown by an empty wave of the hand.

There are three main tempi of Tala—Bilambit (slow), Madh (medium) and Drut (fast). The chief instruments used for Tala are Mridanga and Tabla. The technique of execution and the types of Talas used for these two separate instruments are different from one another as also the physical construction of these two types of drums. The Tablas are smaller and the two drum-heads are on two separate instruments. While played they are held almost vertically. The Mridanga on the other hand has the two drum-heads on the same instrument and is held in a horizontal position. The drums are tuned to the Sa or the first note of the scale of an instrument or song.

Drummers have a curious system of Bolas or drum-words which indicate to them not only the particular kind of Tala to be accompanied but also the strokes of the beats. These Bolas are composed of syllables, e.g., Dha-Dhin-Dhin-Ta, Ta-Dhin-Dhin-Ta, etc.

28

Classical Dances

The classical Indian dance is a truly creative force the ages have bequeathed, a fount of undying inspiration, for all those who are alive to the urgent call of rhythm. **Art and religion in India are so strongly interlinked that they cannot be divorced from each other. Dance and music are a means, among others, of attaining enlightenment of the mind. One can reach God through song, dance and music.** The very conception of the Nataraja elevates the dance art to a high spiritual and philosophical plane, reflecting the essence and inner truth of Indian culture. Sri Krishna is also visualised as the Immortal Dancer. He is the Universal Soul (the "Paramatman") and the *gopis* (the "Jivatman") are human souls, dancing round him and each feeling that the Lord is dancing with her alone.

Bharata Natyam: Of all the classical dance forms, Bharata Natyam is undoubtedly **the most ancient and the richest in content and expression. It is the truest representative of the nation's cultural traditions, with a history as old as civilisation.** It also bears the closest conformity with the timeless tenets laid down by Sage Bharata in his *Natya Sastra,* our oldest treatise on dance and drama.

Divine discontent was the inspiration of this treatise. The legend goes that Indra, king of gods, demanded a form of entertainment that would free his mind from the thoughts and cares of his many arduous duties. So Brahma the Creator produced the Natyaveda, culling the essence of the four older Vedas—Rigveda for words, Samaveda for melody, Yajurveda for the four ideals of *abhinaya* (expressive acting) and Atharvaveda for *rasa* and *bhava* (emotional flavour and intellectual inspiration). He blended them all into this, the fifth Veda, which was later edited and annotated by Bharata, his foremost disciple, for the benefit of mankind.

Tradition also relates that Bharata once produced a play for the delectation of the gods. Siva and Parvati were pleased with his literary excellence and imparted to him the principles of their respective styles of dances. Siva had Tandu, one of his *ganas,* expound his style, and this gained the name of Tandava, noted for its virile strength and masculine force. Parvati taught her style to Usha, daughter of Banasura, the king of Pragjyotisapura, who, in turn, instructed the women of Saurashtra in it. This form of dance was designed as Lasya and expressed the essence of feminity, through the grace, elegance and delicacy of movement.

The *Natya Sastra* of Bharata Muni remains our earliest and most comprehensive treatise on dance and drama. Here, in minute and intricate detail, the various laws governing a proper and aesthetically pleasing dance performance are laid down. It is proof that 2,000 years ago, Bharata Natyam was already a fully evolved and comprehensive art form, which, besides being practised with the utmost precision and dedication, was also meticulously analysed and systematically codified. The precision, clarity and sensibility of this great work has made it the sacred text of the dancer for centuries.

The term Bharata Natyam, however, contrary to popular conception, is not derived from this source, but formed of the initial letters of the three essentials dance—*bhava, raga* and *tala*.

Never in the course of its long history has this art been really lost. At times, like the great subterranean river Phalgu, famed in myth and legend, it has gone underground only to emerge afresh. The *Natya Sastra,* the dance sculptures in the temples and the dedicated Nattuvanars—the traditional dance teachers of the South—have kept alive the glory of the art through all the vicissitudes of history.

In its various postures, rhythmic patterns and movements, Bharata Natyam epitomises the ideals of grace and beauty and has offered our ancient sculptors themes and attitudes to make the temples rich in the glory and grandeur of art—as, for instance, the temple dedicated to Nataraja at Chidambaram.

The Nattuvanars have kept alive Bharata Natyam in their homes, where to the rhythm of the *tattakali*—a small stick used in beating the measure on a block of wood—generations of students have been trained in the time-honoured traditions of this classical art. In a way, their contributions, as teachers, has been immense.

Formerly Bharata Natyam implied the entire generic systems of the Indian classical dance, but it now only connotes the solo dance form that used to be practised by the Devadasis of South India, and in tracing this we have the entire history of the dance from—its first splendour, gradual degeneration and subsequent resurgence.

Till about 750 years ago, Bharata Natyam was the only dance form practised from Kashmir to Kanyakumari. In the Vedic age, it was considered not only an essential feature of religious rites, but also a necessary accomplishment for women of high birth. In the Epic age, it had found its way into the royal courts. The Maurya Empire furnishes evidence of state patronage to the art. Kautilya, the great political thinker and statesman, made it incumbent on the state to provide a livelihood for all those practising the arts. In the Gupta period the coins of Samudra Gupta show him seated on a couch playing the Vina.

But when the Moghul invaders entered India and established their supremacy, though contact with the Arabic and Persian civilisations enriched and remoulded the Hindustani system of classical music, the dance tradition gradually deteriorated and finally disappeared from North India. Eventually **a new dance form was to arise, combining some of the austere notes of the *Natya Sastra* with a lighter, more frivolous and entirely erotic mode of expression that had a greater and more immediate appeal for the Muslim rulers, who were unable to conceive of the dance as a chaste, spontaneous and refined expression of religious ecstasy.** Thus Bharata Natyam came to be confined for the main part to South India, where it grew in beauty, strength and richness, tended by successive generations of kings, chieftains and priests. The devoted care of a gracious, learned, yet rigidly orthodox, people kept intact its pristine purity, and the dance was mainly performed in the precincts of the temple.

Soon a new caste came into being, that of the Devadasis (servants of God). Like the vestal virgins of the Greek shrines, these attendants were young girls dedicated in their childhood to the temple deity. Never suffering widowhood, they were considered ever-auspicious. They had their own special customs, rules of conduct and privileges, and their duties consisted of dancing before the deity during the ritual hour and at the time of sacred processions. Identifying the God with the Beloved and themselves with the Lover, they brought their art a chaste coquetry, a high eroticism and a god-intoxication of a rarefied kind.

But an art that dealt with a theme as delicate and provocative as Divine Love must, sooner or later, face tarnishment. In course of time Bharata Natyam moved on, from the sacred atmosphere of the temples to the pomp and pageantry of royal courts and, finally, to the dust and degradation of the market-place. Eventually, dancing came to be associated with the lewd, the common, and the whole art came under condemnation and was left severely alone by girls from respectable families.

But like the phoenix, it rose from its own ashes: A little over forty years ago, an intrepid soul struggled long and hard to lift this art from the mire of social prejudice. He fought the narrow outlook by learning the art himself and dancing from every available platform in order to reveal to the people its inherent beauty and classicism. He was E. Krishna Iyer, and to him we owe, in a manner, the revival and resuscitation of Bharata Natyam.

After a historic press controversy, his ceaseless campaigns spelt success when artistes from respectable families, like Rukmini Devi, came forward to redeem the dance from disrepute and degradation. They strove to uphold it as one of the most vivid and vital links with the past, containing, as it does, the basic tenets of all arts and the richness of religion and philsophy.

Natyakalavidwan Meenakshi Sundaram Pillai, greatest of all Nattuvanars in recent history, languished many years in his village home in Pandanallur (near Tanjore) before he was "discovered" by E. Krishna Iyer. Coming from a family which gave us the four brothers—Ponnayya, Chinnayya, Sivanandan and Vadivelu—who systematised Bharata Natyam and gave it its present compact form, Meenakshi Sundaram Pillai knew the classical dance art in its purest and most austere form. The later years of his life saw his humble home become a shrine for lovers of the dance. Many and famous are the exponents he trained, some of them gaining world renown. Seeing him one could not imagine that within this frail body rested knowledge so vast and so measureless. Most exacting of task-masters, the rule of his stick during working hours was stern and rigorous. But he was essentially a kind and gentle old man, sightless towards the end, perhaps a little tired of life's unending struggle.

After his death, his son-in-law, Natyakalanidhi Chokkalingam Pillai had been installed as the doyen of Bharata Natyam maestros. Formerly attached to the Kalakshetra, Adyar, and now to the Indian Institute of Fine Arts, Egmore (both in Chennai), he was also a strict disciplinarian.

Natyakalakesari Ramayya Pillai advocated a different school of Bharata Natyam—the Vazhuvoor School. His art was creative, within the framework of tradition, and flexible without overstepping the boundary line. He laid more stress than others on grace, ease of the execution and winsome *abhinaya* (expressive activity), and among his noted pupils was Kamala.

To see Mylapore Gauri Amma interpret a *padam* (song) was to cherish the memory of a lifetime. The delicacy, restraint and sensitivity of her *abhinaya* was beyond compare and, one may say, cannot ever be acquired by anyone. Honoured with a Presidential award she was the oldest among Devadasis.

Balasaraswati is one of those fortunate few who have seen their names become a legend in their own lifetime. Audiences of many kinds and climes have raved over her subtle nuances of expression, the transformation of her ordinary self into a creature of fantasy the moment she steps on to the stage, her ability to convey the entire gamut of feminine emotions. To see her dance is to realise the tantalising charm and the devotional rapture of the old Devadasis.

Rukmini Devi, born in a Brahmin family, had to fight the prejudice of an ignorant public that had tended to look upon Bharata Natyam in terms of licentious entertainment. As a pioneer, she paved the way for a new generation of dancers who, not coming of traditional stock, had found the art a remote star. She has given Bharata Natyam a dignity and sanctity of sentiment, and freed it from an excessive preoccupation of *bhakti bhava* (attitude of devotion). She made her institute, the Kalakshetra, a home of the arts.

Vyjayanthimala, in many ways, answers Bharata's dictates for the ideal danseuse. She proves beyond doubt that the *Kaisiki vrtti* (feminine grace, elegence, dignity) perdominates in this art. A notable contribution on the dance world is her creation of the Thiruppavai ballet. No apter choice could have been made, for it is as if nature and temperament have conspired together to drape on her the mantle of Andal, the girl who chose and won the Lord as her husband.

Nirmala Ramachandran is unusual in having combined the forceful manner of rhythmic sequences (*nritta*) that characterises the Pandanallur school, with the mellow, gracious, suggestive acting (*abhinaya*) that underlines Balasaraswati's style. She has imbibed the best from both.

Bhagavata Mela Nataka: People outside Tamilnadu are mostly familiar with only that form of Bharata Natyam which is performed as a solo recital by one or two female dancers. This, technically known as Sadir Natya, is one of the three forms this dance art has taken, the other two being the Bhagavata Mela dance-drama and the Kuravanji Ballet.

Of these, Bhagavata Mela is still performed annually at the small village of Melattur (near Tanjore), which was given as a gift to 501 Brahmin families by the devout king of Tanjore, Achyutappa Naik, for the express purpose of promoting the fine arts. The exponents of this style believed in the sacred aspects of song, dance and drama.

The performances have always an all-male cast and the dance-dramas usually chosen are those composed by the great Venkatarama Sastriar, who lived about 180 years ago. These dramas are enacted in front of the deity and form part of the annual Narasimha Jayanthi celebrations.

Kuchipudi: This is an early form of dance-drama that flourished in Andhra Pradesh. The village originally called Kuchelapuram, which lent its name to the art, was its home. The residents of this village were all Brahmins, who formed a compact community of dancers. Originally only men performed the Kuchipudi, on such occasions as marriages and temple-festivals. Later women were taught the dance, and a new style was born, known as "Dasi Melam" or "Natuva Melam", the forerunner of the present-day Bharata Natyam.

Andhra culture reached its zenith during the rule of the Vijayanagar Emperors, and with the decline of the empire the dancers migrated to Tanjore, forced to seek their livelihood in the courts of the Naik Kings. At this time the *padas*, composed mostly by Kestrajna and addressed to Venugopala, in a tender, lyrical vein, were greatly in vogue.

Around the 16th century, Siddhendra Yogi made his appearance and changed the form and content of this dance style. Belonging to that cult of Bhaktas who approached their God through ecstatic hymns, and himself a devout Krishna worshipper, he bequeathed to the Kuchipudi tradition his great composition, *Bhama Kalapam*. The dramatic form became popular and has known continuous development. A peculiar and unique characteristic of the Kuchipudi dance-drama is *Vacikabhinaya* (expressive activity through speech), wherein the dancers speak, sometimes a monologue, sometimes a prayer.

Kuchipudi, threatened with near extinction, would have known total annihilation had it not been preserved with love, care and dedication by a small band of traditional exponents, greatest of whom was Vedantam Lakshminarayana Sastri.

Once strictly the preserve of men, it now has a handful of danseuses dedicated to its progress, inspired by the ardent effort of Natyacharya Korada Narasimha Rao, who was the first to dance it outside Andhra. He has also taken it beyond the shores of India, and has instructed many in this appealing dance form.

Outstanding for her part in putting Kuchipudi on the dance map of India is Yamini Krishnamurti. She has helped greatly in its revival by her interpretation of the female roles. Her dance has a vibrant vitality that holds one in thrall throughout the performance. This vitality is part of her being, finding its source in her deep love for the art.

Kathakali: Literally meaning story-play, this dance form of Kerala is intended to enact an incident, an episode or even a saga, with the aid of suggestive gestures, popular enough to convey the meaning even to the uninitiated.

The story regarding the origin of the style centres on the rivalry of two royal devotees of Krishna. The Zamorin of Calicut, it is said, possessed a peacock feather from Krishna's crown. The Raja of the neighbouring state of Kattarakara desired to see this marvellous possession, but the Zamorin not only refused him the favour but insulted and humiliated him. The embittered Raja then sent for Kaplingat Vaidigal, a Brahmin of artistic talent, and asked him to devise a dance style superior to Krishnanattam, which was popular in the Zamorin's court.

The Brahmin went to the temple of Kanyakumari and sat in meditation. On the seventh night the Goddess appeared to him in a dream, and at her bidding he went to the seashore, early next morning. There, before him, in a solemn procession over the waves, passed the characters symbolising the three *gunas* (qualities)—*Sattva* (purity and intelligence), Rajas (activity and passion) and *Tamas* (ignorance and evil). And with this basic idea sprang Ramanattam, as a challenge to Krishnanattam. In the years it developed into the magnificent art of Kathakali which is in actuality the art of mimicry raised to the highest pinnacle of perfection. Only when oneness is achieved between the self and the character portrayed can a performance meet the rigid demands of Kathakali.

Like other classical dance forms, Kathakali, confined to the limits of Kerala, was almost on the verge of disappearance with public and official neglect, before Mahakavi Vallathol took upon the noble task of establishing the Kalamandalam. He and his troupe have done magnificent service to the art by refining and remoulding it for proper representation on the modern stage, at the same time preserving its classic purity and inherent grandeur. This great, noble art, through which the genius of Kerala has found full flowering, still affords the same rich, spiritual experience as before, giving life to drama and drama to life.

In the Kathakali world, Natyacharya Kunchu Kurup is a revered name. He is remembered on the stage in various roles: as Bhakta Kuchela, a humble devotee of Krishna; as Nala, lost in love; and as Ravana, not the fierce demon-king, but in an ardent amorous mood, cajoling the reluctant Mandodari.

Ramankutty Nair, certainly the most brilliant among the next generation of Kathakali dancers, gave memorable renderings of the complex and contrasting roles of

Hanuman and Sisupala—the one, gentle, playful, yet with latent strength, the other, derisive, arrogant, whose might eventually crumbles before Krishna.

Kunchu Nair, versatile master of the art, could awoke all the rasas with equal ease, and had complete command over both the technical and expressive aspects, was another superb artiste.

Manipuri: To the people of Manipur, life is one enchanting song, and death but a continuation of the song, sung to a new rhythm. Accordingly, any ritual, festive occasion, or event that breaks the even cadence of life is celebrated with song and dance.

The Manipuris are chiefly devoted to the cult of Vaisnavism and the episodes from the life of Krishna form an integral part of the dance compositions, which are rendered in a spirit of intense devotional fervour.

Bhagachandra, a former ruler, is credited with the visualisation of the dance style. When his throne was usurped by the King of Moirang, a neighbouring state, he sought refuge with the king of Assam, who granted him asylum on condition that he would tame a wild elephant that was ravaging the country. The Lord Krishna visited the hapless king in the dream and, knowing him to be an ardent devotee, advised him to approach the animal with no other weapon in hand but a rosary. This he did the next morning and the elephant fell at the king's feet. Bhagyachandra eventually reconquered his state, and, in gratitude, consecrated a temple to Krishna. The lord, it is believed, again appeared before the king in a dream and danced the *Bhangi-pareng*, the fountain-head of the Manipuri classical dance system. Even today Bhagyachandra's name is evoked at the beginning of a performance.

In Manipur, among the groups of people in whom

strains of animism of the pre-Hindu religion still persist and who worship certain deified stones and trees, there are other varieties of dance to be witnessed, such as those performed by the worshippers of Siva. But these dances belong to a category altogether different from the *Rasa* of the Vaisnavites.

Guru Athomba Singh, steeped in tradition, orthodox to the core and austere in his technique, was the first to reveal to the world outside Manipur the exquisite beauty of the Manipuri style. Gurudev Tagore took him to Santiniketan and there he started his role as a teacher. Then senior professor at the Manipur Dance College, Athomba Singh continued to impart his vast knowledge to aspiring students.

Guru Amubi Singh, who for many years was in the company of Uday Shanker, was another acknowledged master of the art. Combining traditional knowledge with creative gifts, he evoked images of unsurpassed loveliness in his dance.

Guru Bipin Sinha, who brought Manipuri dance to Bombay and was the teacher of the noted Jhaveri Sisters, was an unusual personality. He had a modern mind that is constantly experimenting and recreating, but not without a sense of the abiding values of the classical dance.

Kathak: The North's contribution to the dance heritage, Kathak is seen at its best in its traditional homes—Lucknow and Jaipur. Youngest of all the dance forms existing in our country, the inspiration for the style came from the "Kathaks", the narrators of Katha, the wandering minstrels who sang of themes both divine and secular, and danced as they sang, embellishing their story and giving it a visible pattern with suitable actions.

As Bharata Natyam gradually disappeared from North India under the impact of the Moghul invasion, Kathak gained a new life from the fusion of Indo-Moghul cultures. Nurtured amidst the pomp and splendour of royal courts, it acquired much glittering paraphernalia but lost its mood of dedication and, deprived of the former inspiration it had found in the *Bhakti Rasa* (devotional mood), it sought a fresh fount in the *Sringara Rasa* (erotic mood). The dance thus came to mean a demonstration of technique, a display of virtuosity, along with a deplorable desire (sometimes predominant) to attract the audience.

Kathak has also gone through the same phase of neglect and misuse that other styles have known. Pandering as it did to the jaded minds of the Moghul rulers—the licence and levity of whose courts were repugnant to Hindu orthodoxy—it also came in for its share of stigma and scandal. With the decline of the Moghuls, it passed on to the house of ill fame, and, out of its ruins, emerged the decadent and crude "nautch."

However, preserved in its classic purity in the families of maestros, such as Kalka, Bindadin and their descendants, Kathak retained its original vitality and vigour. Nothing had been lost, and it needed only the pioneering efforts of Madame Menaka to effect its renaissance.

Shambhu Maharaj and Birju Maharaj, both direct descendants of the renowned family of Kalka and Bindadin, whose art tradition has been the longest and most aristocratic, represent two trends, two generations and two modes of thought. Both have a style that is chaste, precise and in strict conformity with the prescribed tenets of this dance form, but while one is like an ocean, secure in his possession of deep and rare knowledge, the other is like a river, constantly seeking new channels to conquer new horizons.

Birju is creative within the orbit of the tradition and orthodox without being hidebound. Dance was almost a twin of his first consciousness, and, though young in age, he performs with the ease, confidence and finesse of a veteran.

Odissi and Mohini Attam: The recent artistic renaissance that has swept over our country has brought in its wake the revival of some neglected dance styles, that had lain in obscurity all these years. Among such styles to burst their bonds and emerge into the radiance of public acclaim are Odissi of Orissa and Mohini Attam of Kerala.

Apart from references in the Bharata *Natya Sastra,* the sculptured friezes in temples both Saivite and Vaisnavite in Orissa bear evidence to the continuous tradition of Odissi. During the reign of the Ganga dynasty, in the 12th century, it received a great impetus from royal patronage.

Devout followers of Vishnu, the kings maintained a regular staff of *Maharis* (the Oriya version of Devadasis), singers and musicians who were attached to the temples and danced and sang before the deity. Despite degradation and impoverishment they kept the art intact up to the present day. Akin to Bharata Natyam in some ways, yet reminiscent of the Manipuri with its undulating movements, its peculiar features are flexions and deep bends.

Indrani Rahman has made a notable contribution to the Indian dance by being the first professional dancer to perform it outside Orissa—in India and abroad.

Mohini Attam, as its name implies, is the dance of the charmer. Its origin is a matter of conjecture, but it remains a lovely fusion of the parallel streams of dance in the eastern and western regions of South India. Combining the formal grace and elegance of Bharata Natyam with the earthy vigour and dynamism of Kathakali, the petalled *nrtta* hands of the one with the wide stance of the other, the delicate expressions of the one with the stylised eye-movement of the other, it co-ordinates instinct with charm, subtle allure and seductive appeal.

Shanta Rao was well known for her highly individual rendering of this style, while Roshan Vajifdar had lent it an enchantment all her own, investing it with grace, delicacy and passion.

A word, in conclusion, about the efforts that are being made to combine choreography with classicism and fit traditional dance patterns into new moulds. Rukmini Devi, Mrinalini Sarabhai and Birju Maharaj were in the vanguard in this respect, each in his or her own style, but restricting the choices of themes to legendary episodes.

On the other hand, a neo-classical school has sprung up, inspired but not limited by the classical styles. It expresses itself mostly in ballets, the content of which is sometimes ancient and sometimes modern. Uday Shankar pioneered this movement, while Shanti Bardhan, his equally famed disciple, found a supplementary inspiration in the folk dances. The Little Ballet Troupe he established has revealed a world of charm in its creations, bringing a refreshing originality, a delightful naivete and a winsome simplicity to all its productions.

29

Folk Theatre

Every street in an Indian town has its own drama. The bangle-seller hawks his wares in rhyming couplets. The roving conjurer sets up his studio on the pavement and adds a snatch of song every now and then to his performance. There is always a small crowd near at hand to change the place into a small arena. The juggler, the conjurer, the snake-charmer, the monkey man, the bear-tamer—all have something of the actor-producer in them.

Sanskrit drama, addressed to a sophisticated audience of courtiers, used a highly ornate language that did not touch the life of the people. It is the folk theatre in its diverse forms which is the real theatre of the people. It has changed, developed and adapted itself to the changing social conditions. Among the main regional forms of folk theatre are the *Nautanki* of Rajasthan, *Bhavai* of Gujarat, *Ramalila* and *Krishnalila* of Uttar Pradesh, *Swang* or *Naqqal* of North India, *Tamasha* of Maharashtra, *Burrakatha* and *Veedhi Natakam* of Andhra, and *Yatra* of Bengal.

The *Nautanki* troupe generally consists of an old man, his wife, his nephews and his sons. Three of them form the orchestra; one plays a small bowl-shaped drum which he beats with two sticks, sitting on his haunches, another plays a harmonium and the third runs his bow across the hundred strings of the *Sarangi.* The narrator called *Ranga,* which means of the *rang* or stage, is the master of the troupe. Acting as stage manager, director and prompter, he controls the exits and entrances of the players as also the rhythm and tempo of the play and, through his comments, maintains the unity and thread of the plot.

The spectatorsit on all sides of the impromptu stage which is a raised open platform. The story, interspersed with songs, always concerns an old hero, a local Robin Hood or a love romance. The narrative is in the regional dialect and the tunes are unsophisticated folk melodies. Women's roles are invariably played by young boys. A player often stops in the middle of a scene to have a puff at a *hookah* or chew a betel leaf. The spectators ignore these informal interruptions which in no way disturb the continuity of action of the play.

Every *Nautanki* play has its stock character, the buffoon, who caricatures and lampoons persons in authority, even the most exalted among them. While the main action of the play is expressed in verse, the buffoon speaks in prose, improvising all the time, making satirical comments on local big-wigs, exposing social injustices and extemporising on affairs that directly concern the villagers. His favourite targets are monylenders, landlords and corrupt police inspectors.

The players are generally fed and housed by the villagers. Apart from a lump sum which is collected from the people by the village elder, the troupe gets additional contributions during the performance from enthusiastic admirers. When a donation is made the *Ranga* receives it by bowing low and then pays a tribute to the donor with a couplet which announces his name to the public.

Bhavai, popular throughout Gujarat, is a series of playlets which deal with medieval tales of chivalry. It owes its origin to Asahita, a 14th century poet, singer and actor of a high caste Brahmin family, who was boycotted by his community for the crime of eating with a low-caste woman. About three hundred and sixty playlets have come down to us as literary pieces learnt by heart by the actor's families.

The Bhavai actors have to be experts in dance, music and mime. In the 17th century a few *Bhavai* actors secured high posts in the princely courts. In the 18th century the art was vulgarised by players who performed in the court of dissolute princes and pandered to the low taste of those who invited them to perform at wedding parties and in drinking houses.

Normally a *Bhavai* troupe consists of fourteen players. The village headman, who collects a few annas from each family, gathers enough money to entertain the players. Meals and accommodation are given free. The oil in the torches for the show is provided by the village oil-man and the pots by the village potter. The players first draw a small circle of a radius of ten feet on the ground. This area, called *paudh,* is the stage where the musicians sit and sing and the actors perform. Two players blow the *bhungal,* a long-stemmed trumpet, to announce the start of the play. The *bhungal's* shrill notes signify the entry and exit of a player, denote the triumph and victory of a general and mark every abrupt turn and twist of the play. They also signal to the audience to make a small clearing for the actors as they emerge out of the green room, holding two little oil-fed twine torches lighting their faces and the path.

For their make-up the actors use mostly lamp soot, red and white pigments and oil which gives an amber sheen to the face. As the play opens they brandish their torches weaving circles of fire in the air. After this ritual they light a big torch and fix it in the centre of the arena. A chorus of men dressed as women sing and dance and help the actors with properties. If the king is going away the "chorus women" help him with a sword, hold a light to show him the way or flourish torches to add to the grandeur of the moment of departure. They also feed the spluttering flame of the torch with oil from a large metal goblet every now and then. When an actor has to convey an important message they rush to him with flaming torches. As stage hands the "chorus women" are unreal shadows and the audience ignores their presence. They are like the *kurogo* in a Kabuki play who moves like a ghost arranging properties on the stage.

The players use every little gesture to the maximum advantage. The same dance steps, with a different stress, can represent a strutting general, a limping beggar, and a waddling money-lender. Often the costume remains the same but the character of the player changes entirely. The *pagri* with a different tilt can be the head-dress of a peasant or the crown of a king. A slight variation in the way a player carries his *dhoti* makes him a washerman, a merchant or a village headman. The players heighten the idiosyncrasies of the persons they seek to portray with their gestures and the spectators recognise them instantly.

Like all folk plays, *Bhavai* starts at about nine in the evening and lasts the whole night. Sometimes the players continue their show until high noon the next day. By powerful acting, lusty songs, mincing dance steps and whirlwind movements they produce a powerful dramatic impact on the audience.

The *Bhavai* players make use of every opportunity in the play to collect a little money for themselves. When Queen Tara, wife of the great Harishchandra, is reduced to poverty and begs money to pay the cremation toll for her dead son, she moves among the spectators with a begging bowl singing a pathetic song. The drama is projected into reality. In another play a princess who carries seven brass pots on her head, walks for miles and has at last to take a rest. Someone has to take the pots off her head to lighten her burden and has to be paid for his services. The princess beseeches the spectators to pay for her. There is no lack of chivalrous people among the audience. The pot money is paid by them.

Tamasha, the popular folk play form of Maharashtra, is close to *Bhavai* in many ways. In the 18th century, in its endeavour to entertain landlords and local rajas, it came to rely increasingly on lewd gestures and erotic songs and dances. The women players were almost regarded as semi-courtesans and their menfolk were shunned as pariahs. Today they go about carrying their paraphernalia of make-up and costumes in a bundle on their heads. Their plays centre on love stories presented in amorous and passionate scenes with dance and music, or tales of chivalry enacted with lusty vigour.

Ramalila is a spectacle more than a play and as a rule lasts for fourteen days. Songs knit up the narrative which deals with the childhood, marriage, exile and coronation of Rama. The players use rich costumes and elaborate make-up and some of them also appear in masks. The action moves quickly from a city to a forest or from a palace to an *asrama* and the spcctacle, by the help of a cruder version of the kind of multiple set used by Meyerhold in his productions, helps the audience to see two or three parts of the story enacted at the same time. While Rama for instance is giving the final battle to the ten-headed monster Ravana, the audience can also have a close look at Sita who sits as a prisoner in a bower as also at Surpanakha whose nose has been cut off by Lakshamana. The visual spectacle telescopes time and space and achieves at a naive level what some modern producers do by spotlighting different locales in the auditorium and on the stage.

At the end of the celebration huge effigies of Ravana, his younger brother Kumbhakarna, who slept for six months in the year, and Meghanada, which stand high in the open dressed in bright colours, are burnt and the shreds of bamboo and cardboard limps fly about trailing flames. The spectators, thrilled with a sense of moral victory, return home with a feeling of having actually participated in the monsters' destruction.

In *Krishnalila* which depicts Krishna's life, the action of the story is spread over a month. The actors lead a crowd of devout pilgrims, which swells each day, to the woods, hills, temples and streams associated with the exploits of the last *avatar* of Vishnu. The pilgrimage is half drama and half worship.

In sharp contrast to *Ramalila* and *Krishnalila* are plays of a pronounced secular character. *Swang* or *Naqqal* are light farces enacted by *bhands,* the village buffoons. Two buffoons normally constitute a troupe. There are shrewdness and intelligence masked in stupidity. The *compere,* an elderly bedraggled man, holds a triangular leather-folder with which he strikes his partner who plays a woman' role. He initiates the play with a series of questions to his junior partner who gives snappy and evasive replies and leads the *compere* into one absurdity after another.

The topical comments, pungent jokes and mock interviews during the performance are enlivened with delightfully uninhibited and pointed remarks. The comedian playing the female wears no special dress and no make-up. A *chunni* (scarf) draped round the actor's face, barely hiding his moustache, is the magic garment which is supposed to hide his true identity. He plays the bride, the spoiled daughter, the shrewish mother-in-law, all by a deft manipulation of the *chunni* through which he can cast amorous glances as easily as angry scowls.

Typical of the skits acted by the young "woman" are pieces which bear such titles as *I Met the Maharaja, I Went to my Father-in-law's House, I sat in the Chair of the Judge.* She crinkles her nose, pouts, and spurns everything the old man offers. When the audience get curious as to what she wants she makes some absurd demand which makes the old man hit her with his leather-folder and the audience shriek with laughter. In a peformance the compere turned a droll farce into a political joke and *I Met the Maharaja* became *I Met Pandit Nehru!*

Master of wit, the buffoon can improvise on the spot. His is the collective wit of a whole people. With his banter and rapier thrusts of humour he often demolishes his victim with a single phrase. A particularly sharp quip is followed by roars of laughter, hurrahs, cheers, and a shower of coins. If the troupe is invited to perform at the house of a prince or a landord the buffoon always asks for the indulgence of his patrons before he lashes them with his barbed wit. He always carries a rich stock of proverbs, riddles, sayings, quotations and witty remarks at the tip of his tongue.

The *Yatra,* a folk drama peculiar to Bengal, is operatic in form. It deals mostly with religious, heroic and love themes. The chorus is an integral part of the *Yatra.* The rhythmic speech and flowing gestures of the actors are interpreted during the intervals by the chorus which stand up and sings out the scene, giving the actor time to rest. The costumes of the singers are bright, their voices are loud, and their make-up is garish. The action is always stylised and vivid and has the charm of primitive jewellery.

In the 14th century the worship of Kali influenced *Yatra* themes. With the introduction of a heroic element *Yatra* performances became more dynamic. In the 15th century when a wave of Vaisnavism swept over Bengal, *Yatra* performances drew on episodes from the life of Krishna. Prominent actors charged with religious fervour specialise in roles like those of Radha, Krishna's beloved, and Yasoda, his foster mother. The devout singers almost put the people into a state of ecstasy and, reeling, they join in the devotional singing. Though it still remains primarily religious in character, *Yatra* took on a secular colour when the improvisations of the actors and the songs they composed on the spur of the moment imcorporated comments on contemporary life.

Veedhi Natakam, popular all over Andhra, had its source in *Veedhi Bhagavatam*. A group of five or six enact the play on a raised platform. On one side of the platform is a gunny bag enclosure, a sort of pit where the musicians sit. Men play the roles of women while their wives and daughters sit in the pit and sing and supply backstage effects of thunder, battle cries and heavenly voices. The turning of the instruments and the beating of drums start long before the performance. The plays open with an offer of prayers to Ganesha, Shiva, Vishnu and Saraswati.

The commentator often projects old myths into present times by a few pointed remarks. Like the commercial in a television show, he shocks the audience out of a world of fantasy into a work-a-day world. For instance, as Lord Krishna is about to steal the clothes of the milkmaid bathing in the river Jamuna, the commentator may refer caustically to the adulterated milk sold in the market. When Ravana makes overtures to Sita, Kethi-gadu, the clown, somersaults and stands on his head. With his pertinent comments on contemporary life he makes the arena ripple with laughter. The audience puts up with the boring speeches and sermons only to be regaled by Kethi-gadu who is the gay spirit of this folk theatre.

These open-air performances which, on a superficial study, may seem to be lacking in form and structural unity, have in fact plot, movement, action and climax—all the ingredients of drama. Their simple conventions, universally accepted and understood, have been evolved through years of action and reaction of the actors and the audience.

The naked stage in the folk theatre achieves a sort of spacelessness. The narrator, like a film editor, builds up a montage of varied dramatic episodes. The absence of a drop curtain makes the small square a vibrating centre of action where dramatic episodes move with speed and tempo. It is the same spot but it is a different place every time. The hero says, "I must cross the river and meet the princess behind the palace wall." The hero goes round the stage and, cutting a circle, returns to the same plot. "Ah, the palace window is open and I see the princess looking out!" he exclaims. Where a palace stood a minute earlier is now the edge of a forest. Where a river flowed quietly a minute ago is a mountain now. Imagination is the thing!

The folk theatre does not strive to create an "illusion of reality." It breaks the illusion and creates in turn a world of its own. The bareness of the stage is a gain. The actors cannot take shelter behind the wings or seek help from sets and decor but have to depend solely on their art. The lack of a conventional stage lends power to the drama and makes for directness of action and a closer emotional accord between the spectators and the players.

Folk songs have given vitality to contemporary poetry, primitive sculpture has lent power and tension to 20th century sculpture and folk painting has brought colour and vigour to modern painting. The folk theatre has much to offer to the city theatre which is always in danger of losing contact with sreality.

LOTUS CHOICES OF INDIA BOOKVARSITY

INDIA BOOKVARSITY is fast growing as the pioneer publishing program of quality works, old and new, on aspects of indian culture, to inform educate and stimulate the new generation and Indiaspora, as also those interested in Indian religions, philosphies, values, etc,. all over the world. **Editor: Mahendra Kulasrestha**

The Golden Books of Indian Religions

Classics Revived for an Ultra-Modern World

In no other country of the world so many religions were born, all peace-loving, with a variety of philosophies, with God and without God, but all believing in Karman and Rebirth. The Buddha's religion was first world movement for peace, kindness and equality, much liked even today. Every educated Indian and others at large should know about them in the present terror-stricken times. The books are specially planned and produced for the general educated reader.

RIGVEDA

The Golden Book of Rigveda: Humanity's Oldest Scripture

—R. T. H. Griffith

The first book of its kind for the general reader.... selected hymns from a very large collection, arranged subjectwise, translated into easy-to-understand English. Griffith's translations of all the Vedas are famous.

ISBN 81-8382-010-7
Rs. 395/

BUDDHISM

The Golden Book of Buddhism: Humanity's Oldest Religion of Peace

— F. Max Muller, T. W. H. Rhys Davids, Samuel Beal

Buddhism is a much-loved and respected religion of modern times which can play a significant role in overcoming terror. Selected suttas, including Ashvaghosa's *Life of Buddha,* translated from its Chinese version, and *Dhammapada,* the *Gita of Buddhism.*

ISBN 81-8382-011-5
Rs. 395/-

JAINISM

The Golden Book of Jainism: Humanity's Oldest Religion of Non-Violence

— Hermann Jacobi

India's unique religion in philosophical analysis and holy practices, more non-violent than any, and much older to Buddhism.
Selections from *Uttaradhyayana Sutra, Acharanga Sutra, Sutrakritanga*, etc., with *Life and Vows of Mahavira*, Simple English.

ISBN 81-8382-014-X
Rs. 395/-

UPNISHAD

The Golden Book of Upanishads: Humanity's Earliest Philosophical Compositions

— F. Max Muller

Proponents of the concepts of Atman, Brahman, Karman, Prana, etc. Much appreciated in the present day world.Eleven major Upanishads as chosen by Shankaracharya, presented in simple English.

ISBN 81-8382-012-3
Rs. 495/

Aspects of Indan Culture

CULTURE INDIA

Culture India: Philosophy, Religion, Arts, Literature, Society

- Ed. Mahendra Kulasrestha

A classic revived. Special contributions by authorities in their respective areas: Dr. Radha -krishnan, Dr. Suniti Kumar Chatterji, Svetoslav Roerich, Ritha Devi, Priya Chatterji Tandura, Dr. A. D. Pusalkar, Prof. K. A.Nilakanta Sastri, etc. etc. etc.

'...encylopaedia of ancient Indian culture.'
- *Journal of American Oriental Society.*

ISBN 81-8382-013-1
Rs. 495/-

RAJAYOGA

Learn RAJAYOGA from VIVEKANANDA

The first easy-to-understand exposition of India's unique philosophy and practice of perfect health and Godhead by the veteran..... which he made for his American disciples. Easily the best and most authentic.
With commentary on Patanjali's Yoga Sutra; and Yoga references in *Kurma Purana, Samkhya Karika, Shvetashvatara Upanishad, Shankar Bhashya*, and *Vyasa Sutra*, illustrated.

ISBN 81-8382-009-3
Rs. 395/-